THE FLYING WHITE HOUSE

THE FLYING WHITE HOUSE

THE STORY OF AIR FORCE ONE

J. F. ter HORST &
COL. RALPH ALBERTAZZIE

Coward, McCann & Geoghegan, Inc.
New York

Library of Congress Cataloging in Publication Data

terHorst J. F.
　The flying White House.

　Includes index.
　　1.　Government aircraft—United States.
2.　Presidents—United States—Transportation.
I.　Albertazzie, Ralph D., joint author.　II.　Title.
III.　Title:　Air Force One.
TL723.T47　　　973.92　　　78-25556
ISBN 0-698-10930-9

Printed in the United States of America

Contents

Radio Call Signs

Radio call signs and code names used by the White House Communications Agency, the Department of Defense, the Secret Service, presidential aides, and other agencies of government in 1978:

The President	Deacon
Mrs. Rosalynn Carter	Dancer
Amy Carter	Dynamo
The Vice President	Cavalier
Mrs. Joan Mondale	Cameo
Former President Ford	Passkey
Mrs. Betty Ford	Pinafore
Former President Nixon	Searchlight
Mrs. Patricia Nixon	Starlight
Mrs. Lyndon B. Johnson	Victoria
Mrs. Dwight D. Eisenhower	Springtime
Mrs. Harry S. Truman	Sunnyside
House Speaker Thomas P. O'Neill	Flag Day
Secretary of State Cyrus Vance	Fade Away
Secretary of Defense Harold Brown	Finley
Zbigniew Brzezinski, national security adviser	Hawkeye
Dr. William Lukash, White House physician	Sawhorse

Places and Things . . .

The White House	Crown
Air Force One	Angel
Presidential limousine	Stagecoach
Vice President's residence	Clover Leaf
Camp David	Cactus
Carter residence, Plains	Driftwood
Presidential helicopter	Nighthawk
Nixon residence, San Clemente	Storm King
LBJ ranch	Volcano
U.S. Capitol	Punchbowl
Andrews AFB	Acrobat

And in Their Time . . .

Henry A. Kissinger	Woodcutter
H. R. Haldeman	Welcome
John D. Ehrlichman	Wisdom
Gen. Alexander Haig	Clawhammer
Ron Ziegler	Whaleboat
Bebe Rebozo	Christopher
Rose Mary Woods	Strawberry

For the Record

PRESIDENTS	PRIMARY PRESIDENTIAL AIRCRAFT	PRESIDENTIAL PILOTS
Franklin D. Roosevelt	*Sacred Cow* (Douglas DC-4)	Lt. Col. Henry T. Myers, Tifton, Ga. 12 June 1944 to 12 April 1945
Harry S Truman	*Sacred Cow* and *Independence* (Douglas DC-6)	Lt. Col. Henry T. Myers 12 April 1945 to 6 January 1948 Col. Francis W. Williams, Alameda, Calif. 6 January 1948 to 20 January 1953
Dwight D. Eisenhower	*Columbine II* (Lockheed Constellation) and *Columbine III* (Lockheed Super-Constellation)	Col. William G. Draper, Silver Spring, Md. 20 January 1953 to 20 January 1961
John F. Kennedy	*Air Force One** Douglas DC-6 No. 33240 and Boeing 707 No. 26000	Col. James B. Swindal, West Blockton, Ala. 20 January 1961 to 22 November 1963

President	Aircraft	Commander
Lyndon B. Johnson	Boeing 707 No. 26000	Col. James B. Swindal 22 November 1963 to 15 July 1965 Col. James U. Cross, Andalusa, Ala. 15 July 1965 to 18 May 1968 Lt. Col. Paul L. Thornhill, Rossburg, Ohio 18 May 1968 to 20 January 1969
Richard M. Nixon†	Boeing 707 No. 26000 and Boeing 707 No. 27000	Col. Ralph D. Albertazzie, Morgantown, W. Va. 20 January 1969 to 9 August 1974
Gerald R. Ford	Boeing 707 No. 27000	Col. Lester C. McClelland, Masontown, Pa. 9 August 1974 to 20 January 1977
Jimmy Carter	Boeing 707 No. 27000	Col. Lester C. McClelland 20 January 1977–

*Boeing 707 No. 26000 was the first jet to be popularized as *Air Force One*, although this radio call sign for the Air Force aircraft carrying the president was first used aboard *Columbine III*.

†Beginning in 1971, Nixon used the name *Spirit of '76* to designate his primary aircraft, in honor of the nation's bicentennial. President Ford retained the name for that reason, although preferring to call it *Air Force One*.

"So the reporters are calling it the 'Sacred Cow,' eh? Suits me."

—Franklin D. Roosevelt, 1945

"I'm safer up here than on those icy Kansas City streets."

—Harry Truman, 1946

"I settled back in my compartment with the secretary of state and underwent an exhilarating experience—my first jet flight!"

—Dwight D. Eisenhower, 1959

"It's magnificent! I'll take it."

—John F. Kennedy, 1962

"Now, you fellows know I work as hard on this airplane as I do in the White House—maybe harder."

—Lyndon B. Johnson, 1966

"This great plane that took us to China, to Russia . . . this great *Spirit of '76* has got to be remembered."

—Richard M. Nixon, 1974

"When they fly you on *Air Force One,* you know you're the president."

—Gerald R. Ford, 1974

"I thought *Peanut One* was fixed up pretty nicely until I saw this."

—Jimmy Carter, 1976

13

THE FLYING WHITE HOUSE

Preface

This is the story of the very special airplane of a very special American—the President of the United States. There have been seven such aircraft and eight such Americans since the first pairing took place in 1944. Such statistics, however, merely hint at the unusual roles that presidential planes and their crews have played in the lives of Presidents and First Families, and in our own lives. There have been triumphs and tears aboard, as well as fun and games, and events both important and trivial.

The airplane has added a new dimension to the presidency during the last four decades. Today's version, a sleek blue, white, and silver Boeing 707 popularly called *Air Force One*, is the world's most famous aircraft. It has become as much a part of policy making as the Minuteman missile. Nearly every President would sooner do without his Vice President than his special airplane. The big jet can whisk him off to a summit meeting as effortlessly as it can take him home for a weekend of relaxation. And wherever and whenever he flies, *Air Force One*'s elaborate communications system keeps him in touch with Peking and Moscow as readily as with the Pentagon and Miss Lillian.

From the very beginning, the President's airplane has been an

17

elite, one-of-a-kind aircraft, manned by a hand-picked crew and maintained in a manner that only the U.S. Treasury could afford. Franklin Roosevelt used the *Sacred Cow* to impress Stalin in World War II. Lyndon Johnson, as *Time* magazine's Hugh Sidey observed, rode *Air Force One* like a stallion. Richard Nixon's men couldn't wait to get aboard to don their imperial flight jackets. Jimmy Carter can have grits any time he asks. No fabled sultan ever boasted so magic a carpet. Or one so majestic.

In a sense, then, this is a history book, a chronicle of the "Flying White House" from its inception with Roosevelt to its occupancy today by Carter. But "It takes a heap of living to make a house a home," as poet Edgar Guest said, and that applies whether your office and bedroom are at 1600 Pennsylvania Avenue or 40,000 feet over the South Pacific. So this is also an adventure story about airborne presidents and their companions in the sky, their accomplishments and their escapades.

Presidents past and present, along with some members of their staffs, probably will wish we had omitted some episodes and glossed over others. However, ours is not an official, sanitized version of the history of presidential aircraft; it was not authorized by the White House or the U.S. Air Force and does not bear their imprimatur. Rather, this book is the product of the authors' personal experiences on *Air Force One*, many months of research, countless interviews and the help of dozens of persons in and out of government, the aviation industry, and the White House press corps. In many instances, one or both of the authors were either participants in or witnesses to the events recorded here. We obtained some information on a background basis, meaning that we were free to use the data provided we did not reveal the identity of the informants. We attempted to source out all the pertinent material in the process of reconstructing events on the president's airplane.

No book is ever written without sacrifices by some and help from many. We owe special debts to our wives, who encouraged us from the beginning and unstintingly gave up their own claims to our time. We are especially grateful to our colleagues of the press corps, the Air Force, Secret Service, and other agencies, who shared their own experiences on *Air Force One* with us and provided much needed data, records, and photographs.

Several persons made significant contributions to our efforts. Col. Lester McClelland, the presidential pilot for Presidents Ford and Carter, and Chief Master Sgt. William "Joe" Chappell, *Air Force One*'s veteran flight engineer, briefed us on current trip-planning procedures at Andrews Air Force Base. They also helped us conceptualize the next generation of presidential aircraft, as did officials of Boeing, McDonnell Douglas, and Lockheed. Hugh A. Carter, Jr. and Frances Voorde of the White House staff provided valuable insights into President Carter's policies regarding the presidential air fleet. We are grateful to Dr. Henry Kissinger for his cooperation regarding certain key flights during the Nixon and Ford years. And a special debt of gratitude is owed historian Robert C. Mikesh, assistant curator of the Smithsonian's Air and Space Museum, for sharing his painstaking research and files on the early days of presidential air travel.

Our one regret is that time and circumstance did not permit us to talk at length with all of the several hundred former crew members of the presidential airplanes, and the communicators, presidential assistants, and key persons in government agencies whose lives are part of our story. But we salute them, and hope that this book will revive the memories of their own proud days with the "Flying White House."

Obviously, all the opinions—and the errors—are ours.

J. F. terHorst
Ralph D. Albertazzie

Washington, D. C.

Chapter One
The Final Flight

Richard Nixon's pilot was up at 6:30. He had slept fitfully. During breakfast, the radio news and *The Washington Post* conveyed fresh reports of grim decisions being made within the White House. Today, even more than yesterday, there was the unmistakable air of change, of things swirling rapidly and inexorably toward climax in the Nixon presidency.

Col. Ralph Albertazzie sighed. He could not bring himself to believe that the President of the United States was actually thinking of quitting. Nixon quitting? That didn't sound like the Nixon he knew.

Albertazzie glanced at his wristwatch and, as usual, noted the date on its calendar: Thursday, August 8, 1974. It was time to go. He kissed his wife, Carol, and drove the short distance across Andrews Air Force Base from his quarters to the presidential pilot's office.

For several days now, rumors of a presidential resignation had been flying wildly over the big installation, like birds at the end of a much-used runway. Andrews was home base for the presidential air fleet, and Richard Nixon had kept it busier than any Chief Executive in history. But in the absence of any official word, most base personnel did the next best thing—they kept discreet watch on the silver hangars that housed the big Boeing 707 with the tail number of *Air Force One*, 27000, and its nearly identical backup plane, No. 26000.

Albertazzie knew nothing more than what he had read in the papers, as he kept telling everyone who called. The "Washington Switch," his direct line to the Pentagon, had been bristling with queries from the top brass and various support agencies for *Air Force One*, each anxiously checking out the latest rumors regarding Nixon's intentions—and sometimes offering fresh ones. But his priority line, the direct telephone link between the White House and the presidential pilot's office, was the line over which any orders would come. And that one remained silent.

Albertazzie strode into his outer office and greeted his secretary, Staff Sgt. Kim Broyles. She glanced up inquiringly, hoping for a clue. He shook his head and entered his own small office. He felt empty inside, and rather helpless. Things were happening at the White House, yet he did not know if they would also affect him and the crew. Or how. Or when. Still, he told himself, there was no point in moping around. This would have to be like any other day on the ground at Andrews, a time to check out the plane and the proficiency of the crew, to make certain everything was in readiness in case the White House called. Keep busy, he ordered himself. But God, the tension, the uncertainty—it was maddening. And it was building.

Shortly before 9:00, Richard Nixon left the family quarters in the White House and walked through the Rose Garden to the Oval Office. He had slept late, until 8:30, in fact, and had had only three hours of sleep. He worked most of the night on *the* speech, he explained to Alexander Haig, the White House chief of staff.

Haig nodded approvingly; he had surmised as much. Nixon had called him the previous evening to say he finally had persuaded his family that resignation was the proper course. There was no point in waiting for the wheels of impeachment to grind him down. Haig once again assured the President, as he had done the night before, that it was the right decision. Now he studied the man behind the massive desk. Haig had never seen the President so frail, so vulnerable, so weary. But he was calm and resolute. In control.

The President instructed Haig that he would take no phone calls from anyone. Except for seeing Vice President Ford later on, he wanted to devote the rest of the day to the speech he would give over television at 9:00 that night.

Haig was relieved. The days of torment and indecision finally were over; no longer was the President agonizing between defiance one moment and resignation the next. Haig was especially pleased that the President would take no calls. Just the night before, he had reported to Nixon that H. R. "Bob" Haldeman, Haig's disgraced predecessor, had been on the phone again, demanding to talk to the President about obtaining a pardon for his Watergate activities. Haig informed Nixon that Haldeman had been told flatly there would be no presidential pardons. Then, too, John Ehrlichman, once the second-ranking man on the staff, had called Julie Nixon Eisenhower the previous evening to lobby for a pardon for himself.

With the President refusing to take any calls, it would be easier for Haig to shunt aside further demands from Haldeman and Ehrlichman. Above everything else, Haig told himself, it was imperative that nothing should occur during the President's final thirty-six hours to arouse suspicions that the White House was plotting again.

Nixon's decision to resign was firm, but it was still a secret to the outside world and to all in the White House but a few trusted persons. Haig left the President's office to begin the process of easing Nixon's exit. He had already prepared a list of what had to be done.

Albertazzie's phone rang about ten o'clock. It was the Washington Switch line from the Pentagon. The voice was Bob Clifford's, the Air Force lieutenant colonel who handled logistic support for White House travel.

"Ralph, this is on a 'need to know' basis," Clifford was saying. "I just got a call from the Military Office at the White House. They've ordered up a C-141 to transport a twin-pack Huey to El Toro. What the hell's happening?"

"I don't know," Albertazzie replied. "But I'll sure try to find out." He put down the phone, scarcely able to conceal his excitement. Something indeed was happening. But what?

The C-141 is a big Air Force cargo jet, frequently used to ferry vehicles, White House supplies, and Secret Service agents on presidential trips. The Huey Cobra is a two-jet Bell Helicopter, ordinarily used as a support chopper for White House personnel, but not primarily used by the President. Its plushed-up interior could carry six comfortably, eight in a squeeze. On Nixon's extended stays in California or Florida, several Huey Cobras were flown to their destination under their own power. To ship one via C-141 to the El Toro Marine Air Station near San Clemente indicated a sense of urgency, even emergency. What was the White House up to?

Albertazzie leaned into his intercom and spoke to Sergeant Broyles. "Get me Bill Gulley or General Lawson at the White House."

At ten o'clock, the White House switchboard located Milton Pitts for presidential aide Stephen Bull. Pitts, the President's barber, was still at home. "Milt, the President wants to see you at ten-fifteen," Bull told him. "Can you make it?"

Pitts could—and did, as he had been doing on short notice ever since he began trimming the President's hair in 1970. He reached the tiny, one-chair White House barbershop, on the ground floor of the West Wing, just moments before Nixon entered.

The President had scarcely eased himself into the single barber chair when he began thanking Pitts for "your good service over the years."

It's all over for sure, Pitts thought. This was probably the last time he would be cutting Nixon's thick, wavy hair. "It's been my pleasure, sir," Pitts said. He couldn't help noticing how much the President's hair had grayed during the past four years.

As usual, the President did most of the talking. He told Pitts he would be going on television that night. And he promised to see him again in the future, maybe over at Pitts's regular barber shop in the Sheraton Carlton Hotel, two blocks away.

Pitts worked quickly, finishing in twenty-two minutes. He

24

helped Nixon slip on his jacket. The President put out his hand. "Goodbye," he said. At the door, the President paused. "Say goodbye to Mrs. Pitts," he added.

Albertazzie's calls to the White House Military Office were unavailing. "Christ, there are all kinds of rumors." parried Bill Gulley, the administrative aide to Brig. Gen. Richard Lawson, the President's military assistant. "We just don't know what's going on."

Lawson was even more slippery and, Albertazzie thought, deliberately so. He professed to know everything but could not, or would not, say anything.

Albertazzie felt that Lawson particularly enjoyed keeping him dangling. A year earlier, there had been talk of promoting Albertazzie to the job of White House military assistant to the President. Haig had asked him if he was interested and Ron Ziegler, White House press secretary, had urged him to take it. Albertazzie had reservations about handling the White House post along with his job as presidential pilot, but it would have gained him a coveted general's star. Then, quite without explanation, the subject was dropped. Shortly thereafter, Lawson came onto the White House staff to fill the vacancy. And relations began deteriorating between the Military Office and the Special Air Missions unit at Andrews Air Force Base, the parent organization with responsibility for aircraft maintenance, supply, security, and administrative control of the VIP transport fleet, including the presidential aircraft. At Andrews, Lawson was blamed for keeping pilots and crews in the dark about trips until the last moment and for imposing new bureaucratic burdens and unnecessary administrative restrictions.

Albertazzie did not mention that he knew a helicopter was being shipped west to California. Lawson then would have known that he and Bob Clifford had exchanged information—a no-no in Lawson's scheme of operation. The Military Office frowned upon such informal cooperation between support agencies and the presidential pilot's office. Gulley and Lawson wanted all such information to come directly—and only—from them.

But cranking up a C-141 with a 'copter and crew aboard was too big an operation and too significant under the circumstances to be kept a secret. Albertazzie soon got calls from *Air Force One*'s supporting units at El Toro Marine Air Station, the operating base in California whenever the President was at his seaside villa in nearby San Clemente. Priority calls also came in from support units at Homestead Air Force Base in Florida, the operations base whenever Nixon was at his home in Key Biscayne. There was little Albertazzie could say. "The White House isn't saying anything to me," he informed them. "What do you hear?"

Still there were things he could do. The helicopter shipment was a message that couldn't be ignored, even if Lawson wouldn't talk. Albertazzie alerted his co-pilot, Lt. Col. Lester McClelland, and the senior navigator, Lt. Col. Donald McKeown, plus other key members of the crew of *Air Force One*. "We haven't gotten any official word," Albertazzie cautioned, "but something is brewing."

Vice President Ford had a busy morning. At 10:15, in ceremonies at Blair House, just across the street from the White House, he somberly presented Congressional Medals of Honor to the tearful families of seven men killed in the Vietnam War. The growing crowds on Pennsylvania Avenue had cheered Ford's presence and created a momentary traffic jam. When Ford returned to his suite in the Executive Office Building, his staff chief, Robert T. Hartmann, was waiting with a message from Haig. "The President wants to see you," Hartmann said. "Right away."

At 11:01, Steve Bull ushered Ford into the President's office. Nixon was waiting, seated behind his immaculate desk. He began first with small talk, chitchat, as was his custom. Ford, more than Nixon, found it difficult going. The awkward moment was relieved by the entrance of Ollie Atkins, the White House staff photographer, who wanted to record the scene for posterity. He snapped several pictures of the two men together, Ford in the gold-striped chair to the right of the desk, both men leaning toward each other, each with an elbow on the desk and a hand clasped over the opposite wrist.

Nixon and Ford talked for an hour, not about the past and least of all about Watergate, but about their hopes for the future

26

of the country and the government. Finally Nixon got around to the subject, repeating what Haig had already told Ford.

The President would send a letter of resignation the next day to the Secretary of State, as provided by law. It would be effective upon receipt by Kissinger. Then the office of the President would be vacant and the Vice President would be sworn in as Nixon's successor.

"Jerry, I know you'll do a good job," Ford heard Nixon say. They shook hands emotionally, faces taut, tight-lipped. Then Nixon relaxed his grip and Ford left.

At the presidential pilot's office at Andrews, Albertazzie and his staff stayed close to the phones and the radio, waiting, hoping for some definitive information. The Washington stations crackled with a news bulletin, announced by the White House, that Nixon had summoned Ford to the Oval Office. But what the two talked about was only a matter for excited speculation by network correspondents at the White House. If press secretary Ron Ziegler knew the details, he wasn't saying.

And still no telephone call from the White House Military Office. And no further clues for Albertazzie from the Washington Switch line to the Pentagon. The C-141 ground crew, across the way, was busy loading the Huey helicopter for the "secret" flight to California. Beyond that one known fact, everything was pure guesswork.

Albertazzie finally decided to excuse *Air Force One*'s crew members from their usual duties. Except for a skeleton crew, he sent the rest home for the remainder of the day, advising them to stay near their telephones. "I'll call you if I hear any operational news," he told them. The suspense was getting to everybody. Ordinary work had become impossible.

At noon, Haig ordered the presidential correspondence section in the White House to shut off the "Richard Nixon" signature machine. For the first time in five and a half years, the steady flow of White House letters bearing the official facsimile of his handwriting was stopped. From now on, any letters—and Haig knew there wouldn't be many—would have to be signed personally by the President. As Woodward and Bernstein noted

27

in *The Final Days*, "the news spread rapidly through the White House." Loyal staffers who believed in Nixon were surprised and shaken by it.

Nineteen minutes past noon, Ziegler walked into the White House pressroom before live television cameras and a horde of jostling reporters. Struggling to keep his composure, he announced: "Tonight, at nine o'clock Eastern Daylight Time, the President of the United States will address the nation on radio and television from his Oval Office."

Bedlam.

Albertazzie heard Ziegler's announcement via a network news flash. It settled one thing. The President at least would not be going anyplace until after his speech—and probably not even then. Nixon disliked nighttime traveling and rarely did it, particularly not from the White House.

But, of course, the speech might have something to do with that. Albertazzie, along with Americans everywhere, did not know what the President would be saying. He could only surmise, as the news broadcasters were doing, that the speech would deal with resignation. Albertazzie thought of calling the White House Military Office again, but he could almost hear Gulley or Lawson giving him the usual runaround. The hell with it. There was nothing to do but wait.

Waiting was the name of the game for most White House staffers, too. They turned it into a kind of wake. Nixon's speech writers sent out for six-packs of beer. Bottles of scotch and bourbon appeared in the offices of Nixon's lawyers. All afternoon, people strolled up and down the corridors, plastic cups in hand.

"There was emotion, a feeling of closeness," Woodward and Bernstein recorded. "People were shaking hands and hugging each other. At times they tried to act lighthearted. In the White House mess, staffers sat around eating tacos. It was Thursday, Mexican-lunch day.

" . . . In the Military Office in the East Wing, the liquor was flowing. There were bottles and buckets of ice on the desks.

28

Lieutenant Colonel [Jack] Brennan came in even though it was his day off. Everyone had a lot to drink.''

Shortly past three, the White House phone rang in Albertazzie's office. Kim Broyles came on the intercom: "General Lawson for you, sir.''

Lawson's voice was hoarse, almost a whisper. "You have a ten A.M. departure for El Toro tomorrow. Gulley will give you the details later.''

By habit, Albertazzie asked the obvious question. He knew the President frequently remained in California for an extended working vacation. "How long are we staying?''

"You are not staying," Lawson snapped. "You are making a drop. He is announcing his resignation tonight on television.''

Albertazzie put down the phone. So it really was true. It was all over for Nixon. The first presidential resignation in history. Tomorrow there would be a new President. Tomorrow *Air Force One* would bear the departing ruler home, almost like a funeral cortege.

Automatically, Albertazzie picked up the phone and began executing the notification checklist, as he did before every presidential trip. All the support agencies were advised of the itinerary. He called the members of the crew. He worked briskly, smoothly, at his task. Everything went forward without a hitch. Nobody brought up the impending resignation; it was irrelevant to the mechanics of coordinating the next day's flight.

Finally he called Carol, and went home to listen to the President on television.

The morning of Friday, August 9, dawned warm and muggy. By eight o'clock, the orange sun had pierced the sultry haze hanging over the city. Its rays were glinting off the Washington Monument as Haig strode through the Rose Garden toward the East Wing of the White House. He took the elevator to the Nixon family quarters and found the President, dressed and waiting, in the Lincoln Sitting Room.

Nixon glanced over the single piece of White House stationery that Haig handed him. Then he methodically penned his signature below the terse message that would go later in the morning to Secretary of State Kissinger:

> Dear Mr. Secretary,
>   I hearby resign the Office of President of the United States.

Nixon's last official act was done.

By eight o'clock, the big plane was nearly ready. Although technically it and the crew were always prepared to fly at an hour's notice, members of the ground and flight crews had been on hand since six to prepare the plane for its scheduled departure at ten. With two hours still to go, Albertazzie assembled the officers of the crew in his presidential pilot's office to review all procedures. He wanted Nixon's final flight to be as perfect as it could be.

Sergeant Broyles had brewed fresh coffee for everyone. With the radio and television tuned low in the background for any late word from the White House, they began ticking off their checklist of tasks. Co-pilot Les McClelland and navigator Don McKeown reviewed the flight plan with Albertazzie and rechecked the weather forecast. The takeoff and route had been coordinated with all the air traffic control agencies—the Andrews tower, Washington departure control, the Air Force command post, and the command post for Special Air Missions (SAM), their parent organization.

McKeown, much to his chagrin, could not make the trip. He had come down with an ear infection and the Air Force doctors had grounded him temporarily.

Albertazzie sent McClelland and McKeown to the Andrews base operations office to file the flight plan. "Be sure the dispatcher is aware of our impending call sign change," he reminded them.

That would be just one of the exceptions to normal flight procedures on this trip. Sometime around noon, Albertazzie knew, Vice President Ford would be taking his oath of office at the White House as the new Commander-in-Chief. President Nixon would become Citizen Nixon. At that moment, *Air Force One* no longer would be the call sign of the airplane. Without a

30

President aboard, the call sign would revert to the craft's regular designation, SAM 27000.

Albertazzie had calculated that the moment would occur in the skies over Missouri as the plane flew west. So Albertazzie alerted the appropriate air route traffic control center at Kansas City, and notified the Air Defense Command, the Federal Aviation Administration, and the National Military Command Center. It was essential, in a nuclear age, that the transition from one Commander-in-Chief to another be marked with utmost precision by the military and security agencies of the United States.

About nine, the President and Mrs. Nixon made their way to the shaded west end of the wide second-floor hall. Chef Henry Haller's kitchen staff and the maids and butlers under Chief Usher Rex Scouten, had gathered to say goodbye.

Nixon tried to be chipper. He thanked them profusely for their "good care" of his family during their years in residence. Although other countries might have big palaces, and bigger staffs and bigger budgets for such things, he said, they could be proud of working at the White House, for the President of the United States and the First Family. And he was sure they would do their best to make the Fords feel right at home.

Then the Nixons went down the line, shaking hands with each one, adding a personal word of farewell.

Shortly before nine, Albertazzie's phone rang. It was Gulley again, calling from the White House to advise that the president wanted a closed departure. Members of the public were to be discouraged from entering Andrews. There would not be the usual press coverage of *Air Force One*'s takeoff, nor any farewell ceremonies before the Nixons boarded the plane.

Albertazzie did not tell Gulley what he already knew—that nobody on the base was planning a big send-off for the departing President. The spectators would be only those persons living on the base and those having business that morning at the base passenger terminal.

Downstairs in the East Room, members of the White House staff began drifting in early. By the time the Nixons arrived, only

31

standing room was left. The Marine Band struck up "Hail to the Chief," as Nixon entered. He was followed by Mrs. Nixon, Julie and David Eisenhower, Tricia and Edward Cox. As the loud applause died away, the President stepped forward to the microphones and began talking to all who had worked so loyally for him through the years.

"This is one of those spontaneous things that we always arrange whenever the President comes to speak, and it will be so reported in the press, and we don't mind because they have to call it as they see it."

He spoke of his mother and his father, his early days in California, his five and a half years in the White House. Now, at last, the moment of farewell was at hand.

Nixon's voice was thick with emotion, his chest was heaving. Many in the room were sobbing. Some wondered if the President would give way, too—crack up right there over live television. But he took a deep breath and plunged on to the finish.

" . . . and so, we leave with high hopes and good spirits," he said, "and with deep humility and with very much gratefulness. . . ."

The television cameras followed Nixon to the door. He was gone. It was over.

Albertazzie was ready to head for the airplane about nine-fifteen. He glanced in the long mirror behind his office door for a final once-over. His shoes were shiny and so were the silver buttons on his blue tunic. The tips of his epaulets were properly tucked under his collar. He put on his hat with the scrambled-egg visor. He picked up his pilot's briefcase and opened the door.

"See you later," he said to Sergeant Broyles.

"Have a good trip, sir," she said.

The walk from the presidential pilot's office to *Air Force One* was about 800 yards, a brisk four-minute trek. The sky was bright and nearly cloudless. It was going to be a hot August day. As he rounded the corner of the passenger terminal, he could see spectators already gathered along the waist-high fence at the edge of the tarmac. An Air Police officer and a Secret Service agent waved him through the gate.

Hc headed diagonally across the ramp toward the plane, its freshly waxed wings gleaming in the sunlight. He was aware of being watched by those along the fence as he made his solitary way the last hundred paces. Funny, he thought, the mystique that non-pilots accord aviators. He had walked this stretch countless times before, but he was self-conscious about it this morning.

Chief Master Sgt. Joe Lopez, the boss of *Air Force One*'s guards, saluted Albertazzie as he approached the front boarding stairs. Albertazzie handed him copies of the manifest bearing the names of all persons who would be on the flight.

"We've already got some people on board," Lopez said. "I checked with the office first to see if they were okay."

Albertazzie nodded approval and climbed up the stairs. Co-pilot Les McClelland was already in the cockpit. The two flight engineers, Chief Master Sgts. Joe Chappell and Danny Daniels, were busily loading the inertial navigation system, putting in the coordinates of the various checkpoints on the ground that the plane would traverse as it crossed the country.

Chappell took Albertazzie's pilot case and placed it in its customary position to the left of the pilot's seat. He took Albertazzie's headset and plugged it in. Albertazzie noted that the instrument approach plates already were in the holder on the pilot's wheel. The navigation charts had been folded and placed in their retainer at the pilot's right knee. Chappell had computed all the airplane performance data and had put the information on the TOLD (Take-off and Landing Data) card; it was in place near the flight instruments. McClelland had verified the computations.

Albertazzie was proud of his crew. He had picked them himself, and they had been forged into an organized, disciplined, highly professional team. They were the best in the Air Force, and once again they had justified his pride in them. With everything going smoothly up front, he went out to check the rest of the airplane.

Chief flight steward Charles Palmer and Staff Sgt. Terry Yamada were setting up the food service in the front galley, which served the First Family.

"What's for lunch?" Albertazzie asked.

"Roast beef, sir," replied Palmer.

33

Across the aisle in the communications center, the teletypes were clacking furiously. Master Sgts. "Van" Van Valkenburg and Ray Johnson, headsets on, were readying the plane's electronic and avionic equipment, the autopilot, the telephones, the navigation aids, and the air-to-ground communications systems. Johnson looked up and said, "The President is on television—in the stateroom."

The presidential suite, designed to Nixon's tastes, dominated the forward section of *Air Force One*. It was laid out in the manner of a railroad compartment and consisted of three rooms, the first one for the President, then a sitting room for the First Lady, and, to the rear of a lavatory, the lounge or conference room. To ensure privacy, the entire suite could be bypassed by an aisle running along the left side of the plane.

The door into the President's private office—designated by the gold and blue presidential seal—was open. Albertazzie entered and found all in readiness. The desk was polished. Atop was a fresh pad of yellow paper, a briar pipe Nixon liked to smoke occasionally, plus a pouch of the tobacco mixture put up for him by Garfinckel's, the Washington tobacconist.

The President's leather chair, facing forward, was matched by another on the other side of the desk. Each chair could swivel, recline, slide forward and back or laterally toward the right wall.

Although Nixon rarely invited more than one person into his office at a time, there was a sofa for three along the right wall. The couch, like the one in the First Lady's room, could be converted into a single bed. But Albertazzie could not remember that Nixon had ever used it for more than a brief nap. In the five and a half years of his presidency, Nixon had never traveled overnight in the plane. He preferred to stop en route if it was a long trip.

Albertazzie inspected the lighting options, the table lamps, and desk and reading spotlights, all controlled from a switch panel to the right of the presidential chair. At fingertip level there was a panel for operating a stereo music system. The President could listen to any available radio station simply by asking the communicators to tune him in. While there was no built-in television set in the Nixon office—he never watched it in flight anyway—the plane carried four portable sets that could be plugged in there and at other locations aboard. A white telephone rested on the right of Nixon's desk. Thanks to satellite communication, he could talk to any place on earth.

Master Sgt. Lee Simmons, the President's personal steward, had done his usual good job of anticipating the First Family's needs. The latest magazines and the day's newspapers were in Mrs. Nixon's compartment. So were several ash trays and an ample supply of cigarettes.

Mrs. Nixon refrained from lighting up in public, but aboard *Air Force One* she smoked incessantly. That was one of the little secrets she shared with the crew. Sometimes, after a flight, the stewards good-naturedly counted the butts to see who had consumed the most cigarettes—Mrs. Nixon or the President's chain-smoking physician, Major Gen. Walter Tkach. The doctor invariably won, but not by much.

Albertazzie checked out the lavatory, too, but Simmons had put it in spotless condition. He knew Albertazzie was a nitpicker about airplane cleanliness.

Simmons was standing inside the lounge, near the doorway, when Albertazzie came in. A large color television set was mounted on the forward wall in a recess above a clothing compartment. Like the other sets on the airplane, it was a Sony, but the nameplate had been removed. Although the Sony was considered superior to American makes, the White House did not want to call attention to the fact that *Air Force One* sported Japanese television sets.

Simmons was watching the President on television. Nixon was winding up his farewell remarks to the staff. Diane Sawyer and Anne Grier, two of Ron Ziegler's press assistants, were sitting on the lounge's couch. They had been crying. Albertazzie glanced quickly about and moved on to check the remaining compartments for the staff. He noted another exception to this flight. There would be no pool of news correspondents aboard.

In the rear galley, he gave a copy of the passenger manifest and seating plan to Master Sgt. Russ Reid and his assistant stewards, Master Sgt. John Haynes and Staff Sgt. John Palmer. Then Albertazzie put on his hat and clambered down the rear stairs to the ground. Master Sgt. Bill Kimmer and Tech. Sgt. Willie Hill, two Air Force guards, were stationed there along with a Secret

Service agent. They went over the manifest together, Albertazzie verifying the names of those already on the plane and those who would arrive shortly with Nixon.

Standing there beneath the plane, he gave the underside a quick once-over, wing tip to wing tip, tail to nose, looking for anything unusual. It was a cursory inspection. He had done it hundreds, maybe thousands, of times. The ground crew had done its job, too. Nothing was amiss.

Albertazzie strolled back to the fence that separated the terminal from the field and determined which Secret Service agent was in charge of airport security for the President's departure. Consistent with Nixon's order, several predeparture arrangements had been canceled.

For once, there would be no "press fence." It was a mobile affair that formed a box fifty feet square, and it was customarily rolled into place near the front stairs that the President and ranking passengers use to enter or leave *Air Force One*. Inside the barricade, guarded by Secret Service and Air Police, members of the news services and networks were herded to perform their duties of observing the President's departure or arrival, and reporting any remarks he might make. The box is an elaborate one, complete with telephone lines, electric power plugs for cameras and microphones, and, if necessary, for floodlights at night.

Nixon was not fond of reporters but press coverage of *Air Force One* ceremonies was useful to him. At Andrews, arrangements provided by the Air Force were superior to those at any other field in the world.

Today, however, the press would not be useful to Nixon; so they were "dis-invited." Similarly, the small box for VIPs was dispensed with. The customary contingent of Andrews brass would not be gathered to see Nixon off.

Albertazzie returned to the plane and went directly to the flight deck.

"How are we doing?" he asked.

"We're ready to start engines," Chappell said.

It was nearly ten o'clock, the scheduled departure time. Albertazzie went back to the lounge to see how Nixon's farewell speech was progressing. Diane Sawyer and Anne Grier were still crying. The President seemed to be winding it up. Tears were in his eyes too.

Albertazzie watched silently until Nixon concluded. Then he went up to the cockpit and took the pilot's seat.

"He ought to be on the way soon," Albertazzie advised McClelland. He asked the co-pilot to notify the Andrews ground controller in the tower.

"Andrews, *Air Force One*," McClelland spoke into his mike.

"Roger, *Air Force One*."

"It looks like about a fifteen-minute delay for us this morning. Over."

"Roger, *Air Force One*. Call when ready to taxi."

"Roger," acknowledged McClelland, flipping off the radio switch.

There was nothing to do now but wait for the White House signal board to flash word that Nixon was en route.

The President, accompanied by his family, was escorted by the Secret Service and a few key aides from the East Room to the Diplomatic Reception Room downstairs. Pat Nixon thought it was one of the cheeriest in the White House, especially when morning sunlight bathed the south front of the mansion.

Gerald and Betty Ford were waiting to say goodbye.

Nixon grasped Ford's hand and their eyes met. "Well, Mr. President," Nixon said to Ford, "Good luck. I know you'll do a fine job."

Mrs. Ford put her hand on Nixon's arm and groped for a parting word. "Have a good flight, Dick," she said. Impulsively, she reached for Mrs. Nixon and hugged her.

Mrs. Nixon did not respond, but closed her eyes tightly for a moment. Then she clasped the hands of several weeping staff members.

Nixon stepped back from Ford and looked around. "Well, it's time to go," he said in a loud voice.

He took Mrs. Nixon's elbow and they led everybody out to the South Portico and down the red carpet across the lawn, past the honor guard, to the waiting Army helicopter.

Suddenly, about ten o'clock, in the cockpit of *Air Force One*, the communications loudspeaker blared: "All cars and stations, Signal, five and nine Charlie! All cars and stations, Signal, five and nine Charlie!"

It was the White House signal board, alerting everyone who monitored the frequencies that the President had physically left the White House and was going to another point. It might be Camp David, Andrews Air Force Base, a speech site in Washington, anyplace. Whenever or whatever the occasion, the Secret Service would instantly notify the White House Communications Agency (WHCA, usually pronounced "Wahcah"). It, in turn, would immediately put out the preliminary notice of a presidential exit from 1600 Pennsylvania Avenue. "Charlie" designated the main FM communication channel for further conversation. The message also told everyone not involved to stay off that channel except for emergency calls.

At 10:06, the speaker blared again. "All cars and stations, Signal—depart, depart!" The President's helicopter was lifting off the White House lawn.

Ray Johnson, the *Air Force One* communicator, came on the intercom to Albertazzie in the cockpit. "We have a departure," he confirmed. Nixon was on his way to the airport. He would be there in eight minutes.

"Thanks, Ray," Albertazzie replied.

"Sir?" It was Johnson again. "Sir, Mr. Haldeman called and asked to speak to the President the minute he arrives here. What should I do?"

"Don't bother the President," Albertazzie ordered. "Give the message to Ziegler or Bull when they arrive. Let them decide."

Albertazzie marveled at Haldeman's audacity. It was fifteen months since he had run the White House staff, but he kept in touch with people there. Haldeman must have something important on his mind to call Nixon from California at a time like this. Could it be about a Watergate pardon for himself? Rumors of that had been in the papers. But Albertazzie didn't feel he owed Haldeman any special favors. So let him talk to the staff, just as he used to insist everyone else had to do. Albertazzie relished the irony.

He glanced out the cockpit window to his left. There was a lot of activity along the fence as word of the President's imminent arrival traveled up and down the line. Agents closed the gates to the field. Air Police stopped vehicle traffic on the terminal ramp. In the Andrews tower, the ground controller halted aircraft movement on the field.

The base operations duty officer and senior Secret Service agent began their customary final sweep of the runway in an Air Force station wagon, checking for debris or anything suspicious. Meanwhile Air Police with dogs patrolled the wooded area near the taxiways. All across the field, at predetermined locations, other Air Police waited in their vehicles.

Fire trucks, ambulances with medical personnel, and other rescue equipment were in position to assist in case of an emergency. An evacuation helicopter hovered near the end of the runway to lend assistance if a crash occurred during takeoff.

All eyes in the cockpit, Albertazzie's included, kept scanning the western horizon for the first glimpse of the President's chopper, *Army One*. Flight engineer Daniels was the first to spot it.

"There he is," said Daniels, pointing west of the tower. Nixon was closer than expected.

Army One passed south of the tower and swung around to make its final approach in a northerly direction. That would bring it parallel to *Air Force One*, but off to the right about 300 yards to the helicopter landing zone marked with a crosshatch.

The chopper's pilot, Lt. Col. Gene Boyer, set the wheels on the runway and made a left turn toward *Air Force One*. The ramp coordinator was standing near the 'copter's assigned parking spot, his arms upraised.

The big olive green and white Sikorsky whirred to a stop about a hundred feet to the left of the airplane's nose. The ramp coordinator clenched his fists. The big rotor blades began slowing as Boyer applied the brakes.

In the picture window on the left side of the helicopter, Nixon was now visible. So was his daughter Tricia, Ron Ziegler, Steve Bull, and the accompanying pair of Secret Service men.

Brig. Gen. Clarence Douglas, commander of the First Composite Wing at Andrews, walked briskly toward the door of the helicopter. It swung down, forming a short stairway to the ground. An Army sergeant bounded out, snapped to attention, and froze in a salute. Mrs. Nixon was the first passenger to descend, followed by Tricia. Several minutes elapsed. The President was struggling to regain his composure. Then he, too, appeared in the doorway, followed by a Secret Service agent.

As Nixon stepped onto the concrete, he held out his hand to Douglas. The surprised general abandoned his salute and thrust out his own hand. They shook quickly and the President, scarcely pausing, moved on toward *Air Force One*.

Sensing Nixon's haste, the rest of the passengers—Dr. Tkach, Manolo Sanchez, Nixon's valet, and the remaining aides—hurtled out of the rear helicopter door and broke into a trot toward the plane's stairway. They bounded aboard ahead of the First Family and quickly moved down the aisle toward the rear of the craft.

Mrs. Nixon glanced up silently at Albertazzie as she boarded. The pilot waited for the President's customary nod of recognition and greeting. Today there was none.

Nixon, the last aboard, paused for a moment at the top of the stairs, and flung a quick wave—the familiar arms-uplifted double V wave—to the small crowd at the fence. Then he moved on to his private compartment, ignoring Daniels' "Good morning, sir."

As soon as the President's foot had touched the boarding stairs, Albertazzie had barked an order to McClelland: "Start three." The co-pilot depressed the start switch for the number three engine. The air valve opened and Albertazzie could hear the swish of air through the motor. "Rotation!" McClelland called back.

"Start four," Albertazzie said. Again the swish of air, McClelland's "Rotation!" and the jump of the tachometer needle on the console. The two jet engines on the right wing were idling perfectly.

Behind him, Albertazzie heard Daniels close the cabin door and lock it. He glanced out to his left. The mobile stairs were clearing the left wing. Over the interphone, he heard communicator Van Valkenburg saying, "Remove telephones, remove telephones." He had established his air-to-ground link.

Albertazzie passed the signal outside to Master Sgt. Freeman Klier, the ground crew chief, by pointing his left thumb down. Klier relayed the signal to a crewman under the nose, who disconnected the external telephone and emerged to display the lines and his headset.

"Start number one and two," Albertazzie ordered. McClelland depressed the starter switches simultaneously. Outside, Klier tossed a salute, indicating all was clear. Albertazzie released the brakes and the plane rolled forward.

40

McClelland spoke into his microphone to ground control. *"Air Force One* taxiing."

"Roger, *Air Force One,*" came the reply.

Albertazzie glanced at the time. It was 10:15 plus thirty seconds. Only a minute had passed since Nixon left the helicopter. Everything was going beautifully. As he taxied east and then south toward the runway, Albertazzie and the flight crew ran through their predeparture checklists. No problems.

McClelland contacted the tower, which came back instantly:

"Air Force One, cleared for takeoff. Contact Departure Control one-nineteen-seven when airborne. Best wishes to the President."

"Roger," McClelland said.

Albertazzie had been steadily increasing power from the moment the plane moved onto the runway. As he neared the limit of the thrust lever, he called out, "Max power!" and released the brakes. Instantly, *Air Force One* began gathering speed—eighty knots, one hundred knots. With a gentleness surprising for such a powerfully built man, he eased back on the yoke and lifted the big Boeing off the runway. *Air Force One* was airborne at 10:17. Richard Nixon had begun his final flight as President of the United States.

With Nixon gone, the White House seethed with anticipation of a new President.

Vice President and Mrs. Ford had gone directly to Ford's old suite in the Executive Office Building, overlooking the White House grounds. While she rested, he chatted briefly with close aides, gulped a cup of coffee, lit his pipe, and settled down to polish the speech he would give after the swearing-in ceremonies.

In the now-deserted East Room, custodians busily rearranged the chairs for that event. In the Oval Office, unused since Nixon's televised address the night before, the presidential desk was carefully dusted and rubbed to a high gloss under the eyes of a Secret Service agent.

The White House pressroom was roaring with excitement. Reporters, photographers, and camera crews were wall to wall. Nixon's farewell talk had been transmitted; now the press noisily awaited the next news events—Ford's taking office, his

41

speech, and whatever else an incoming President might do on his first day.

Conversation in the cockpit was unusually muted. Ordinarily on such trips, Albertazzie, McClelland, and Chappell whiled away the hours with lighthearted banter, swapping golf and fishing yarns, tips on good restaurants in southern California, and stories about their families. Today there was none of that. Nobody wanted to talk. They concentrated instead on the routine business of the flight, and between chores they fell into silent contemplation.

Albertazzie found himself reflecting on his five and a half years as presidential pilot. They had been good years, he decided. He had often told press interviewers that flying *Air Force One* was "the best job in the Air Force." He had meant it, too, in spite of all the guff and petty harassment he had received from the Nixon staff at the White House, especially in the last few years. He liked the excitement, the glamor, the prestige, the fun of traveling the world with the President of the United States. And he had acquired many new friends, too, particularly around San Clemente and Key Biscayne, where Nixon had flown frequently for extended stays.

It sometimes seemed as if Nixon were perpetually airborne. When he returned June 19 from his Middle East trip aboard *Air Force One*, Nixon had chalked up another of those "historic firsts" he loved to brag about. He had visited more countries—28—and traveled more miles outside the United States—137,500—than any previous President.

In addition to his foreign travels, Nixon had been constantly on the go between Washington and his homes in California and Florida, not to mention the campaign swing of 1972. The past year had been unusually busy for *Air Force One*, even by Nixon's peripatetic standards. Five days after the Mideast trip, Albertazzie had flown Nixon to Moscow, his second visit there in two years. On July 12, Nixon had gone west again to California, remaining at Casa Pacifica and the Western White House until July 28. And now, eleven days later, this flight.

The route was one Albertazzie had selected early in the Nixon presidency as the best between Washington and San Clemente.

It was almost a straight line, taking *Air Force One* over central West Virginia, past Cincinnati, St. Louis, Wichita, and Liberal, Kansas; on to Gallup, New Mexico, over Palm Springs, California, and then an easy approach and landing at El Toro Marine Corps Air Station near Santa Anna. It was the shortest route, therefore the swiftest, and it avoided most of the heavy air traffic over the big commercial terminals between the east and west coasts.

An hour out of Washington, *Air Force One* was 35,000 feet over Ohio and cruising flawlessly at 600 miles an hour. Albertazzie decided it was time to check into the "tempo" of the trip. What was happening behind the cockpit? What was the cabin temperature? Who was telephoning the plane? Who on board was calling out? How was lunch coming along? While ordinarily he would be wondering if everybody was happy, this time he wondered if they at least were comfortable. That was part of the responsibility of a presidential pilot.

There were thirty-four passengers. Albertazzie and his crew knew most of them. Four were members of the First Family— the President, Mrs. Nixon, daughter Tricia, and husband Eddie Cox. Daughter Julie, the President's staunchest defender, and her husband, David Eisenhower, had remained in Washington where David was attending school.

Fourteen on the passenger list were Secret Service agents being assigned to protective duty with the soon-to-be-former President. There were two military clerks, two baggage handlers, plus a couple of valets to assist Manolo and Fina Sanchez, the Nixons' personal servants. The rest were White House staffers going to California to assist in Nixon's transition to private life. Besides his doctor, Major Gen. Walter Tkach, they included Ron Ziegler, Steve Bull, Marine Lt. Col. Jack Brennan, the military aide, three secretaries—Jeanne Quinlin, Diane Sawyer, Anne Grier—and the White House photographer, Ollie Atkins.

Albertazzie made his first "tempo" check with Van Valkenburg, the aircraft's veteran communicator. The trip had begun differently, it turned out, even while *Air Force One* was on the ground at Andrews. There was no black box aboard—the closely guarded box containing that secret set of codes that only a President could activate in event of a nuclear attack. If ever our radar

43

or satellites detected incoming nuclear missiles, a Commander-in-Chief would have about fifteen minutes before the enemy rockets would strike. In that time, he could select one of several forms of nuclear retaliation. The black box, carried by a military aide, ordinarily was never far from the president's hands. It traveled with him wherever he went—even to Peking and Moscow.

Whenever the president boarded *Air Force One*, the black box customarily would be entrusted to Van Valkenburg, who would place it for safe-keeping in a specially provided safe in the communications section, just forward of the President's compartment. Whenever the President left the plane, the military aide would retrieve it from Van Valkenburg.

Just before he went on television the previous evening, Nixon had met in the Cabinet Room with a group of his most loyal supporters in Congress to apprise them in advance of his decision to quit. Those present remember Nixon reminiscing over his foreign policy successes and warning of the dangers for America that still lurked in the world.

"As I am winging my way to California tomorrow," they quoted him as saying, "I will still have the black box aboard the plane up to the moment of transition."

But the top secret file had not accompanied Nixon this morning when he entered *Air Force One*. Lt. Col. Brennan had nothing to hand to Van Valkenburg for safekeeping.

Its absence brought to mind a controversial news report that had surfaced three days before in Washington. There had been considerable concern that the embattled Commander-in-Chief might try to use the military establishment to retain his office or create a pseudo-emergency. To forestall any such eventuality, Secretary of Defense James Schlesinger had warned all military commands to accept no direct orders from the White House or from any other source without the countersignature of the Defense Secretary himself.

Thus, in the final few hours of his presidency, winging westward aboard *Air Force One*, Richard Nixon's constitutional power as Commander-in-Chief had already been emasculated. He no longer held the ultimate authority to decide America's response to any national security emergency that might arise in the waning moments of his presidency. That power, without his knowledge, had already shifted to Vice President Ford back at the White House. The black box was there, not with the President.

About eleven o'clock, Van Valkenburg came on the interphone to inform Albertazzie that Bob Haldeman was still trying to talk to Nixon. Haldeman had twice telephoned the White House. The signal board had put him through to the airplane. As instructed, Van Valkenburg had given both calls to Ron Ziegler in the staff compartment. The President had not talked to Haldeman.

Albertazzie flipped up the switch on his own jackbox in the cockpit to monitor the communications link with the ground. He heard Diane Sawyer talking to a tearful secretary back in the White House press office.

"You can't imagine what's happening," the distraught voice was saying. "They're literally throwing us out. It's awful."

Moments later, Ziegler put through a call to Gerald Warren, the deputy press secretary who had remained behind to handle the press transition from Ziegler to Jerry terHorst, Ford's man. Warren confirmed that some of the incoming President's press aides and secretaries already were moving into some of the desks, even though Ford had not yet taken the oath of office.

"That's contrary to my understanding," Ziegler fumed. "For Christ's sake, we're still President!"

"I know," Warren acknowledged, "but what is there to do?" TerHorst, he said, was not there. He was waiting in the EOB with the other Ford transition men.

At 11:35, a brief letter on White House stationery was handed to Secretary of State Kissinger. It was Richard Nixon's resignation. In accordance with the Constitution, the way was now officially clear for the installation of a new President, the thirty-eighth in America's history, the first ever selected under the emergency provisions of the Twenty-fifth Amendment.

At 11:35, *Air Force One* was moving flawlessly at 35,000 feet, eight miles northwest of Salem, Illinois, about 82 miles east of

45

St. Louis, Missouri. Shortly after crossing the Mississippi River, the plane encountered air turbulence. With lunch hour approaching and wishing to avoid any further buffeting of his passengers, Albertazzie took the plane up to 39,000 feet. There he found smooth air.

Things were not so smooth among the passengers.

"It's really quite sad back in the lounge and the staff area," steward Lee Simmons reported to the cockpit. "People are crying."

Usually the Nixon staff had plenty of work to do aboard. Today there was little of that; there was almost nothing that could be done except reflect on the past—which was too painful—or look ahead to the next day at San Clemente—which loomed empty and bleak.

Steve Bull, long the keeper of the door to Nixon's Oval Office, slumped deep in his seat. He felt drained, emotionally and physically spent. Loyal to Nixon, yet without the burning personal ambition that drove so many of the other clean-shaven young Nixon aides, Bull tried to manage an air of detachment. He signaled a steward for the first of several stiff drinks.

Jack Brennan, Nixon's Marine aide, was still wearing his dress white uniform, resplendent with the gold braid of his office. To others aboard, it seemed to be a defiant display of his devotion to the 37th President of the United States. Colonel Brennan, too, was exhausted, but he was also angry and bitter over the events that had led to this moment.

He had wanted Nixon to stay on, to tough it out, to tell the opposition to go to hell. But now they were here, aboard *Air Force One*, retreating westward to California. Well, to hell with Washington. Deep in his heart, Jack Brennan knew he would stay with Nixon as long as the President wanted him.

Ron Ziegler had a hard time remaining in his seat. On past trips, there always had been so much that needed doing. Presidential statements had to be drafted, revised, edited, and run through the photocopy machine. There were schedules to review and policy positions to be gone over with Haig, Kissinger, or the President. And, of course, the half dozen members of the White House press pool, quartered in the rear of the plane, always expected to be briefed on what was happening aboard or was likely to occur upon landing.

But now there was none of that to do. Nobody was expecting anything further from this President. All the action, all the attention was centered back in Washington, at the White House, on the incoming President.

On Nixon's orders, Ziegler had dropped the usual press contingent from the *Air Force One* manifest; Secret Service agents were occupying the correspondents' seats on this trip. Nor was there any "press plane," the chartered aircraft that the White House press customarily employed to convey reporters accompanying a traveling Chief Executive.

Ziegler snorted pleasurably. The press wouldn't have Nixon to kick around any longer. And from now on Ziegler wouldn't have to worry about doing those Godawful daily White House news briefings.

The calls from Haldeman roused Ziegler from his musings. Nixon's former chief aide, unexpectedly blocked from talking to the President at the White House, was doggedly determined to get through to him now. It was Haldeman's final chance to obtain a presidential pardon that could erase his criminal indictment.

Ziegler did as he had been ordered. *I'm sorry, Bob,* he found himself telling his old mentor. *Sorry, but the President is not taking any calls. That's right, Bob. I can't put you through. I know it's rough. But that's the way it is, Bob. You understand. The President? Yeah, he's bearing up, but it's been tough, real tough. Sure, Bob, sure. You hang in there too.*

Ziegler handled Haldeman's second call the same way.

Edward Cox emerged from Mrs. Nixon's compartment, where he and Tricia had been sitting with the First Lady. He was relieved the ordeal was over.

Cox had never relished the White House spotlight, not even in the good times. Neither had Tricia. The unremitting public attention on the First Family had a way of imprisoning each of its members. And the disasters of the last few months had been grinding, psychologically and physically. Perhaps now, out in California, they could gain some much-needed privacy and be-

47

gin anew to rebuild their lives. At Mrs. Nixon's urging, he and Tricia had agreed to stay for a while in San Clemente to keep them company and to assist in the transition, the decompression from life in the White House to life on the Pacific shore. He strolled back to the staff compartment.

The sight of the President's son-in-law reminded Bull of the work they planned to do on the plane. During the last few days, Cox had been assisting Rex Scouten, the boss of the White House domestic staff, in packing up the Nixon belongings and separating the family's things from those that were owned by the government. The sorting had been incomplete. The packing had been done in great haste. Bull, meanwhile, had taken on the task of gathering up the President's personal effects, the memorabilia, books, and other materials from the Oval Office and his private study in the West Wing, as well as from his office in the EOB.

"Let me bring you up to speed on where things stand," Bull told Cox.

He had an inventory of the presidential items in the belly of *Air Force One*, as well as what probably would be arriving later from Washington. Nixon would need some things immediately at his home in San Clemente. Other things could be held in storage, in Washington or in California, until the Nixon library was built. Since Cox was going to remain in California indefinitely, he would be the family member responsible for coordinating the process with the Ford White House.

"I'm quitting," Bull said to no one in particular. "I'm going to see if I can make a living out there in the cold cruel world." A steward replenished his drink.

Shortly before noon, Sgt. Simmons was called to the President's private compartment. He entered not knowing quite what to say—or what to expect.

"Is that clock right?" Nixon asked, pointing to the wall. There were three digital clocks for the President's convenience, one that showed Washington time, another with the local time on the earth below, and a third that gave the time at *Air Force One*'s destination point, in this instance, California.

"Yes, sir," Simmons assured him. "It's exactly right." It was

48

a few minutes before twelve back at the White House. Ford's swearing-in ceremonies were about to begin.

Simmons busied himself momentarily, straightening up things for the President he had served for the last four years. Nixon was still wearing his blue suit coat. He had not put on the comfortable red houndstooth sport jacket he kept aboard *Air Force One* for leisurely moments. He looked weary to Simmons, but not nearly so drawn and haggard as he had appeared on television from the White House a couple of hours earlier. He seemed quite composed, even relaxed. Simmons marveled to himself and quickly launched into the little speech he had steeled himself to say.

"Mr. President," he began, "I'm really sad about all this and I hope you and Mrs. Nixon and the fam—."

"Now, Lee," Nixon interrupted, "I've been wanting to tell you how much I appreciate all the good care and all the nice things you've done for me and Pat."

The President kept talking, pleasantly, almost cheerily. Simmons was astounded.

Just remember, Nixon was saying, *just remember that tomorrow is a new day. You can't let things get you down. You can't stay down, you have to pick yourself up and keep going. Life goes on.*

Later when he recounted the conversation to Albertazzie, Simmons couldn't get over it. "I went in to cheer him up, but there he was, cheering me up instead. Life goes on."

Nixon summoned the steward a second time. "Can I get you anything, sir?" Simmons asked.

"I think I'd like a martini," the President said. "Ask Ron to come in. Better fix one for him, too. After that I'll have my lunch."

Simmons went out to do the President's bidding, closing the door behind him.

Nixon was a light drinker on *Air Force One*, and rarely had any liquor in the middle of the day. When he did indulge, he usually asked for scotch. His favorite was a thirty-year-old Ballantine. The White House regularly sent out a bottle or two to be kept aboard the aircraft. But Bebe Rebozo liked martinis and whenever the President's friend from Florida was aboard, Nixon would join in. Often the two would go into the presidential lounge, more spacious than Nixon's private compartment. There they could put up their feet and relax.

Chief steward Chuck Palmer fashioned the martinis with a practiced hand. Two chilled glasses packed with ice. A whisper of dry vermouth. Then gin to the brim and twists of lemon peel, rubbed lightly around the edges and deftly dropped atop the ice. A quick stir and onto a silver tray bearing the monogram AIR FORCE ONE.

Simmons picked up the tray and returned to the President's compartment. Ziegler was already there. Simmons informed them that the communications section had selected a good, clear radio channel over which they could hear the presidential installation ceremonies at the White House. He adjusted the sound system for Nixon, served the martinis, and departed. The digital clock blinked steadily on toward noon.

In the East Room, everybody was waiting for Ford.

The Speaker of the House, the Democratic and Republican leaders of both House and Senate, and dozens of Ford's old friends in Congress had gathered to witness the oath taking. Most of the others who crowded the ornate chamber were cabinet officers and senior government officials who had served Nixon and would now serve the new President. The Fords' four children waited intently in the front row, as their parents entered.

The Vice President and Mrs. Ford took their places on the same podium and before the same television cameras that had displayed the Nixon family to the nation just two hours earlier. Chief Justice Warren Burger, who had flown back hurriedly from Europe by military jet, stood before the microphones to administer the oath of office. Gerald Ford put his hand on the Bible held by his wife and soberly repeated the lines from the Constitution that had been uttered by each of his thirty-seven predecessors, including Nixon:

"I do solemnly swear that I will faithfully execute the office of President of the United States, and will to the best of my ability, preserve, protect, and defend the Constitution of the United States."

50

Then the new President began a brief and moving speech to the nation:

"My fellow Americans, our long national nightmare is over. Our Constitution works; our great Republic is a government of laws and not of men. . . . May our former President, who brought peace to millions, find it for himself. . . ."

Co-pilot Les McClelland's earphones were tuned to the same radio channel that carried the voices of the Chief Justice and Gerald Ford into the passenger compartments of *Air Force One*. As Ford finished his oath of office, McClelland punched the "position hold" button of the inertial navigation system, marking for history the precise location of the aircraft.

The position was 38° 35.5′ N, 92° 26.6′ W. *Air Force One* was 39,000 feet over a point thirteen miles southwest of Jefferson City, Missouri. The time was three minutes and twenty-five seconds past noon.

Nixon and Ziegler finished their martinis.

Albertazzie picked up his microphone and spoke to ground control:

"Kansas City, this was *Air Force One*. Will you change our call sign to SAM 27000?"

Back came the reply: "Roger, SAM 27000. Good luck to the President."

"Roger, 27000."

It was done. Richard Nixon was now the nation's only living former President. He was now a guest aboard an airplane on loan from President Ford.

Steward Terry Yamada came into the cockpit moments later. "Ready to eat?" he asked.

"Fine," said Albertazzie. "Start feeding everyone else but hold mine. I'm going to take a walk through the plane."

He slipped on his jacket and moved aft. In the forward galley, chief steward Chuck Palmer was putting the final touches on lunch: shrimp cocktail, prime ribs, baked potato, green beans, tossed salad, rolls, and coffee, tea, or milk. Dessert would be cheesecake.

The door to the President's compartment was closed. Nixon

and Ziegler were still together. Mrs. Nixon and Tricia were in the First Lady's compartment. Albertazzie passed the lounge and entered the staff section. Ed Cox, Steve Bull, and Jack Brennan were discussing arrangements for transferring Nixon's effects to his home at San Clemente.

Albertazzie reminded Brennan that the plane and its crew were under orders to return to Washington later in the day. "How much ground time do you figure you'll need at El Toro?" he asked the military aide.

"Well, we'll have to unload the plane and transport all the family's personal belongings to Casa Pacifica," said Brennan. Supervising that task would be the responsibility of Master Sgt. Herb Oldenburg, *Air Force One*'s baggage manager. "When Oldenburg gets that done and returns to the plane, why, you'll be free to depart," Brennan told Albertazzie.

Albertazzie did a quick calculation. The plane would land at noon, Pacific time. Four hours on the ground ought to be sufficient to accomplish everything that needed to be done. Allowing five hours flying time, and taking into account the fact that Washington was three hours ahead on the clock, it would be nearly midnight in the East when the plane returned to Andrews Air Force Base.

"What do you plan to do about all the 'Richard Nixon' items in our inventory at Andrews?" he asked Brennan. Albertazzie was referring to the stock of ash trays, candy dishes, playing cards, matchbooks, cocktail napkins, and notepads, all imprinted "Richard Nixon," that were customarily distributed around the plane. Presidential guests, even high-ranking officials and members of Congress, loved to pocket them as status symbols.

"Somebody back at the White House, probably Bill Gulley, will have to arrange to ship them out to us," Brennan told him. "I don't think the Ford bunch will want them."

Tricia came out of the First Lady's compartment and ordered lunch for her mother from Lee Simmons—"something light." She said Mrs. Nixon would be eating with Ed and herself, and asked that her mother's tray be brought into the lounge where they would be sitting.

Simmons was momentarily sorry to hear that. He had been

52

waiting for Mrs. Nixon's call. She had always been pleasant to him and frequently took time to chat. Simmons had been hoping he would have a chance to talk to her on this flight, to wish her well for the future. Now he might not have that private moment. Perhaps one would arise before the trip was over.

Steve Bull was amused by Ziegler. The press secretary had ordered his secretarial assistants to obtain the verbatim text of Ford's speech in the East Room. He wanted it immediately. Diane Sawyer and Anne Grier were on the phone to the White House press office, taking it down in shorthand and typing it up in transcript form at the typing stations in the rear of the staff compartment.

The whole exercise struck Bull as ironic. Who could care now, aboard this dismal plane, what Jerry Ford was saying back in Washington? Why did the girls have to work so furiously? What bothered Bull was that Ziegler was carrying on as though things still mattered, as though Richard Nixon were still President and still had to know instantly what was transpiring someplace else. Bull wondered how much longer the charade would continue.

For Ziegler, the need for a Ford transcript was eminently practical. The Air Force advance agent at El Toro had gotten word to the plane that Citizen Nixon could expect to find a large and friendly crowd when he landed in California.

The news pleased Ziegler. It pleased Nixon even more. He would take the time to give a short speech there, perhaps the last one he would make in public for some time. It would not be a direct response to the Ford speech at the White House, but it still would be an important moment, on camera and before the press, for Richard Nixon. Ziegler wanted Nixon to know exactly what Ford had said—and how he had said it.

Ziegler was in the aisle when Albertazzie finished talking with Brennan. "Who's flying this airplane?" he joked.

Albertazzie told Ziegler of the plane's geographic position at the time Ford was sworn in. "We're now called SAM 27000," he added. Ziegler nodded without commenting. Albertazzie turned to complete his stroll through the rest of the plane when something up front caught his eye.

53

It was Nixon. He had left his private compartment and was coming down the aisle into the staff section.

He was wearing the same attire he had worn all day: a dark slate-blue suit with a white shirt and a red-and-blue patterned tie. He looked strained, but he was smiling and rolling his hands together, one over the other. Albertazzie had seen him do that a thousand times before.

Nixon glanced around at all of them—Brennan, Ziegler, Bull, Cox, and Albertazzie.

"Well!" he exclaimed, rolling his hands. "Is everybody enjoying the trip?"

No one spoke. Nixon looked at Albertazzie.

"Ralph," he said, "when we get to El Toro I'd like some pictures. You know, me and the crew. Then I'd like some of Mrs. Nixon and me and the crew, and of Mrs. Nixon, you and me—and if you've got the time, one of just you and me. Think you can arrange that?"

"Of course, Mr. President," Albertazzie responded.

Nixon kept talking. "I'll have to make some remarks when we get there. And there'll be some people to visit with. But before we get on the helicopter, we'll get some pictures."

Turning to Brennan, he added, "Jack, make sure Ollie [Ollie Atkins, the White House photographer] knows about this. Make sure he gets a lot of pictures."

"Yes, sir!" snapped Brennan, emphasizing the last word in Marine fashion.

Nixon returned to Albertazzie. "Ralph, you know before we went to China, I told you that when we got back, I'd make you a general. I really meant to do that. But like so many other things I meant to do—."

His voice trailed off momentarily, and then came back strongly once again. "I'll just have to leave them all undone. I'm sorry."

"I understand, Mr. President," Albertazzie replied.

Nixon walked back to the VIP lounge in the center of the plane. Albertazzie headed back to the flight deck. Then Nixon, accompanied by Ziegler and Bull, decided to stroll the length of the plane, pausing here and there to speak to members of the staff and the stewards. At the rear, Nixon noted that Secret

54

Service agents were occupying the section usually reserved for members of the White House press pool.

"Well!" he said jocularly. "It certainly smells better back here."

Everyone laughed, including Nixon. Then he turned on his heel and strode back to his private compartment and shut the door. He did not venture out again the rest of the flight.

Strapped up once more in his pilot's seat, Albertazzie got a fill-in from McClelland on the progress of the flight. The plane had just passed over Liberal, Kansas. Gallup, New Mexico, would be next. They were making good time. In fact, they had made up the seventeen minutes lost on departure from Andrews.

Terry Yamada brought in Albertazzie's lunch. As he ate, he thought about the future—his own, not Nixon's. A year before, he had seriously contemplated retirement from the service, particularly after General Lawson had come in as the White House military assistant. Relations between the White House Military Office and Albertazzie's office became strained, unfriendly, and, he felt, quite unprofessional. Lawson seemed to delight in keeping him in the dark about the President's travel plans until the last possible moment. Some of the new rules were petty, childish. Then, too, the Watergate affair had steadily sharpened staff tensions on nearly every flight following Nixon's reelection in 1972. There was a lot of backbiting among the White House people and a lot of nitpicking at members of *Air Force One*'s crew. The Nixon staff had become very hard to please. The "fun" of flying the President had long since disappeared.

But Watergate had kept him on the job, too. Albertazzie felt that his departure during the height of the turmoil would have been misunderstood by the Nixon crowd as well as by the press and the public. He decided he would have to stay on and see it through.

Now, however, with Nixon's resignation, it might be a good time to think about retirement. Besides, President Ford might prefer a new pilot. That was a presidential prerogative, Albertazzie reminded himself.

His reverie was interrupted by a call from the Air Force advance man, Wayne Bradley, at El Toro Marine Air Station.

The weather on the ground was clear, with a westerly wind of 15 knots and a temperature of 82 degrees. The plane would land on runway 34 right. Albertazzie should taxi to the usual parking spot. There was a sizable crowd on hand, Bradley advised. And it was growing.

The call reminded Albertazzie that there had been a noticeable lack of telephone communication between the plane and the ground during the flight. His somber passengers had little to say now, and almost no one on the ground, it seemed, wanted to talk to them. The seat of power was back at the White House, not aboard the plane. It was not *Air Force One* now, only SAM 27000.

The arrival route in California had been worked out with Los Angeles Control Center back in 1970, shortly after Nixon had acquired the San Clemente property. The approach began at Thermal, just north of the Salton Sea, proceeded on a southwesterly course to Oceanside, and then on a northwesterly leg up the coastline and into El Toro Marine Air Station. The route kept the presidential plane away from the high-density approach and departure corridors of Los Angeles International Airport. From Thermal, it was a gradual, continuous descent until the wheels touched the runway at El Toro. Albertazzie had traversed it often. It was as familiar as his own driveway back home.

Still, the smooth landing of a Boeing 707, a man-made bird weighing 105 tons, is not something to be done with one hand on the wheel and an elbow on the window ledge. In good weather or bad, in daylight or dark, the task calls for the utmost coordination of human skill with the aircraft's electronic guidance systems. Albertazzie and McClelland soon were deeply engaged in that mission.

Eighty miles east of Thermal, Los Angeles Center came on the radio. "Sam 27000, you are cleared to flight level two-four-oh. Descend at pilot's discretion. Advise leaving three-nine-oh."

McClelland acknowledged. Fifty miles from Thermal, Albertazzie slowly retarded the plane's thrust. It began descending from 39,000 feet toward the assigned altitude of 24,000 feet. McClelland spoke into his microphone again:

56

"Los Angeles, SAM 27000 out of three-nine-oh."

"Roger, SAM 27000," replied the ground controller, simultaneously providing a new radio frequency. "Contact Los Angeles Center, one-twenty-three point two. Over."

"Roger, one-twenty-three point two," confirmed McClelland.

So it went, one controller "handing off" the airplane to another with every change in direction and altitude. Each controller change was accompanied by a change in radio frequency.

It was a specialty of Albertazzie's to descend with as little noticeable change in altitude and engine sound as possible. The passengers thus would be almost unaware of any difference in the airplane's angle or speed. Frequently the first indication would be the thump of the landing gear as it moved down into locked position on approach to the runway.

Albertazzie's technique involved retarding the two outboard engines only, plus delicate use of the outboard speed brakes to "spoil" the lift created by the airflow over the wings.

At 15,000 feet, Albertazzie called for the descent checklist. The crew went through its customary briefing on approach procedures. Everything was in order. The plane was passing every checkpoint on time.

As the aircraft flew above Oceanside and out over the Pacific to begin its right turn northerly up the coast toward El Toro, Albertazzie could see San Clemente and Casa Pacifica, Nixon's home. It was built on a promontory overlooking the sea, adjacent to a cluster of stark white Coast Guard buildings that had served Nixon as the Western White House. On the inland side, Albertazzie spotted the large square helipad to which Nixon soon would be flying from El Toro.

Now the Marine Air Station tower was on the horn. "SAM 27000, you are cleared to descend to two thousand five hundred feet and cleared for your approach. The altimeter is three-zero-one-one. Sky is clear, visibility more than one-zero; wind west-northwest at one-five. Report field in sight."

Just off Laguna Beach, Albertazzie could see the Surf 'n Sand Hotel, where the White House press had stayed when covering Nixon in San Clemente. To the right, in the valley, was the Laguna Niguel Country Club. Albertazzie wondered if he would ever play golf there again.

The plane passed the outer marker of the runway approach at 160 miles an hour. The blue marker light began to flash on the cockpit panel. The landing gear was down and locked, the flaps were set at forty degrees.

The plane swooped low over Number Twelve tee on the base golf course. Marine military police had halted auto traffic in both directions on the base road that ran beneath the flight path. SAM 27000 crossed the runway threshold at 140 miles an hour. Albertazzie moved the thrust levers to OFF, slowly eased back on the yoke, and lowered the left wing to counteract a slight crosswind from that direction. The wheels touched down at 125 miles an hour. It was a smooth landing. Richard Nixon was on the ground in California.

Mrs. Nixon was the first of the family to appear in the aisle, followed quickly by Tricia and Ed Cox. As Mrs. Nixon passed steward Lee Simmons, she reached out impulsively and hugged him, saying not a word. Nixon joined the family group in the doorway just as the mobile stairs butted against the fuselage. Danny Daniels stepped back out of the way.

The family quickly deplaned, Nixon pausing on the platform. He lifted his face to the crowd, smiled broadly, and raised both arms high in a waggling V-for-victory greeting.

People cheered, applauded. Some wept. More than 5,000 persons had turned out for Nixon's homecoming. Unlike the closed departure Nixon had decreed from Andrews Air Force Base back at Washington, he had authorized an open arrival at El Toro, something that had occurred infrequently in the past. Many of Nixon's loyal supporters had driven for miles to be on hand, to show they were still behind him, still believed in him.

Nixon came down the plane's stairs, still smiling, savoring the outpouring of sentiment and affection. He shook hands vigorously with El Toro's Marine commander and walked immediately over to the airfield fence to shake more hands, to let the jostling crowd touch him, and to draw strength from their approval.

From under the fuselage, where he had gone to claim his luggage from the already busy baggage handlers, Steve Bull heard something that at first he couldn't believe. He stopped to listen. By God, people were singing "God Bless America!" It had started at one end of the crowd and was spreading, like a spontaneous wave, along the fence to the far side. It wasn't organized, it wasn't overwhelming, and it was off key. But, by God, people were greeting Richard Nixon with a song. And all on their own.

Bull was overcome, for the first time on the trip. The sincerity of the crowd and the singing washed over the anger and the bitterness inside him. Bull pulled himself erect and went busily from one member of the plane crew to another, saying goodbye, saying thanks and good luck, until he came to Lee Simmons. Simmons had been his favorite, the understanding steward who so often had quietly poured bourbon in his white coffee cup whenever Bull needed to escape the Haldeman-Ehrlichman-Haig pressures aboard *Air Force One*. Bull looked at Simmons—and clutched him wordlessly, sobs silently wracking his body.

Now Nixon was standing before the microphones on the ramp. The crowd was hushed, expectant. Behind the crowd, on a raised platform, the television cameras and crews were massed.

"Many statements have been made," he began, "and this is not the time to bore you with another one." Nixon's hands were clasped tightly in front. Mrs. Nixon, impassive as ever, stood on his left. Tricia and Ed Cox were on his right. A soft noontime breeze played with Tricia's blond tresses and ruffled the women's skirts.

"Having completed one task does not mean we will just sit and enjoy this marvelous California climate and do nothing," Nixon was saying.

The crowd broke into prolonged cheering at the mention of California. Nixon, ever mindful of his locale, tried another. He declared that of all the sustaining messages he had received during his five and a half years as president, "believe me, the ones that meant the most were from right here in California."

He talked of America as the land of freedom and opportunity. He talked not at all of Watergate, his tapes, his taxes, the impeachment hearings, or of the resignation that had brought him to this moment in this place.

"With all the time that I have which could be useful, I am going to continue to work for peace among all the world," Nixon

59

vowed. "I intend to continue to work for opportunity and understanding among the people here in America."

He spoke of *Air Force One*, the sleek jet on the ramp behind him, the ultimate symbol of the power and majesty of the president of the United States.

"This great plane that took us to China, to Russia on two occasions, to the Middle East, this great *Spirit of '76* has got to be remembered because of those trips."

Nixon paused, as if wondering whether to elaborate, or perhaps whether to correct himself. The plane to his rear, SAM 27000, had never been to China and only once to Russia. He had confused it with its twin, SAM 26000. But who in the crowd would know the difference? They had come out because they believed in him, not an airplane. Nixon proceeded swiftly to a cheer-rousing conclusion:

"And so I am going to continue—we are all going to continue—to be proud of the fact that we, too, are Californians and we're home again."

Nixon took his wife's elbow and guided her back toward the airplane. The crew was waiting for the promised picture-taking session.

The two Nixons and Albertazzie formed a threesome in front of the others. Ollie Atkins took several group shots, then photos of the trio. They stood stiffly, seriously, posing just below the handsome presidential seal on the fuselage beside the forward door.

The helicopter was waiting, the twin-pack Huey Cobra that had been shipped out from Andrews the day before. Albertazzie escorted the Nixons to the chopper. Some of the staffers already were on board.

Dr. Tkach thought Nixon was limping again, favoring his painful left leg and its phlebitic condition. All the walking and standing on the concrete had not done him any good.

At the helicopter's stairs, Nixon turned to Albertazzie and took his hand. Atkins snapped the picture.

"We covered a lot of miles together, you and I," Nixon said. "I'm sorry it's ending this way."

"I am, too, Mr. President," Albertazzie said. "Good luck. Goodbye."

Nixon waved once more to the crowd lingering back at the fence, then entered the helicopter. Marine Lt. Col. David Pirie revved the engines to full power. The wide blades churned the air, building lift. The machine slowly rose from the ground and hovered.

Nixon looked out the left window at the magnificent blue and white airplane on the ramp. He could see the impressive signature emblazoned along its fuselage: "United States of America." Then he looked down at the pilot still standing there. Nixon waved. Albertazzie saluted.

The helicopter turned away, gaining speed and altitude for the fourteen-mile hop to San Clemente. Soon it was just a speck in the sky. Then it was gone altogether.

Richard Nixon had come home. It was time to get President Gerald Ford's airplane back to Washington.

Chapter Two
The Magic Carpet

There is a special magic about *Air Force One*. It enchants Presidents, fascinates royalty, and awes voters. No conveyance on earth offers power and pleasure quite so irresistibly.

Only a President rides in such majesty and authority. *Air Force One* is his winged stallion, extending his reach far beyond that of any ancient Caesar. It serves as an instrument of national purpose, a symbol of the United States as authentic as the Statue of Liberty. Soaring aloft like a magnificent Pegasus or thundering in for a feather landing, it arouses the emotions as grandly as the flag on the Fourth of July.

But *Air Force One* is also the joy of Presidents, bringing delights and adventures that surpass all other fringe benefits of the White House. His big Boeing liberates him from the grind of the Oval Office. It can whisk him away to a distant land as easily as it takes him home to the piney woods of Georgia.

Only seven airplanes have borne the designation "presidential aircraft." The first one, the legendary *Sacred Cow*, rolled out of the Douglas plant at Santa Monica, California, in wartime 1944. Five of these elite planes were propeller-driven; the remaining

63

two constitute the presidential aircraft of today—a handsome pair of virtually identical Boeing 707 intercontinental jets.

Together the jets have served the five most recent Presidents over a remarkable span of sixteen years, sharing moments of personal triumph and national tragedy, opening up new vistas of American interest and shrinking the distance between Washington and once-forbidden places like Peking and Moscow. Each of these glistening airplanes has carried that most prestigious of titles, *Air Force One*, across the seas and the skies of seven continents.

No President traveled abroad until Theodore Roosevelt sailed to Panama in 1906. For the first 117 years of the Republic, the twenty-five presidents were homebodies, never venturing beyond our national boundaries. And no President before Franklin D. Roosevelt traveled outside the continental limits of the United States more than once.

It was not lack of curiosity but duty that kept Chief Executives at home. For most of American history, Presidents were expected to stay on American soil, as close as possible to the nation's capital. Teddy Roosevelt muted public criticism for his precedent-making trip to Panama by traveling on an American ship and remaining outside United States waters for only a few hours.

Woodrow Wilson, the first President to cross the seas, ran into a storm of criticism when he announced he would attend the Paris Peace Conference after World War I. Senator Lawrence Y. Sherman from Illinois introduced a resolution to declare the presidency vacant whenever the occupant left American soil. Sherman's authority was the Act of 1790 that established the seat of national government in the District of Columbia and decreed that all powers should "cease to be exercised elsewhere."

Fortunately for Wilson, Sherman's resolution lacked sufficient support in Congress. But the controversy continued in newspapers and magazines of the time. Objectors were upset not only because Wilson would be traveling beyond the Western Hemisphere but would be absent from Washington for an extended period. He would lack the direct physical protection of home territory, and would be engaging in high-level international negotiations on his own.

Wilson went anyway, becoming the first President to engage in summit diplomacy. But the Senate refused to ratify the Treaty of Versailles and its League of Nations proposal that Wilson brought back from Europe. There was little doubt that his absence made him lose touch with important domestic issues and impaired the effectiveness of the executive branch.

Nearly a quarter century passed before another President dared go abroad. He was Franklin Roosevelt, who journeyed to Casablanca in 1943 for a wartime conference with Prime Minister Winston Churchhill of Great Britain. But FDR made that trip without prior announcement—and he went by air.

That made all the difference.

The interval between Roosevelt's "borrowed" Pan American airliner and the first Boeing 707 presidential aircraft encompasses less than twenty years. Yet in terms of transporting a President, the jump from the *Dixie Clipper* to today's *Air Force One* is almost as remarkable as the change from foot travel to chariot.

The name, *Air Force One,* demands explanation. For while it aptly and admirably designates the world's best-known airplane, the name is also the subject of much confusion and misunderstanding.

To begin with, *Air Force One* is not, in the strictest sense, the specific name of a specific aircraft. Rather, it is the radio call sign of any Air Force plane carrying the President of the United States. To be even more exact, it attaches itself to him, not to the air vehicle.

In the early days of presidential flight, the President's airplane had both a name and a call sign. The name could be almost anything that struck the fancy of the Chief Executive, his pilot, or, sometimes, the press corps. The call sign was its official designation, its permanent "license number."

Roosevelt's first official plane was dubbed the *Sacred Cow,* but its call sign was the last four digits of its registered tail number, 42–107451. The call sign was preceded by the prefix "Army" whenever it was on a routine flight (the prefix was changed to "Air Force" in 1947); if a ranking VIP was aboard, the prefix became "Special Flight," or its phonetic initials, "Sam Fox." Thus the *Sacred Cow*'s crew, in all radio communication, used either the call sign "Air Force 7451" or "Sam Fox 7451." Similarly, Harry Truman's airplane was a DC-6 named the *Independence*, but the call sign on his trips was "Sam Fox 6505," although later the prefix was shortened to "Sam" or simply the tail number. And while President Eisenhower successively flew two Lockheed Constellations, their call signs at the outset were "Sam 8610" and "Sam 7885."

The tail number call sign is used today by ordinary military aircraft, private planes, and commercial airliners. But during the Eisenhower presidency in the mid-fifties, it was deemed to be inadequate for quick and positive identification of an airplane bearing the President of the United States. And so "Air Force One" was created as his personal radio call sign. There was ample justification for making the change.

In an age of nuclear missiles, with potential devastation only minutes away, the Commander-in-Chief alone can order the American response to enemy rockets. For this primary reason, plus matters of protocol and prestige, it became vitally important to not only know the location of the presidential airplane but to know instantly whether the President was on board or on the ground. The old, traditional call signs could not do that.

The signature *Air Force One* does it beautifully. It designates the President's presence on *any* Air Force plane he may be using. And it is a permanent signature. Presidents may change, along with presidential aircraft, but the call sign now remains unchanged. From the moment a Chief Executive boards an Air Force plane until the moment he leaves that specific craft bears the call sign *Air Force One.*

A similar procedure, by the way, applies whenever the President travels on an aircraft of one of the other military services. The helicopters that shuttle a President from the White House lawn to Andrews Air Force Base, for example, become *Marine One* or *Army One* when he is aboard. If he traveled on a Navy craft, its temporary call sign would be *Navy One.* The call sign is recognized not only by the Department of Defense and the Pentagon tracking agencies for presidential flights but equally by civilian aviation authorities and air traffic control centers in this country and generally abroad.

There is only one other radio call sign that is similar to *Air Force One.* It is, logically enough, *Air Force Two*, the call sign for the Vice President of the United States. Identical rules of usage apply. Whenever the Vice President is aboard any Air Force craft, that plane temporarily becomes known as *Air Force Two*; whenever he boards an Army helicopter, it is called *Army Two*. Although the press occasionally has tried to extend the system to the Secretary of State by dubbing his aircraft *Air Force Three*, it is well to remember that there is no such call sign. Whenever any American official below the rank of Vice President commandeers an airplane of the Special Air Missions (SAM) unit, its call sign is simply the prefix SAM followed by the tail number.

Unfortunately for purists, the *Air Force One* radio signature was simply too catchy to remain the exclusive property of airway communicators. President Kennedy may have contributed to the theft by failing to christen his airplanes with special names, as his predecessors had done (and as he himself had done with the Kennedy family's private twin-engine Convair, the *Caroline*). So the nation's press filched the call sign of the President and made it the name of his presidential airplane as well. Some Air Force officials tried to discourage the practice, but it was no use. *Air Force One* had a ring to it. It captured the public fancy. Before long it became the popular name for the primary presidential airplane. Oddly, the moniker failed to attach itself to the initial presidential plane used by Kennedy. It was a four-engine Douglas DC-6, a reliable propeller craft already in the SAM inventory and bearing the serial number 53–3240. But Kennedy used "3240" only sporadically during his first year, and then mainly for short hops from Washington to New York. The name *Air Force One* sprang into public prominence only late in 1962 with the delivery of the first jet transport to be assigned specifically for the use of the President. It was a beauty—and still is.

That the elected head of a democratic nation could have—or even desire—an airplane as magnificent as *Air Force One* is a measure of the contradictions of the presidency. Thomas Jefferson understood the anomaly even back in his day when a spanking horse-drawn carriage was about as much royal luxury as the office afforded. His life as President, said Jefferson, was a "life of splendid misery."

The misery, of course, is a dimension of the problems we im-

67

pose on a President, problems that confine him physically and wear him mentally, and often turn the White House into a pillared prison.

But the splendor, especially for modern Presidents, is the luxury with which we surround them and tend them. A First Family leads the sort of life that no multimillionaire could afford and no monarch can surpass. Who but an American President has a personal fleet of plush turbojet helicopters at his disposal and available on a few minutes' notice? Where reigns the king or dictator with a pool of jet aircraft of various sizes and speeds to accommodate his official needs or personal whims? But imperial splendor is standard equipment on the President's airplane. It comes with the office.

It would be erroneous to assume that the primary purpose of *Air Force One* is to serve as an airborne Oval Office, and equally inaccurate to assume that Presidents work as hard aloft or perform the same kinds of tasks that occupy them at 1600 Pennsylvania Avenue. No President yet has taken to the air because he works better with his head above the clouds than with his feet on the ground.

The problem for every President is that he can never escape the responsibilities of his office. They are his alone, twenty-four hours a day, every day he occupies the presidency. Wherever he goes, they go, too. That is why, since the inception of presidential air travel in Franklin Roosevelt's time, every presidential plane has been crammed with the latest in communications equipment, plus desks, typewriters, and working space for key members of his staff.

Although decisions of national policy have been made aloft in the thirty-five years that Presidents have been flying in airplanes, that has been more a matter of necessity than design. The President's plane is not adequate to serve as an alternate White House. It is, at best, a traveling substitute of limited use for a temporary period. The primary purpose of *Air Force One*, quite obviously, is to transport a President as swiftly and conveniently as possible, with the least disruption to his daily duties.

When he is airborne, a President is en route to a place where his mind and heart already may be, a vacation place away from the rigors of Washington, his hometown, a political gathering of importance to him and his party, or a foreign country where matters of ceremonial or diplomatic significance await. So while the atmosphere around the White House focuses on attention to duty, the atmosphere aboard *Air Force One* crackles with anticipation. The mood shapes the nature of the work that engages an airborne President. To a great extent, it also determines the composition of the group that flies with him.

If the President is off on a political trip, the speeches he must give are of critical importance. He may spend most of his time going over the final drafts, making last-minute changes, demanding more data and rewriting by the speech writers traveling with him.

A traveling President also likes to bring along key senators and representatives of the states where he will appear. It is a form of mutual back scratching. A President usually spends a good deal of time talking to them, getting substantive information and tidbits he can work into his opening remarks—a funny story, a sports rivalry, political gossip—intended to demonstrate to the audience that he keeps abreast of local events. A politician's reward for helping him is the opportunity to step off *Air Force One* in the company of the President of the United States, in full view of the press and his constituents. Even the lowliest politician thus gets a moment to look like an important statesman. And for weeks thereafter, he will be able to regale his public with lines like, "When I was traveling with the President, I told him. . . ."

When the President flies abroad, the entourage will include senior American diplomats and perhaps a general or two to lend the right touch of pomp and circumstance. On such flights, the President will not be so much concerned with his arrival statement—usually brief, trite, and canned in advance—as with topics that will come up in private meetings with foreign heads of state. He will spend hours reviewing the thick briefing books prepared by the State Department, the National Security Council staff, and the CIA. And he may call in his interpreter to help him memorize a few catchy phrases in the foreign language of the country to which he is flying. John Kennedy, for example, en route to West Berlin in 1963, practiced mightily aboard *Air Force One* to teach his stubborn Boston tongue to say, in passable German, *"Ich bin ein Berliner!"*

Presidents work least aboard *Air Force One* when flying off on vacation or for a few days' rest at home. Of course, they rarely admit they are going anyplace just to relax or to shake off the dust of Washington. Such trips usually are called "working vacations" or "working weekends."

And they work hard on the appearance of work. Lyndon Johnson even resented stories that said he was on a working vacation. "This is no vacation," he would complain. "I'm working all the time, as hard as if I were in the White House."

To preserve the fiction of the working vacation, White House aides dutifully load the plane with briefcases full of paperwork requiring presidential attention. Courier planes arrive daily with a fresh batch of Washington officials and more documents. But the fact is that on most such presidential trips—to Independence, Missouri, or to the golf links at Augusta, Georgia, to Cape Cod, Texas, Key Biscayne, Vail, or Plains—the presidential plane is more like a Winnebago in the sky than a flying office. On such occasions, *Air Force One* becomes the world's most luxurious recreational vehicle.

Little of the presidential "work" aboard *Air Force One* can legitimately be termed historic. Most often it involves consultation with key staff members or perhaps with visiting foreign dignitaries or members of Congress. The presidential suite is ideal for small conferences; the telephone rarely rings, secretaries seldom intrude, and no one has a pressing appointment in another office or another place.

But there have been occasions when notable actions took place on the presidential airplane. Aboard the *Sacred Cow*, Harry Truman signed the National Security Act of 1947, the legislation unifying the armed services under a Department of Defense. Dwight Eisenhower put the final touches to his "Atoms For Peace" address at the United Nations in December 1953, while flying *Columbine II* from Bermuda to New York. (Ike asked pilot Bill Draper to circle Manhattan an extra thirty minutes while Secretary of State John Foster Dulles, Atomic Energy Commission Chairman Lewis Strauss, and speech writer C. O. Jackson ran it through the mimeograph machine and stapled the copies.)

In October 1963, despite the misgivings of his political advisers and Vice President Johnson, President Kennedy decided on

Air Force One to sell American wheat to the Soviet Union as a positive step on the road to improved relations between the superpowers. The agreement was consummated in the skies between Milwaukee and Minneapolis as Kennedy and Senators Mike Mansfield and Hubert Humphrey flew to a fund-raising dinner for Senator Eugene McCarthy.

If John Dean is correct, the scandal that became Watergate had its inception aboard *Air Force One* on January 14, 1971, as Nixon sped across America's heartland to the University of Nebraska to deliver a speech far from antiwar demonstrators in the East. Into his IBM dictating machine, the President spoke a memo that was typed up by secretary Rose Mary Woods and passed on to H. R. Haldeman, the White House staff chief:

> It would seem that the time is approaching when Larry O'Brien [Democratic national chairman] is held accountable for his retainer with [Howard] Hughes. Bebe [Rebozo] has some information on this, although it is, of course, not solid. But there is no question that one of Hughes's people did have O'Brien on a very heavy retainer for "services rendered" in the past. Perhaps [Charles] Colson should check on this.

Haldeman discussed it a day later with Nixon, suggesting that instead of Colson it be an assignment for Dean, the young White House legal counsel. Nixon agreed.

Writing later in his Watergate book *Blind Ambition*, Dean observed "At the time I did not know I was handling a matter of intense interest to the President, but years later this assignment would help me understand the chain of events that destroyed the Nixon Presidency." As Dean viewed it, the memo Nixon had dictated at 35,000 feet was an instigation for the break-in at the Watergate offices of the Democratic National Committee in the spring of 1972.

And it was in March 1976, as *Air Force One* carried President Ford from Illinois to North Carolina for a primary campaign appearance that former secretary of the Army, Howard "Bo" Callaway, notified the President of his decision to resign as campaign chairman to avoid embarrassing him over allegations of impropriety concerning a Callaway ski resort in Colorado. Then

71

Callaway retreated to the guest lounge and wept. The allegations later turned out to be unfounded.

As much as President Ford relished flying on *Air Force One,* the presidential plane inadvertently played a contributing role in creating the impression that he was a clumsy man, perhaps even mentally inept. For Jerry Ford, the unfortunate perception probably began that day in May 1975 when he stumbled on the plane stairs while arriving at Salzburg, Austria, in clear view of the dignitaries, correspondents, and the ever-present photographers. Then, later the same day, en route to a meeting with Egyptian President Anwar Sadat, Ford stumbled again on the long, wet stairs leading into Salzburg's Residenz Palace.

By nightfall, the traveling White House press corps was certain something was seriously wrong with the President. Reporters bombarded press secretary Ron Nessen for an explanation.

Was Ford tired? Was he off balance because he was exhausted from the trip? Or—? Nessen failed to provide a reassuring answer.

The photographs of the airport tumble showed Ford landing on both hands and one knee, then straightening himself instantly. One UPI account said Ford "toppled over and, for a moment, lay spread-eagled at the bottom of the airplane ramp." In its account of the Palace incident, AP reported that only the alertness of accompanying aides had saved Ford from tumbling down twenty steps.

In the memoirs of his White House years, Nessen attributed the President's missteps to the lack of a good rest—the fault of a too-short, too-hard bed the Spanish government had provided him during his previous night's stay in Madrid. Nessen believes the stumbling was caused by "fatigue, compounding the usual stiffness in his knees from old football injuries."

Whatever the reason, the nation's press thereafter stayed on the alert for every presidential stumble, verbal as well as physical. There began a series of photographs and word pictures of Ford bumping his head on helicopter doors, falling down on his skis, catching his heel on a sidewalk, getting tangled in the leashes of his dogs. And each time, such episodes somehow seemed to justify Lyndon Johnson's graphic cracks about Ford's intelligence, that he was unable "to walk and chew gum at the same time," or had "played football too long without a helmet." After Salzburg, Nessen lamented, "The image of Ford as a klutz would never fade away."

While news is generated aboard, more frequent are the occasions when decisive news clatters into *Air Force One* by teletype.

Kennedy was returning from a weekend at Cape Cod on September 18, 1961, when he was handed the grim message that UN Secretary-General Dag Hammarskjöld had been killed in a plane crash in the Congo. Flying to New York several days later to speak at the UN General Assembly, Kennedy and speech writer Ted Sorenson squatted on the floor in the passageway, comparing speech drafts and sorting pages, because the presidential compartment was too crowded.

Lyndon Johnson was streaking across the Pacific skies in mid-1967 when he got word that North Vietnam's Ho Chi Minh had released and publicly rejected LBJ's secret letter of peace. On *Air Force One,* while flying to California in 1969, Richard Nixon learned that his nominee for Chief Justice of the Supreme Court, Warren Burger, had been approved by the Senate Judiciary Committee.

Aboard *Air Force One,* jetting west to Palm Springs for a golfing holiday over the weekend of Easter 1975, Gerald Ford was handed a brown envelope from the radio operator with the terse message "Danang has fallen." Vietnam was in its death throes.

High over the Amazon jungles in the spring of 1978, Jimmy Carter learned that American steel companies had decided to raise prices in spite of his efforts to keep a lid on inflation. Carter, understandably, raised a Baptist's version of hell.

Regardless of who happens to be President, there is a certain regimen about *Air Force One* flights that is rarely altered. A President may change the appearance of his airplane, select a new pilot and crew, or vary the ceremonial arrangements for his arrivals and departures. But flight and security procedures have been constant from one administration to the next, and every President wisely leaves those decisions to the persons responsible for executing them. Occasionally, even a security officer suffers a memory lapse.

As soon as the President boards the airplane, for example, the ever-present black box, or "football," as it is sometimes called—the briefcase containing the codes for ordering a nuclear strike—is deposited in *Air Force One*'s safe near the cockpit. There it remains until the President deplanes, when the briefcase is retrieved by the military aide accompanying him. The briefcase was inadvertently left aboard in November 1975 when President Ford landed at Paris. As soon as the military aide discovered his error, he radioed the plane crew and the ultra-secret briefcase was rushed to the President's location in another car. But for about an hour, Ron Nessen said in his memoirs, *It Sure Looks Different From The Inside*, the President was without the codes he would have needed in order to respond to a nuclear emergency.

No presidential journey occurs without an accompanying press plane or two, the arrangements for which are the responsibility of the White House Transportation Office. Presidents and White House aides may complain loudly about press coverage, but they also know they can't survive politically without the public attention the media commands.

To help a President while away his hours aloft, the flight crew makes certain he has an ample supply of the latest magazines and newspapers. Presidents are voracious consumers of the printed word, especially those that concern themselves—even when they do not like what they read.

John Kennedy occasionally would snort at a news story and, if the offending reporter was in the press pool, would send Press Secretary Pierre Salinger back to complain. Lyndon Johnson would scoop up the entire newspaper, crush it like a bug, and toss it to an aide with a bellow: "Get rid of this damned thing!"

Richard Nixon did a slow burn and usually said nothing at the time, although a peevish memo might turn up later for the attention of Haldeman and Press Secretary Ron Ziegler. Via the ever-present chain of command, pilot Ralph Albertazzie once got a message, scrawled on the back of an *Air Force One* seat assignment card by Lt. Col. William L. Golden, Nixon's Army aide, and forwarded through Brig. Gen. Richard Lawson, Nixon's senior military assistant: "Col. A—Verbal to me from Ron Ziegler: 'Never put the *Washington Post* or the *New York Times* in the First Family Lounge.' "

74

But, of course, both papers were on the airplane in any event; the staff needed to know what they were saying. And there was always an odd chance that Nixon might want to find out for himself.

Nixon once told Ziegler to pick the four most anti-administration reporters he knew and put them into the *Air Force One* pool on a certain trip.

"But why?" asked the startled Ziegler.

"So that when you get them on this plane, I can go over and ride the press plane," Nixon cracked. Members of the press pool are confined to a tight compartment in the rear of *Air Force One.* They are not permitted to roam about freely, as do their companions traveling aboard the press charters. Nixon sometimes complained it "smelled bad" back there.

White House correspondents snort derisively whenever outsiders refer to the "lucky few" traveling as pool members on the President's airplane. A pool assignment is a working assignment under fairly austere circumstances, often with little or no opportunity to make contact with the President and his important guests up front. On most long flights, veterans of the press corps prefer the ambience and the camaraderie of the press planes to the restrictive press space on *Air Force One.*

The term "press plane" is something of a misnomer, since members of the White House press office and other presidential aides also travel aboard. A ninety-seat jet aircraft is chartered by the Transportation Office from the regular airlines, usually Pan American and TWA for overseas trips, with the cost prorated among the news organizations sending correspondents, photographers, and technicians on the journey.

The news media also pay for the air travel of the White House press staff, so a trip costs a journalist or a television newsperson about 25 to 50 percent more than first-class air fare. The theory behind the arrangement, says Transportation Office chief Bob Manning, is that the press office staff goes along on trips to help the news media, not to help the President.

The practice began back in Harry Truman's time when White House telegrapher Dewey Long took over the responsibility of operating the press plane for the nation's first air-minded President. Since then, the White House Transportation Office has made all plane, hotel, bus, baggage, and ancillary arrangements for newspersons covering the President on domestic and foreign trips.

Many times, when *Air Force One* trips come up on short notice or the schedule is changed, press arrangements have to be put together with frantic overseas calls, Scotch tape, long hours, and Excedrin. Preparing for Lyndon Johnson's world tour of 1966, Ray Zook, Transportation Chief, arrived in Wellington, New Zealand, to discover that there was a shortage of hotel space for the LBJ staff and the press.

"In desperation we negotiated to rent an overnight ferry that formerly made the run to North Island," Zook later told *Parade* editor Lloyd Shearer. When the press and the Secret Service agents and staff got aboard, the ferry began to list badly and was promptly dubbed the "Tiltin' Hilton." Added Zook: "We stayed aboard one night and then fortunately left. I say 'fortunately' because, about a week later, the ferry sank."

In the early days of VIP flight service by the Air Force, mealtime was a spartan experience. Food was a matter of sustenance, not enjoyment, and galleys on military transports hardly merited the name.

Food service on Special Air Missions planes gradually improved as the planes themselves improved. With the acquisition of Boeing 707 jets, the increased space and advances in food service technology made it possible to provide better meals for VIP travelers. The primary presidential planes, SAM 26000 and SAM 27000, are equipped with two ultra-modern galleys. Ovens, broilers, and microwave units give the stewards a chance to prepare food in flight, reducing the plane's dependence on precooked meals from flight kitchens on Air Force bases. Both planes also have deep-freeze units in their cargo compartments, where all manner of meats, frozen vegetables, and fruits can be kept. Dishwashers in the galleys also make it possible to serve meals on handsome *Air Force One* china, along with fine glassware and silver.

The selection of on-board menus always varies from one presidency to another. During the Kennedy years, it was generally decided by the chief flight steward and the pilot. In the Nixon era, the White House staff insisted on the right to approve or reject menu ideas, but took so long to clear the paperwork that Albertazzie finally intervened.

"Since we needed at least twenty-four hours to do the buying and the preparing, we eventually resorted to telling the White House what we planned to serve each day and hoped they wouldn't object."

For Jimmy Carter, says appointments aide Frances Voorde, who alternates as trip director, menus aren't a worrisome thing. "We may send some suggestions from the White House mess or the First Lady's office, but we leave it pretty much up to *Air Force One*'s crew."

Presidents and members of their families, from Roosevelt to Carter, have generally proved to be the least-demanding air passengers. Truman would devour whatever was set before him. Eisenhower was a hearty eater but, after his 1956 abdominal surgery, never traveled without bottled Mountain Valley spring water—doctor's orders. Kennedy had a craving for fish chowder and Johnson wanted steak and diet soda. Nixon and Ford preferred cottage cheese for lunch but never, stewards grimaced, with ketchup—thereby debunking a popular myth. President Carter may be among the least finicky.

But First Family members always get special attention in any event, so if one of them demands special food service on board *Air Force One*, the stewards make sure that their desires are met. Tricia Nixon Cox, for example, usually developed a yen for hot dogs when the others were having steak, roast leg of lamb, baked chicken, or filet of sole. Chief steward Vernon "Red" Shell usually managed to rustle up a wiener or two.

All others aboard are expected to eat identical meals. Except for a choice of beverage, there is little catering to individual tastes. When President Carter, Rosalynn, Amy, Secretary of State Cyrus Vance, a planeful of staffers, and a handful of newsmen took off on *Air Force One* about dawn on March 28, 1978, to begin a week's safari to Latin America and black Africa, the flight stewards came around with gold-embossed menu cards that offered just about everything one might order for a bon voyage breakfast except hominy grits and Bloody Marys. The menu:

* * *

Orange Juice
Melon Balls
French Toast
Scrambled Eggs
Sausage
Blueberry Muffins
Butter/Jelly/Syrup
Choice of Beverage

Just for the record, we checked during that breakfast to find out what was offered up front in the presidential cabin. The President, Rosalynn, and Amy had been served the same bill of fare. But Jimmy Carter, as usual, settled for juice and coffee.

But a mass-produced meal, even on *Air Force One,* is still a mass-produced meal. During the years that he was Nixon's pilot, Albertazzie never pretended that his crew was serving gourmet food at 40,000 feet. But some of Nixon's staff thought they deserved it.

There were four flight stewards on SAM 26000, the first Boeing *Air Force One,* but the complement was increased to six stewards with Nixon's acquisition of SAM 27000. "It didn't ease the work load because the Nixon staff had become so demanding," Shell said. "Even on one-hour flights, say to New York, they wanted full meal service. And they insisted on getting involved in the menus and the wine selections. In the Nixon years, it seemed like everybody was into the food business."

Preparing to return from a twelve-day stay in California on July 18,1971, for example, the Nixon staff changed the menu at the last minute. Haldeman wanted Mexican food for dinner on the flight to Washington, although everyone had had nearly two weeks to gorge on southern California's specialty. Lacking oven space aboard *Air Force One* to prepare it in time, chief flight steward Shell scratched the prime rib dinner he had planned and dashed out to a top Mexican restaurant to purchase the required number of tacos, enchiladas, refried beans, and assorted sauces and salads. It was a time-consuming process, since security regulations require that flight stewards watch the food preparations whenever meals are "catered" from outside kitchens.

Larry Higby, Haldeman's chief assistant in the White House,

78

functioned as Haldeman's Haldeman on *Air Force One* matters. Higby once fired off a long memo to the military liaison office in the White House, demanding to know why food service aboard the President's plane wasn't comparable to the "Trader Vic" fare then being offered first-class passengers by United Airlines.

It was a subtle tactic. Although there was no hint that the memo was drafted at the suggestion of the President, it was commonly known that the Nixons relished the Polynesian and Chinese cuisine of Trader Vic's restaurant in Washington. Sometimes they slipped out of the White House to dine at Trader Vic's eatery in the Capitol Hilton Hotel, two blocks away.

William Gulley, the retired Marine sergeant-major who handled administrative detail for the White House military office, drafted a tart rejoinder to Higby's memo and forwarded it to Albertazzie for approval. The rebuttal noted that Trader Vic meals on United flights were built into the extra cost of first-class tickets, but that *Air Force One*'s crew would try to match Trader Vic's menu if the "cheap bastards" on the White House staff were willing to pay the extra cost. General James Hughes, the President's Air Force aide, thought the proposed reply a bit too blunt. So it never was sent.

But that was the crux of the problem. Nixon's staffers wanted fancy meals aboard, but they were unwilling to pick up the tab. On one trip, Haldeman brought along his wife and two children, taking advantage of the greatly reduced cost of dependents' travel on a nearly empty plane. Later he complained loudly when the Air Force billed him $24 for four prime steak dinners that would have cost twice as much at any good restaurant.

Another gripe of *Air Force One*'s passengers is that reporters traveling on the chartered press planes receive tastier food and better beverage service. One of the most vocal complainers on the Nixon staff was John Scali, the ABC correspondent who then was serving as special assistant to the President. After hearing Scali sound off on three successive trips, Albertazzie counterattacked on the next flight. It happened to be a journey from Washington to Florida, where Nixon planned to spend a few days at Key Biscayne.

"Before we left Washington, I had one of my stewards go over to the press plane and pick up one of their meal trays for dinner that night. As I remember, it was a baked chicken dish. It had been prepared in the airline's New York kitchens earlier in the day. And, by now, it was five or six hours old. Well, we served everybody on *Air Force One* a nice steak that night, but gave Scali his press plane meal. I never heard a gripe from him again."

Nitpickers on the Nixon staff also suspected that the crew was eating better than the passengers. Albertazzie recalls a Thanksgiving day flight to Florida on which the dinner menu featured traditional holiday fare, complete with pumpkin pie for dessert. It so happened that the wife of a Secret Service agent had baked a pecan pie that day and had sent along a piece for the pilot.

"Higby came into the cockpit to inquire about something just as I was eating my piece of pecan pie," Albertazzie said. "He didn't say anything then, but a few days later I got a memo that he sent to the Military Office. He demanded to know why the President's pilot could have pecan pie when the President's staff hadn't gotten any."

Flight steward Lee Simmons found the Fords much more informal than the Nixon family. "The President and Mrs. Ford always ate their meals together in his suite and they were very easy to please. At mealtime, I just served them the same entree that everyone else was getting—that's the way they wanted it.

"Mr. Ford was more relaxed than Mr. Nixon. And he did less work during flights. He kept the door to his cabin open and staff people and guests were in and out of there all the time. He seemed to like that."

Still, travel aboard *Air Force One* is persistently downgraded by those in position to make a frequent judgment: members of the press who function as pool reporters on one leg of a presidential trip and then switch to the press plane for other segments of the journey.

Air Force One's crew is quick to acknowledge one glaring difference: airline stewardesses serve the food on the planes chartered by the press, whereas meals on the President's plane are served by businesslike Air Force males.

But the basic reason for the grumbling about food on the President's plane may have more to do with the difference in atmosphere and accommodations. On *Air Force One*, the paramount

80

function of the crew is not to serve the press pool but the President, the First Family, White House staffers, and VIP guests. The crews of the press charters have just one function: catering to the taste buds and comfort of the reporters and photographers aboard. And they deserve to be fussed over. Their news organizations are paying almost 50 percent more than first-class air fare for every seat on the press planes.

Much of what passes as the "perks" of the President is rooted in his constitutional capacity as Commander-in-Chief of the armed forces, not as elected civilian leader of the nation or executor of its foreign policy. It is this military responsibility, this requirement that he be always in position to command and in contact with his military subordinates and the weaponry of a nuclear age, that serves as justification for many of the benefits associated with the office.

As civilian head of state, for example, he may merit a costly and beautiful limousine, the modern equivalent of a royal coach. But it is only as the supreme military commander that he rates something as special as *Air Force One*. The funds for it and all the other command facets of the presidency come out of the Defense Department budget, not the congressional appropriation for defraying the civilian expenses of the White House and the Executive Office of the President.

The White House Communications Agency, which lays in special telephone lines and a sophisticated communication system wherever he is on the face of the earth, is funded by the U.S. Army. So is the signal board at the White House, the motor pool, and Fort Ritchie, the "underground White House" in the Maryland mountains. The U.S. Navy maintains the presidential retreat, Camp David, and operates the White House staff mess, and any vessel or naval refuge for the President. The Marine Corps provides helicopters for his use (notably *Marine One*), a function the Army shared until President Carter decided he could get along with a smaller chopper fleet. The U.S. Air Force quite logically provides all fixed-wing transportation for the President, including the presidential Boeings and executive Jetstars.

If all these costs were lumped together into one presidential

81

budget instead of being spread throughout the military establishment, they would add up to a fantastic allocation of money and manpower that a President would have to seek from Congress. Perhaps that is why none has had the political temerity to suggest it. No elected President or leader of Congress has been anxious to publicize how much it really costs to support the nation's Chief Executive in the style to which America is accustomed.

Still the taxpayers are not saddled with every cent of *Air Force One*'s operations. To avoid public outcry over traveling extravagance, the expenses of a plane trip are pro-rated between "official" and "political" uses of the aircraft—with "personal" use remaining a very gray area. The procedure for determining the breakdown is not exactly scientific, for it's not easy to determine precisely what part of a trip falls into which category when the uses so often overlap.

An exception would be a presidential campaign flight solely on behalf of his own reelection or the election of candidates for Congress. The sticky part involves a mixed *Air Force One* trip, during which a President not only speaks at a campaign rally but, say, christens a new aircraft carrier, inspects a federal project, and holds a bona fide news conference. Or, to cite a case that government auditors will be arguing over for a long time, how much of the air transportation for the Carter family's western rafting, fishing, and sightseeing vacation in August 1978 constituted an official expense of the presidency? How little of it (the approach usually taken by any White House occupant) should be borne by the First Family?

Constant scrutiny by the press and the opposition party has made it useful for a President to insist that suitable portions of mixed and personal *Air Force One* flights be billed to him, to his campaign committee, or to the headquarters of his political party, as the case may be. And if a President errs on the side of allocating expenses to the cost of doing business, any Internal Revenue Service auditor will tell you that he is merely doing what countless other individuals do at income tax time.

The rate of reimbursement for unofficial *Air Force One* flights is computed at least once a year by the Air Force comptroller's office. It is a limited rate, based upon fuel, maintenance, and depreciation costs attributable to the aircraft. The rate excludes crew members' salaries, since they are career personnel who would be paid by the Air Force regardless of their duties.

At the end of the Johnson presidency, the cost of using *Air Force One* was pegged at $1,995 an hour. It gradually drifted downward during the Nixon years to a low of $1,195 an hour and then up again. The principal variable is the price of jet fuel. While Gerald Ford was in the White House, the hourly rate hovered around the $2,000 mark. Six months into the Carter presidency, it had risen to $2,327. On business or pleasure, flying *Air Force One* is obviously not a low-budget matter.

On one occasion, the Nixons wanted to have dinner with daughter Julie and her husband, David Eisenhower, who was then studying at Amherst College. To avoid massive publicity, the President ordered Press Secretary Ron Ziegler to hold the announcement until just before departure, thereby effectively limiting press coverage to the handful of pool reporters who travel aboard *Air Force One*. The Nixons left at 5:18 P.M. and landed at Westover Air Force Base in Massachusetts forty-five minutes later. They were back at Andrews by 10:27 P.M., and fifteen minutes later their helicopter deposited them again on the south lawn of the White House.

But even for such a modest undertaking, all the presidential, Pentagon, and aviation security agencies had to be brought into play. Merely counting *Air Force One*'s flying time at the 1970 rate of $1,995 an hour, the presidential dinner in Julie and David's apartment cost $2,992.50. Fortunately, Julie is said to be a very good cook.

Increasing public concern over government spending and public propriety led to other changes in *Air Force One* finances during the Nixon days. A decision was made to bill individual members of the White House staff for their in-flight meals and drinks (seventy-five cents a shot). Even crew members' meals were tallied and charged to their per diem travel allowances. Officials from other agencies who happened to be on board also were billed, as were members of the media who comprised the press pool on *Air Force One*.

One of the bonuses of an overseas trip, at least for members of the official presidential party, is the presence of the State Department disbursing agent or "bag man." And this is an appropriate point to note that when it comes to personal expenses, the government of the United States, in the name of the taxpayer, discriminates against *Air Force One*'s crew, Secret Service agents, White House Communications Agency specialists, and others below the rank of White House assistant.

Whenever a President travels at home or abroad, the entourage customarily is put up at a fashionable hostelry. Expenses usually are borne by the White House or the host government for members of the official party. All others whose job assignments require close proximity to the President have to defray their bills out of a modest, not to say paltry, daily allowance.

"On domestic trips, it's not unusual for crew members to go in the red to pay for their rooms and food," said Albertazzie. "Overseas, it's a bit better because a special per diem allowance is available." The same holds true for other government employees, including the President's bodyguards.

But the State Department's bag man eases the expenses of those who rank high on the presidential manifest. In many countries, the government can draw on "counterpart funds," coin of the local realm belonging to the U.S. Treasury but not permitted to leave the host country. In countries where that does not pertain, the bag man provides American dollars or foreign currency to help presidential party members meet "unusual" expenses, which, of course, are rarely itemized or expected to be.

Albertazzie said he first learned of the practice, during an early Nixon trip, from Gen. James Hughes, the White House military aide. Hughes handed him $100 "to buy a few drinks for the crew." Another time, said Albertazzie, a presidential physician casually mentioned that "the money they pass out here is a good deal, isn't it?"

"I nodded agreement, but I didn't let on that none of us on the crew ever got any."

Commercial airlines and manufacturers of various products have generously contributed to the quality of life aboard SAM 27000 and SAM 26000, the two primary Boeings serving the White House.

During the Nixon years, Pan American Airways and Corning Glass provided the special china service that fits *Air Force One*'s serving trays. Lufthansa, the German airline, came through with a supply of its own superior plastic trays. Hamilton Tailoring Company of Cincinnati, Ohio, donated the sky-blue blazers worn by the flight stewards.

"We had gone to each of them, intending to buy what we needed," Albertazzie said. "In each instance, they refused payments. I guess it was the honor of being able to do something nice for the President."

One source of amusement on *Air Force One* is the acquisitive nature of presidential guests. "It isn't unusual for us to lose a dozen crystal glasses during a short flight," observed a steward for President Carter.

In the Nixon years, Albertazzie said, "People would have a cocktail and then walk off with one of our *Air Force One* tumblers, bearing the seal of the President."

Coming back from a presidential trip to Norfolk with the Virginia congressional delegation, Republican Senator William Scott told Nixon he wanted one of the brass ash trays in the presidential suite for a souvenir. It was a handmade item, produced especially for *Air Force One* at a cost of $60 a copy, inscribed with Richard Nixon's signature and the words AIR FORCE ONE.

Nixon hesitated, then pushed an ash tray toward Scott, who seized it with both hands and walked away. Back in Washington the following day, White House congressional liaison chief William Timmons urgently contacted the military office. Six Virginia congressmen, he said, also wanted *Air Force One* ash trays.

"I demurred, noting that would be $360 worth of brass ash trays and asked who was going to pay for it," Albertazzie said. "Finally, after three weeks of back-and-forth conversation, I was told in no uncertain terms to bundle up six airplane ash trays and send them down to the White House. Well, then I had to get them replaced—and discovered the cost had gone up to $107 per ash tray."

There are many little things on the President's plane that the crew expects to find missing after a trip, matchbooks and notepads inscribed *Air Force One* and packages of cigarettes with a special cellophane wrapper marked with the presidential seal and *Air Force One*. The cigarettes are donated by the major to-

85

bacco companies; the other items are written off as part of the cost of presidential travel.

The Carter administration, determined to save money, has limited the number of candy dishes and crystal glasses aboard the President's plane, favoring plastic containers and paper cups. That policy has sharply reduced the pilferage by presidential guests.

Lyndon Johnson, on the other hand, looked upon airborne acts of petty larceny as evidence of pride in his presidency. "It was useful to him to have people brag about flying with LBJ— and to have a souvenir with which to prove it," observed George Christian, his White House Press Secretary.

Presidents get political hives anytime there is a public hint that an *Air Force One* trip may be a waste of money. Gerald Ford, vacationing in Vail, Colorado, was incensed by a CBS report that thousands of gallons of jet fuel were expended to assemble his energy advisers at the ski resort to ponder ways of conserving fuel. Another time, Ford wanted so badly to play golf in Florida that a speaking opportunity was quickly arranged to provide an excuse for the *Air Force One* trip. The government naturally picked up the tab.

Unlike other Presidents, Jimmy Carter keeps a personal eye on the number of aircraft and staff persons assigned to accompany *Air Force One*. "He likes a lean trip," said Hugh Carter, Jr., the President's young cousin, who functions as his White House cost cutter.

Besides reducing the number of television sets and chauffeured autos serving White House aides, the President has authorized cutbacks in helicopter service and support aircraft for Special Air Missions, the parent organization of the presidential planes.

"The President told us to minimize our travel assets," Hugh Carter said. "So we use the phrase 'necessary minimum' to decide which personnel and what equipment is necessary to get the job done."

Before every trip, President Carter goes over the detailed manifest with Appointments Secretary Phil Wise and his deputy

Frances Voorde and sometimes bumps people off the trip when not convinced their presence is needed.

Jimmy Carter once bumped an entire hotel off the schedule—the Claridge in London, one of the most fashionable hostelries in Europe and a traditional stopping place for international bigwigs. About 50 of its rooms had apparently been reserved by the American Embassy in London as soon as Carter's visit in May 1977 was announced. But Carter took a look at the prices—$135 a day for a suite and $68 for a room—and at the last minute decreed that Secretary of State Cyrus Vance, Treasury Secretary Michael Blumenthal, and top White House aides had to find cheaper accommodations.

The Carter aides ended up at the less expensive Britannia Hotel, but the flap created a lot of embarrassing publicity. Press Secretary Jody Powell shrugged it away by saying the new President was "tight as a tick"—although Carter himself stayed at the fancy Hutton mansion, a gift to the U.S. government.

Frugality in the enjoyment of *Air Force One* cuts both ways. Jimmy Carter's penchant for putting off interior changes and his decision to cut back the number of aircraft on call by the White House are moves calculated to save taxpayers' money and reap the political credit. Yet the Associated Press reported a cost to the government of at least $100,000 when the Carter family went on its western mountain vacation in the summer of 1978, even though the president paid the equivalent of first-class air fares for himself, Mrs. Carter, and each of the children.

During the winter of 1974, President and Mrs. Ford were irked by an Internal Revenue Service ruling, stemming from the Nixon era, that personal travel on *Air Force One* either be reimbursed to the Air Force on the basis of first-class fare or it would be added to his presidential income for tax purposes. The Fords briefly considered buying tourist-class tickets on a commercial airliner for their annual Christmas skiing vacation in Colorado, but the Secret Service persuaded the President that such a move would greatly complicate security protection.

Perhaps the most controversial case of all was Nixon's decision, after days of agonizing, to shy away from using the presidential plane to fly home to California during the Christmas holidays of 1973. Anxious to set a good example of fuel conservation and not be inconsistent with his administration's demand for public curtailment of unessential travel, Nixon even debated going by special train. But the media said that would be even more fuel-costly than an *Air Force One* flight. In the end, he surprised everybody, including his presidential pilot, by putting himself and the First Family, plus a contingent of Secret Service agents, aboard a regular United Airlines DC-10 flight from Washington to Los Angeles.

"We had concluded that if he went at all, he would use his own plane," said Albertazzie. "We weren't sure it would be to Florida or California, but we were standing by to go."

Then, after Christmas, Albertazzie got a call from General Hughes, the White House military assistant, saying "The President is going commercial! I'll call you back when he's left."

Actually, the White House signal board beat Hughes to the call. With Nixon already boarding the United jetliner at Dulles International Airport, there was nothing for Albertazzie and the crew to do but "button up" the President's own plane at Andrews Air Force Base.

In the end, it is doubtful that Nixon saved fuel or money by leaving his presidential airplane behind. Staff members and security and communications personnel had to be flown out by other government aircraft to the Western White House in San Clemente since it was a "working" vacation for the President. As luck would have it, a Special Air Missions Jetstar was out in California undergoing repair. Albertazzie suggested a crew "deadhead" out there to fly the President and First Family back to Washington when he ended his stay on the Pacific. Nixon jumped at the chance, although everyone had to be wedged in tightly during the five-hour return flight aboard the small aircraft. It was so crowded that the lone flight steward had to sit in the lavatory. As *The Washington Post* editorialized, giving up the presidential Boeing "with all the built-in and time-tested security arrangements it provides . . . would seem to amount to one of those penny-wise, pound-foolish ventures."

Chapter Three

"You Have A Bomb Aboard"

Security for the two presidential planes, SAM 27000 and SAM 26000, is a round-the-clock process. It begins, actually, with the construction of the craft.

From the moment the contract is placed with the manufacturer, special inspectors are assigned to keep watch over the project. Once the airframe is built, it is moved to a secluded area in the plant for completion. Thereafter guards never leave it. The airplane manufacturer knows his reputation is at stake, as well as the safety of the President. The plant's most skilled workmen are put on the job. Only the finest structural components are used, for no expense is spared to produce as perfect a plane as men and machinery can devise. The manufacturer appreciates the honor of having his product chosen for the President's use, but that is usually his only profit. The contract price for a presidential plane has rarely covered all the extra costs incurred in its production. That was true when Douglas Aircraft built the *Sacred Cow* for Franklin Roosevelt in 1943, and when Boeing constructed today's primary *Air Force One* in 1972.

An airplane's wings must be flexible—they must be able to bend or give with the stresses inflicted by varying air pressures and turbulence at high speeds. On a Boeing 707, like *Air Force One*, the wing tips may flex as much as three feet during flight turbulence. This is not the result of flimsy construction or metal fatigue but a safety factor, built into the wings through the use of metal alloys possessing flexing capability. Wing rigidity is a liability, not an asset.

In the same way, the fuselage of an airplane must be able to withstand the tremendous expansion and contraction that results from varying atmospheric temperatures and pressures. At sea level, an aircraft's body tends to shrink because of the greater air pressures. Aloft, at cruising altitudes of 31,000 feet or more, the body actually swells because cold air is "thinner."

The necessity of maintaining sea level air pressure, so that crews and passengers can fly without oxygen masks or heated clothing, creates an added problem. At different altitudes, the skin of *Air Force One* may expand up to six inches or shrink as much as three inches, a nine-inch gap that must be anticipated and compensated for during construction. The variables of pressurization and temperature also affect the working parts of the engines, the hydraulic and electrical systems, the aircraft controls, and the doors, windows, seats, desks, medicine cabinets, galley drawers, and everything that is attached to the airframe.

"While all these problems theoretically have been ironed out in the factory before delivery, you can't really be sure until you've had a chance to check it out in flight under actual conditions of use," Albertazzie observed. "That's why *Air Force One* pilots and crews like to take a new plane up for about a hundred hours of shakedown and 'cold-soaking' at very high altitudes and extremely low temperatures. Instead of passengers, we take along a group of Air Force mechanics who can work on eliminating the technical bugs, plus the stuck doors and what-have-you before the plane is really ready for service. We try to make sure that when the President of the United States gets on board his airplane, everything will be functioning as perfectly as we can make it."

In the big hangar that houses the two presidential planes at Andrews Air Force Base, no one is permitted to go aboard—not even the pilots—without checking in with the Air Police security detachment. The security guards themselves are rigidly screened by the Air Force (and by the FBI) before selection.

Pilot Les McClelland, chief flight engineer Joe Chappell, and senior radio operator Earl Van Valkenburg select the air crew from the best talent in the Air Force, and each candidate undergoes security screening before assignment. Screening is also used for the thirty-three crack maintenance men who work full time on the big Boeings. One security precaution is the use of a "buddy system": no lone workman is ever allowed near the airplanes.

Each of the presidential planes gets an annual physical checkup at E-Systems, Inc., a special Defense Department contractor at Greenville, Texas. "Each year, the inspection concentrates on one of the plane's systems," McClelland said. "Every five years, each plane undergoes a full overhaul. Even the interior is stripped out so that tests can be conducted for stress and metal fatigue. Major modifications are made at that time. But, of course, if anything needs repair or replacement at any time, we have that done immediately."

At Andrews, a special spare-parts stockroom for the presidential planes is maintained within the hangar complex. Even a spare set of jet engines is kept on hand. After several unexplained cuts showed up recently in the tires drawn from the main base supply room, McClelland made the decision to stock *Air Force One*'s tires in a separate, secure room at the hangar.

But a security system is only as good as its ability to thwart penetration by potential saboteurs, hijackers, or assassins. Two "penetrations" occurred during the Nixon years, and one of them gave everybody a fit.

"You have a bomb aboard the President's plane!"

That startling message came to Col. Jay Wallace, commander of the 89th Air Force Wing at Andrews Air Force Base, from an agent of the Inspector General's Office. The bomb, he said, had been planted on the aircraft the previous day during a crew proficiency flight.

"Impossible!" Albertazzie told Wallace. He turned to *Air Force One*'s flight engineer, Joe Chappell. Chappell's face suddenly lit up.

"That explains that package of cigarettes," he said with a grin.

It was a hoax—an official one, perpetrated by a pair of Air

91

Force security investigators who had taken advantage of Albertazzie's hospitality.

During their examination of the 89th Wing, the parent organization for *Air Force One*, two members of the Inspector General's staff had asked Albertazzie for permission to accompany the crew on one of its regular proficiency trips over the Washington area.

"We like to have fellow officers observe our training procedures, so we agreed," Albertazzie said.

During the flight, one of the inspector agents quietly slipped a pack of cigarettes into the pocket behind Chappell's seat. During the critique for Col. Wallace the next day, the inspector contended he could have been an enemy agent or someone set on sabotaging the President's plane. The cigarette pack, he said, could have been a bomb.

What he didn't know was that Chappell, policing up after the flight, had found the cigarettes and removed them.

"They didn't belong to anybody on the flight crew so I gave them to one of the ground maintenance men," Chappell said. "I like a neat airplane."

On another occasion, a man wearing the insignia of an Air Force brigadier general and identifying himself as Robert Smart, executive director of the Air Force Association, presented himself at 89th Wing headquarters. He said he was serving his two-week active duty stint as a reservist and asked if he might have permission to tour the President's plane while waiting for a flight out of Andrews. As was customary, Col. James Keel, the Wing's vice-commander, telephoned Albertazzie to obtain his approval.

"I assumed the visitor was a friend of Keel's, so I gave my permission," said Albertazzie. "Personal identification of prospective visitors was our best method of ensuring that they were who they purported to be."

Accompanied by Col. Keel, Smart was logged in on the *Air Force One* security book, and given a tour of the aircraft. The next day, the Air Force Office of Security and Intelligence boasted it had scored a penetration of the security barrier around the presidential airplane. "General Smart" turned out to be an OSI agent using phony credentials to bluff his way into Keel's confidence.

"Although the imposter had never left the sight of Col. Keel and had hidden nothing on board, it took reams of paperwork to refute the OSI's claim of a penetration," Albertazzie said.

"After these two attempts to discredit our security, we adopted a new rule: we would in the future give no more tours or rides to members of the OSI or the Inspector General's staff."

Actually, there has never been a covert penetration of *Air Force One*'s security system, according to pilots and crew members of the presidential fleet. But there have been other incidents. *The Washington Star,* in a 1968 feature story about Col. James Cross, President Johnson's pilot, recounted one during the Eisenhower years that turned out to be more bizarre than serious.

Air Force police and Secret Service agents picked up a shabbily dressed man and woman loitering near the runway at Andrews Air Force Base shortly before Ike was scheduled to take off. In the man's pocket was a water pistol. The couple told interrogators they had planned to dash toward the President's plane as it began to move, with the man waving his toy gun. Their hope was that they would be shot down and killed by Air Force guards—a suicide pact that would garner them headlines in the papers. They represented no cause and had no intention of harming the President. As it turned out, they didn't even get the desired publicity because the incident was kept secret. "We didn't want to give other people any ideas," an Air Force official explained.

On a Nixon visit to Plattsburgh, N.Y. in June 1969, authorities apprehended a man carrying a high-powered rifle in the vicinity of the runway shortly before the President's departure. Secret Service agents questioned him at length and later released him. He insisted he was merely a hunter looking for game.

But the threat of assassination, of course, is very real.

President Ford's ability to take stress in his stride was especially noticed on the return flight to Washington after narrowly escaping the assassination attempt by Lynette "Squeaky" Fromme in Sacramento during early September 1975.

As *Air Force One* hurtled homeward through the skies, pool reporters in the rear of the plane imagined a brooding President, probably nursing a martini, sitting alone in his cabin and reflecting quietly on his narrow escape from death. But, as Dennis Far-

93

ney of *The Wall Street Journal* later noted, that notion was absolutely wrong.

"Somewhere over Indiana the President ambled back into a staff compartment in the middle of the plane and it was immediately apparent that he wasn't in a brooding mood at all. He was puffing contentedly on a pipe. He was smiling broadly. He was, it seemed, in the mood for a party."

Indeed he was. Drinks were passed, jokes were told, and everybody laughed, with Ford sharing the fun. Press Secretary Ron Nessen said the President recounted his memories of the incident again and again, even demonstrating how his Secret Service bodyguards had doubled him over and hustled him away as other agents wrestled Fromme to the ground and took away her .45 caliber pistol. The White House Communications Agency transmitted to *Air Force One* the sound track of NBC's news coverage of the episode; Ford listened to it intently.

"As usual, Ford kept his deepest emotions to himself," Nessen observed in his White House memoir. "It was no calculated façade."

Seventeen days later the incident repeated itself in San Francisco, only this time the would-be assassin, Sara Jane Moore, actually fired a shot that narrowly missed Ford. The Secret Service raced him to the airport in his limousine. But before boarding *Air Force One,* the President insisted on shaking hands with members of the San Francisco motorcycle escort and ordered agent Ron Pontius to radio his thanks to all the security men involved in protecting him during his visit.

Ford went straight to his compartment as soon as he boarded the plane, followed by Dr. William Lukash, Nessen, senior aides Don Rumsfeld and Bob Hartmann, and David Kennerly, the White House photographer. A steward was waiting with a frosty martini. Ford took a deep gulp and grinned. The rest ordered drinks, too.

Betty Ford had been visiting out on the Monterey peninsula, so another round of drinks was consumed while *Air Force One* waited her return. She walked in, smiling sweetly. It was instantly obvious that she hadn't heard a thing about the assassination attempt. "I watched her face intently to see what her reaction would be," Nessen said. "She never changed her expression. She just kept smiling and took a sip of her drink."

On the homeward flight this time, the Ford staff was tense and filled with foreboding. There had been two attempts on Ford's life in less than three weeks. What was going on out there? Some staffers, deeply shaken, drank too much. Once again, Ford remained calm. He telephoned daughter Susan and son Jack to assure them he was fine, wolfed down a steak, and went promptly to sleep. Back in the White House just before midnight, Ford went before the television cameras to praise San Francisco's hospitality and tell the American people he intended to continue traveling around the country. But at Secret Service insistence, thereafter he agreed to wear a lightweight bulletproof "undershirt" beneath his clothing.

Sometimes nature poses a threat as real as any devised by man. Deer have had to be shooed off the runways at Andrews Air Force Base, and India's sacred cows were a runway worry when President Eisenhower visited there. Nixon's air crew fretted about the big gooney birds that wander everywhere on Midway Island. On the night of August 18, 1970, taking off from New York Naval Air Station, *Air Force One*'s No. 4 engine burped loudly, then stabilized itself to permit the flight to continue to Andrews. Safely on the ground, the crew discovered the engine had ingested two large seagulls.

Communications aboard the President's plane are more advanced than any in the world, but still not ideal. A President has really but one secure system for sending and receiving secret messages—a teletype system that automatically encodes or decodes cable traffic between *Air Force One* and the White House Situation Room or the National Military Command Center in the Pentagon.

During Lyndon Johnson's presidency, communications experts came up with a scheme they said would provide equal security for voice communication by radio phone from *Air Force One*. An airborne President, it was claimed, would be able to speak secretly with the Secretary of State or the Secretary of Defense from any point on earth. His voice transmission would automatically be "scrambled," much as can be done on voice communications over ground line telephones to foil eavesdropping. But on the receiving end, the President's voice would be clearly audible to his designated listener, and vice versa.

95

The vaunted new system, called the High Frequency Scope-safe and developed at a cost of $25,000,000, was installed aboard *Air Force One*. Lyndon Johnson, with his love for the telephone, could hardly wait to use it. There was only one slight problem. It didn't work.

During the Nixon years, Albertazzie kept nagging Air Force headquarters to make the High Frequency Scopesafe system reliable enough to trust. "We never could get more than a couple of minutes of intelligible conversation out of it," he said. Albertazzie was determined to make Scopesafe operational or get rid of it. It weighed 1,700 pounds and occupied valuable space in *Air Force One*'s belly.

So the presidential plane took off one day for Europe with a high-ranking galaxy of electronics and communications experts, plus a two-star general and a covey of Air Force colonels.

"We put Scopesafe to a total test," Albertazzie said. "We flew to Madrid and then to Athens. Then back to Madrid and home to Washington via the South Atlantic. The purpose was to check out the ground support systems in Spain, Ethiopia, Germany, and the Caribbean. We wanted to check all of them, so nobody in the Pentagon could say, 'Well, it was the fault of the ground station in Spain,' or Germany, or wherever. We were in the air seventeen hours and forty minutes. In all that time, we were able to keep Scopesafe in a secure mode just slightly over three minutes. When we got back home, we dismantled the darned thing and took it out of the airplane."

Physical security for the President begins with the interior design of his special quarters aboard his plane. As far back as Franklin Roosevelt's *Sacred Cow*, the Secret Service has insisted that the President be seated on the side of the aircraft away from the doors. That keeps his windows out of view of the crowds at airport ramps and helps foil anyone with a rifle who might be lurking in the vicinity, awaiting an opportunity to take a pot shot.

Airfield security measures are elaborate whenever the President is aboard *Air Force One*. On military and civilian airports, armed guards are stationed at strategic points along the runway; other guards with K-9 dogs patrol wooded areas in the vicinity.

96

Moments before takeoff or landing, a Secret Service vehicle drives slowly along the runway to make sure there is no debris or foreign object that might damage the President's plane. Fire trucks, ambulances, and rescue helicopters are positioned for any emergency. And it is customary for airport flight controllers to briefly suspend other air traffic whenever the President arrives or departs.

Air Force One may be physically out of Washington's sight whenever the President flies, but it is never out of Washington's electronic mind. Its flight plan and whereabouts are constantly monitored by a host of security support agencies strung around the globe. The National Military Command Center, which controls the Boeing 747 "Doomsday" aircraft that serves as a President's command post in event of a nuclear emergency, keeps in close touch with President Carter's *Air Force One* pilot, Col. McClelland.

Whether aloft or on the ground in this country or abroad, McClelland also keeps in steady touch with a special weather team at Andrews Air Force Base, which provides the latest weather information on a global basis for *Air Force One*. The presidential weather watch is mounted by Air Force Capt. Lowell Aires. "When we're in the air," said McClelland, "Aires is always on duty back at Andrews, keeping the same hours as the flight crew, no matter what country or time zone we're flying in. You might say Aires is a crew member in absentia. We may not see him but we're in radio contact all the time."

One of *Air Force One*'s requirements is to be ready to fly the President back to Washington at a moment's notice. "The first thing we do after landing is to prepare the aircraft for immediate departure—just in case," McClelland said.

When Carter landed at Bonn, West Germany, in July 1978 to attend the economic summit meeting of free world leaders, McClelland had only to flash Andrews Air Force Base to obtain an immediate flight plan for a fast return to Washington. Called a "no-notice flight plan," it is kept up-to-the-minute and stored in the computers at Andrews for instant use.

From Washington, the hush-hush National Security Agency (NSA), with its global network of spy satellites and exotic electronics, also keeps watch over the skies that the Commander-in-

97

Chief traverses. In 1972 for example, as Nixon's plane departed Warsaw on the long flight back to Washington, NSA suddenly flashed a warning. An unidentified plane, bearing fighter characteristics and coming from East Germany, was hurtling toward *Air Force One*. It was on a collision course and was closing fast. NSA kept Albertazzie apprised with a tense countdown: "Fifty miles . . . forty miles . . . thirty-five miles—and now he's turning away from you! Have a safe trip." Albertazzie, ready to take evasive action, sighed with relief. At the speed the unidentified plane was approaching, it would have intercepted *Air Force One* in three more minutes.

On overseas flights, *Air Force One* is constantly protected by a fleet of guardian angels, although the Air Force has given them an ignominious sobriquet—"Duck Butts." These planes of the Air Rescue Service are specially modified cargo aircraft, carrying rubber life rafts and medical teams ready to parachute to assist persons aboard the President's plane if it is forced down at sea. The air rescue system has recently replaced the several dozen U.S. Navy and Coast Guard vessels that were strung across the ocean at hundred-mile intervals along the route of the President's airplane.

In 1950, when President Truman flew the *Independence* to Wake Island for his historic meeting with Gen. Douglas MacArthur, an air and sea armada accompanied him. Air Force B-29s and B-17s flew escort part of the way. Four Navy destroyers, the USS *Carpenter*, USS *Perkins*, USS *Rogers*, USS *Cabezon*, and three Coast Guard cutters, the *Iroquois*, *Escanaba*, and *Wachusetts* cruised at spaced intervals along the route from San Francisco to Hawaii and Wake. The vessels offered rescue service if the *Independence* ran into trouble over the ocean. They also kept pilot Frenchie Williams abreast of the latest weather conditions.

"It takes only three or four Duck Butts to shepherd *Air Force One* across the Atlantic," said Albertazzie. "As soon as the plane clears the eastern seaboard, for example, Duck Butt Alpha picks it up with its radar and then flies alongside until the President's plane begins to outdistance him. Then he hands *Air Force One* on to Duck Butt Bravo, who in turn passes it along to Duck Butt Coco, and so on until *Air Force One* is over Europe."

During over-water trips, the plane's radio operator stays in constant communication with each of the air rescue planes monitoring the President's position. On long flights over the Pacific, the polar icecap, or in troubled regions of the world, the air rescue fleet may be augmented with ships at sea, and, if necessary, *Air Force One* can instantly command a fighter plane escort. By tradition, however, Presidents in peacetime shy away from heavy emphasis on military security, preferring their flights to be treated as civilian trips under the international rules of the air. So while the Defense Department and the Secret Service are determined to take no chances with the safety of the Commander-in-Chief, in deference to his wishes, they endeavor to keep security at a low profile.

There are always exceptions, however. Some of the most extraordinary security measures ever undertaken to protect a traveling President occurred in late February 1964, scarcely three months after the assassination of John F. Kennedy, when President Lyndon Johnson decided to fly to Florida.

The occasion was a major Democratic fund-raising dinner at the Fontainebleau Hotel in Miami Beach on February 27, with an en route stop at Palatka, Florida. There LBJ was scheduled to dedicate the new Cross-Florida Barge Canal.

Not until the following day, with the President safely back in the White House, did the world learn that the government had wrapped Lyndon Johnson in a security blanket unmatched since the secret wartime trips of Franklin Roosevelt and Harry Truman. The reason? The FBI's intelligence network had picked up a report that one of Fidel Castro's pilots, flying out of Cuba, might attempt to ram *Air Force One* or shoot it down over Florida.

With Dallas only thirteen weeks past and on everyone's mind, U.S. security agencies were taking no chances. Their first priority, of course, was to protect LBJ from harm. But if an attempt was made on his life, even an unsuccessful one, security officials wanted to nab the attacker, dead or alive. And if he were a pilot flying a Cuban plane, that just might yield important evidence on the Kennedy assassination, then being investigated by the Warren Commission. Cuba's links to Moscow, and Lee Harvey Oswald's puzzling connections with both communist capitals, were of great concern and much speculation within the intelligence community.

So while every effort was made to capture a potential attacker, elaborate precautions were taken to ensure that his mission would fail.

At Andrews Air Force Base, where the flight began, reporters noted that the President was not boarding the regular *Air Force One*, SAM 26000, but the similar backup Boeing, SAM 970. Only this time the tail number had been painted over. Inquiring reporters were told only that the regular plane was being overhauled. No explanation was forthcoming about the missing tail number.

Correspondents aboard SAM 970 with the President and his family noticed something else that didn't normally occur on a routine domestic flight. Among the passengers was James J. Rowley, chief of the Secret Service.

En route from Washington, the big Boeing did not climb high into the clear skies as it always did. It stayed low, in the heavy cloud cover. The initial destination was Jacksonville Naval Air Station, where LBJ transferred to a waiting helicopter for the short hop to Palatka and the canal ceremony. When the pool of reporters returned to board the President's plane again at Jacksonville, they discovered the next stop would not be Miami after all. President Johnson, they were informed, had decided to stop first at West Palm Beach to pay an unannounced visit to Joseph P. Kennedy, the father of the slain President. He had suffered a paralytic stroke and was convalescing at his oceanside home there.

Back at West Palm Beach airport after the visit, reporters were surprised to see the presidential plane take off without LBJ (it flew to Homestead Air Force Base outside Miami as a decoy). Instead, they and LBJ were placed aboard a fleet of ordinary military helicopters for a 67-mile hedge-hopping flight to the fairways of the Bayshore Country Club in Miami. There Johnson transferred to a closed limousine for the short drive to the Fontainebleau Hotel, with an Army helicopter flying less than a hundred feet overhead. The next morning, shortly after dawn, LBJ was secretly driven to Homestead Air Base, where he boarded SAM 970 for an unannounced flight back to Washington.

The tip about a possible attack on Johnson's plane had proven false, but the Secret Service had taken no chances. Only then were inquiring reporters briefed on some of the other security precautions. On the flight from Washington to Miami, two Boeing 707s identical to SAM 970, their tail numbers also painted over, had flown beside the President's plane so as to confuse any would-be attacker. Air Force fighters flew high cover, and armed Navy ships patrolled the coastal waters off Miami.

If the First Family felt any concern, it was masked as carefully as the flight itself. Lady Bird joshed her husband as the "star performer" of the Democratic Party. LBJ, seeking privacy for a political huddle with accompanying senators, was chagrined to find his quarters occupied by a napping daughter Luci. Instead, he conferred with them in the aisle, dictated some memos to his secretary, Juanita Roberts, made several calls on the radio telephone to Washington, and gulped down a lunch of vegetable soup, tuna sandwich, and Sanka coffee. Then he shed his shoes in the corridor and clambered into a curtained bunk for a short nap. Col. James B. Swindal, the cool presidential pilot, chalked it up as another day's work. As it turned out, he said later, it had been "almost routine."

Reports and rumors of potential attacks on an airborne President are not uncommon. It is then, while flying high in the skies in an unarmed and very visible airplane, that he may be most vulnerable to a hostile country or a crazed aviator. Fortunately, most such rumors are precisely that and no more; inventive minds leap easily to them. But when the price of such a horrendous deed is considered, even the most fanatic of adversaries has had the wisdom to push the notion aside as self-defeating. Even in a ruthless world, self-preservation is still more important than the destruction of a perceived enemy.

Shortly before President Nixon's trip to Peking in February 1972, Mao Tse-tung's agents in Paris relayed information to American authorities that the unhappy Nationalist Chinese regime on Taiwan would attempt to shoot down *Air Force One* as it approached the People's Republic of China. Peking would not vouch for the report's validity but felt the President should know about it. The information, of course, turned out to be false. Perhaps Mao was merely testing Nixon's mettle.

101

Such incidents, even when they turn out to be false alarms, would be unnerving were it not for the constant drilling that *Air Force One*'s pilots and crew members undergo during periods when they are not actually flying the President. The standard term, "crew proficiency flights," does not adequately describe the gamut of responsibilities with which the crew is charged. It ranges from handling mechanical emergencies of the aircraft itself to detailed procedures, some of them secret, for safeguarding the President and members of the First Family in event of a forced landing or crash.

Over and over, literally hundreds of times, the crew practices takeoffs, landings, instrument approaches, and every imaginable type of simulated in-flight emergency. *Air Force One* (SAM 27000) and its primary backup (SAM 26000) have made scores of landings with only two or three engines operating—although, of course, never with the President on board. Just as repeatedly, the crews rehearse takeoff situations in which an engine or two may fail moments after the big Boeing has left the ground.

Similar precautionary measures are taken by the ground maintenance team that tends the presidential planes. Fuel, for example, is selected at random from various storage facilities to make sure that no saboteur could know, in advance, which one contains the fuel to be used in *Air Force One*. It is analyzed for contaminants and then, after approval, placed in refueling truck tanks, which are then sealed and placed under guard for twenty-four hours, until the fuel is pumped into the aircraft.

Guarding the presidential planes, the special hangar, spare-parts lockers, and tools is the responsibility of an elite Air Police unit assigned full time to the task. Top members of the security force, headed in 1978 by Chief Master Sgt. Jose Lopez, undergo training by the FBI and Secret Service. No person or item is allowed aboard the presidential aircraft without security screening. Lopez and three members of the security guard are part of the air crew of *Air Force One* and accompany the President wherever he flies. Whenever the plane is on the ground, the guards obtain the assistance of local police and the Secret Service in mounting a wide security perimeter around the aircraft, but the close-in barrier is always maintained by the veteran

Lopez and his men. They happen to be crack pistol shots.

Keeping unauthorized persons away from *Air Force One* is simpler than avoiding the insidious threat of sabotage. So the guards and crew members are regularly briefed on what to watch for by specialists in countersabotage.

"Some of the saboteur's methods and tools are pretty exotic," said Albertazzie. "For example, we were shown a marking pencil that looks innocent enough on the outside—the kind anybody might use. But this particular one contained a ferocious acid, not detectable by sight or smell, that could cause 'fatigue' in metal within a few hours of application. Imagine what might happen if it were applied to an integral part of the airplane—a wing span or a flight control mechanism—just before the President took off on a long flight."

Every time the President flies, the stewards make sure the latest magazines, newspapers, and periodicals are within handy reach in his cabin. When he stops in an American city, the local papers frequently are added to his library. But even such material can be transformed into a lethal weapon.

"Countersabotage agents demonstrated to us how a killing application of a special nerve gas could be surreptitiously applied to a newspaper," Albertazzie said. "When the reader opens it up, he is instantly overcome by the fumes.

"There is also a deadly liquid which can be applied to spanking clean sheets and pillow cases. After it dries, you can hardly detect its presence. But the heat from a user's body would be sufficient to release a poisonous gas that is usually fatal. Imagine what might happen if a President decided to take a nap!"

As a result, *Air Force One*'s flight stewards take extraordinary precautions to ensure that all personal supplies brought aboard—from reading matter to linens, food, and bathroom tissue—are free of contaminants. Even cigarettes, cigars, candy, notepads, and pencils undergo special attention to avoid what the crew calls "clandestine sabotage."

One of the most useful ways to thwart sabotage is through a deliberate policy of random procurement. Foodstuffs acquired for *Air Force One* are never obtained from a single source. Sometimes food items are drawn from Air Force kitchens,

103

sometimes from the White House, and frequently from local supermarkets and specialty grocers. The flight stewards personally select the food and deliver it to the airplane.

"By shopping around, we make it nearly impossible for anyone to deliberately tamper with our food supplies and other items," said Colonel McClelland, pilot for Presidents Ford and Carter. "Whenever our linens come back from our own laundry, the flight stewards open up, examine, and refold every piece. We can test it if necessary. And, of course, once we have ascertained that everything is all right, we lock it away and keep it under 24-hour guard—just like the plane."

The security system is pervasive. A special kitchen for preparing the First Family's food is housed within *Air Force One*'s hangar complex at Andrews Air Force Base. Not only is the kitchen itself kept locked, even when in use, but individual cupboard units, refrigerators, and freezers are locked as well. "It takes a little longer to prepare the meals, but it guarantees security," said Chief flight steward Palmer, the presidential chef and keeper of the keys.

The Secret Service, ever concerned about bombs hidden in or near *Air Force One*, assists the plane's security force in screening personal luggage, briefcases, and all other items put on board the aircraft. Airport support equipment—boarding stairs, auxiliary power units, fuel trucks, and public address systems—is closely examined before every presidential arrival or departure by a special explosive ordnance team. The bomb squad's biggest worry is that a powerful device might be electronically detonated from a distance just as the President stepped on the stairs or walked past some innocent-appearing object.

Skyjacking became a new concern for *Air Force One*'s crew during the Johnson years. Given the tight security, the risk of the President's airplane being successfully seized by armed intruders seemed overblown to many persons in government and even to the staff of the White House. But with hijackers becoming an increasing problem on commercial air flights, and international terrorism on the increase in Europe, the Middle East, and Africa, the Defense Department and the Secret Service instituted special precautions at home and abroad for safeguarding the President's aircraft.

The greatest risk obviously is not from a lone gunman who might come aboard as a passenger; that possibility is precluded by the fact that strangers are never admitted to the elite company of those who fly on *Air Force One*. The real worry is that an armed group of terrorists might attempt to seize the President's plane while it was on the ground at some airport in the United States or a foreign capital. The prevention of such an armed attack is basically the responsibility of local authorities wherever the President lands, plus the intelligence-gathering services of federal and foreign agencies.

The crew leaves such larger matters of security to those who must handle it, but they have instituted extra security measures for themselves and the airplane they are responsible for safeguarding. They have undergone special anti-hijacking training by the Secret Service and the Air Force. In the Nixon era, key members of the air crew were encouraged to carry personal firearms, although such close-up protection of the President and his plane remains the prime responsibility of the large Secret Service contingent that always accompanies the Chief Executive and his family. But there were occasions when Albertazzie, flying a member of the President's family on one of the smaller Jetstars, discreetly tucked a .25 caliber automatic pistol into the top of his right stocking before takeoff. "Just in case," he said.

As of this writing, no attempt to seize the President's plane— on the ground or in the air—has ever occurred. Nor have any such plots been reported. But the vigilance continues. "Knowing what I know," observed McClelland, "it would be extremely unhealthy for anybody who tried."

There have been scary moments in the sky, however. Breaking out of heavy clouds on an approach to Manila Airport in July 1969, Albertazzie was startled to find *Air Force One* surrounded by Philippine jet fighters. "My God, they were up there in the clouds with us and we never knew they were that close! We might have collided."

Co-pilot John Schutes immediately radioed the Manila tower and demanded that the fighters break off. On the ground, Albertazzie protested to the commanding general of the Philippine Air Force that his planes had violated international rules of the air. "It scared hell out of the passengers and alarmed me that any group of planes would fly that close to the airplane of a chief of state without advance permission and coordination."

The White House and the Pentagon, in fact, have a worldwide prohibition against fighter escorts for presidential flights. In peaceful regions there is always the problem of airborne coordination, selecting the time and place for rendezvous, and possibly overcoming a language barrier. And there is the risk of collision. Even in combat zones such as Vietnam, an escort serves to call unnecessary attention to *Air Force One*'s presence. It was deemed safer to slip in unannounced and, with luck, unnoticed. Beyond all these practical reasons, a fighter escort is objectionable because it lends a martial atmosphere to a presidential visit. Every President of the United States wants to be perceived abroad as a man of peace and good will, not as the commander-in-chief of a military superpower.

During Nixon's nine-day swing through the Mideast in June 1974, Albertazzie got word from the Air Force advance party in Damascus that the Syrians wanted to provide Nixon with an escort of Russian-made fighter planes. There was some reason for the recommendation. Syria's propaganda machine had only recently ceased spewing vitriol and hatred against America, the champion of Israel. Syria was the hard-line Arab state on Israel's border, the most resistant to Kissinger's diplomatic blandishments for peace. There was concern that some rebellious antiaircraft unit, or some fanatic pilot, inflamed with an Islamic sense of *jehad* (holy war), might try to kill Nixon and thereby save Syria from any peaceful accommodation with Israel. That very morning, even as Nixon prepared to fly to Damascus, leaflets had suddenly appeared throughout the poorer districts of the city: "Was all the war, all the blood that was shed under American bombs, all the dead we suffered, so that Nixon and the prophet of imperialism, Kissinger, could visit Damascus and give us a hundred million dollars?"

Albertazzie, under orders, relayed word back to the advance party in Damascus that President Assad's offer of an escort should be turned down firmly, with thanks. *Air Force One* would come in alone, unattended, following the chartered press planes that would land first. The arrival would be governed, as was customary for civilian aircraft, by the procedures of the International Civil Aviation Organization.

106

Twenty minutes away from Damascus, with his craft already down to 15,000 feet, Albertazzie got the shock of his life. Four camouflaged jets were closing fast. They were Soviet-built MIGs. "My God!" he said and barked orders to the co-pilot, Lt. Col. Frank Hughes. "Call Damascus and find out what's up."

In the staff section over the wing, Major George Joulwan, Haig's deputy, spotted the planes at almost the same instant. "Look—we've got fighters on the left!"

Another staffer spotted another pair of jets moving in from the right. William Henkel, the trip coordinator, started up toward the cockpit to investigate. He knew a fighter escort was not supposed to be out there.

As Henkel moved into the aisle, Albertazzie suddenly pushed *Air Force One* into a dive, banking sharply. Henkel was tossed across the aisle and fell into a seat next to Lt. Gen. Brent Scowcroft, Kissinger's assistant for national security affairs. Scowcroft was bracing his legs and clutching the arms of his chair. "Wouldn't this be a helluva ending," he was saying softly.

For nearly eight minutes Albertazzie put the big Boeing 707 through an erratic pattern of steep turns and evasive maneuvers while Hughes sought an explanation from the Damascus tower. Kissinger struggled forward to the flight deck. "Albertazzie, what's happening?" Finally assured the Syrian fighters were not hostile—although unscheduled, Albertazzie leveled out the plane and continued his landing approach toward Damascus. On the ground, Syrian Air Force officials apologized for the incident, explaining that the fighters were after all, only students. Kissinger told the Syrian air marshal, "That's worse yet." Nixon, who had remained safely in his suite during the episode, made no mention of it to Albertazzie or the Syrians.

Flying a President in peacetime is a piece of cake compared to the flying assignments that periodically came during the Vietnam War. For McClelland, the most memorable trip was the first American flight into North Vietnam in February 1973.

Hanoi was the destination and Henry Kissinger the primary passenger when McClelland lifted the big Boeing, emblazoned with "United States of America," off the runway at Andrews Air Force Base. North Vietnam and the United States had signed the Paris protocols ending the Vietnam War. Now it was

Kissinger's turn to shift the focus "from hostility to normalization." As promised in the Paris accords, the United States was prepared to contribute to repairing the ravages of the B-52 bombing raids and to general reconstruction. But Kissinger also wanted to remind Premier Pham Van Dong that the Congress and the President could do nothing unless Hanoi stopped violating the cease-fire in the South and used its influence to terminate the fighting in Cambodia and Laos.

Flying an unarmed plane into hitherto enemy territory was not exactly routine. And, as McClelland discovered, the North Vietnamese were not very cooperative. "We had the name of the field that served Hanoi, but we got word back from them that there was no such airport," he recalls. "Finally, after much checking, we discovered the field was there, but the name had been changed. They just wouldn't tell us."

McClelland put the 707 down on a runway pockmarked with B-52 bomb craters. North Vietnamese officials were on hand to greet Kissinger and escort him away. After posting an Air Force guard around the airplane, McClelland and the crew were bused to a hotel in downtown Hanoi.

"The B-52s had done an amazingly accurate job of bombing right up to the city limits," McClelland said. "But the North Vietnamese figured out how to work around it. They kept their truck convoys inside the city limits at night, when the bombers were overhead, and moved them south during the daytime."

McClelland and the crew were instructed not to leave their hotel except under official escort. Whether it would have been unsafe to walk the streets is sheer conjecture. During Kissinger's stay, the presidential air crew was taken on two trips by bus, once to a shopping area and another time to a museum. "Almost as if on signal, people on the streets began beating our bus with clubs," McClelland recalls.

McClelland remembers Hanoi most vividly for two reasons.

One was the sight of American POWs being bused to the airport, where C-141 transport planes were waiting to take them back to the United States. "I wanted to rush over to greet them," he said, "but of course that wasn't permitted."

And then there was the night he woke up in his hotel room to discover an intruder near his bed.

"I sat up and flailed at the mosquito netting," he recounted. "The moment I did that, the stranger fled silently out of the room."

McClelland, a former pro football player, moved swiftly to the door and flung it open. The hallway was deserted. In a room across the hall, members of his crew were still up, playing cards. But they had not seen or heard anyone in the corridor.

"I finally went back to bed and fell asleep again, wondering if I had imagined the whole thing. But the next day I knew it really had happened. Out of the blue, my interpreter apologized to me for 'the intrusion of last evening.' He said someone had entered my room by mistake."

McClelland is skeptical of that explanation. He remembers feeling uncomfortable and listless during his brief Hanoi stay, "almost as though I were drugged." But neither he nor Air Force medics could explain it. In any event, the sensation wore off quickly and McClelland flew Kissinger on the rest of the Asian journey, first to British-controlled Hong Kong and then to Peking via Canton. "That was the first time we were allowed to enter the People's Republic of China from Hong Kong," he observed.

On a presidential trip, coordination of assignments and equipment—the determination of who does what, when, and where—becomes a logistical exercise that almost defies description. Every detail is set out in advance in the trip "bible." Even for a routine jaunt, making up the bible is a formidable task. For a one-stop trip to Columbia, Missouri, made by Carter, for instance, it ran three pages and was crammed with footnotes and parenthetical advisories for the President, staffers, and reporters. For a major trip, covering many days and events in many countries, the bible may grow fat as a catalog. For ease of handling on such occasions, it is usually put into a large looseleaf notebook, very much like the kind that teenagers take to school, with individual copies for the several hundred persons accompanying the President. Elite staffers get a pocket-size edition in fine print.

It is one thing for a presidential entourage to know what it wants to do on reaching a foreign capital but quite another thing

109

to dovetail a President's requirements with what is expected by his hosts. The trip bible thus reflects not only the gospel according to the White House but also the diplomatic liturgy of the country inviting him.

Such things are complicated enough when a President visits a Western nation—Britain, France, West Germany, or Australia. They become infinitely more complex on journeys to totalitarian lands like the Soviet Union and those in Eastern Europe and the Middle East. The trip bible for Nixon's week-long China visit stands as the most elaborate ever issued. It ran 114 pages in length, with twelve subsections, a special rundown on Mrs. Nixon's itinerary, and a chart for converting Peking time into the correct date and time in Washington, Honolulu, and Guam.

But thin or thick, the trip bible is the distillation of hundreds of hours of advance work by an incredible number of persons in many federal agencies. Moving a President constitutes an accomplishment in timing, coordination, detailed planning, and scrupulous preparation. The process amazes even those who have been doing it for years.

Several weeks before a major presidential journey, the President's plane embarks on an advance trip to give the crew and members of the White House staff and supporting agencies an opportunity to inspect the facilities the President will use and to make final plans with the host countries for his actual visit. Some of those on board—Secret Service men, State Department protocol officers, specialists from the White House Communications Agency—are dropped off at various points to perform their tasks and await the President's arrival.

Each trip, naturally, commences with the President himself. Once he accepts an invitation, his scheduling staff at the White House begins constructing a tentative scenario around the target dates of departure and return, drawing in his political and press advisers (and the State Department's protocol officer for foreign trips) and the key support agencies—Secret Service, Department of Defense, National Security Council, White House Communications Agency, and the White House Military Office.

The procedure varies little from President to President. Appointments secretary Phil Wise and deputy Frances Voorde serve alternately as trip director for Carter's journeys, coor-

110

dinating the preparatory work of the agencies involved in the venture. What complicates the task, of course, is the constitutional nature of the presidency, since its duties follow the occupant wherever he goes. When Jimmy Carter went rafting in Idaho on the Salmon River in August 1978, the black box containing the secret nuclear codes was carried aboard an accompanying rubber craft. That requirement alone stipulates great care in planning, and adequate planning requires considerable advance time. For Carter's trip to Bonn and West Berlin in July 1978, Voorde flew to Germany over Memorial Day weekend to confer with officials of the German government and to traverse the President's prospective route before submitting a rough itinerary for his approval. "As soon as he signed off on the outline, we began filling in the details," she said.

For the presidential pilot and the crew of *Air Force One*, the first hint of an upcoming trip usually is a White House request for information about flying times between Washington and various cities in the United States or abroad.

"We have a rule of thumb that has applied for years," said McClelland. "We can put *Air Force One* into the sky with one hour's notice. If they want to eat a meal, we like two hours' notice. But the fact is, we rarely get less than a day's warning. On overseas trips, we're clued in at least four or five weeks in advance, frequently longer. And well in advance of public announcement."

Sufficient notice was especially critical for the crews of presidents who seemed always to be on the move—Lyndon Johnson and Richard Nixon. Some presidential journeys have been almost back-to-back, with little more than a day to ready the aircraft for the second trip.

During the five and a half years of the Nixon presidency, presidential pilot Ralph Albertazzie was never alerted less than seventeen hours in advance of a presidential flight. But that is insufficient time to prepare adequately for an extended journey, and Albertazzie found himself pressing the White House for earlier notice.

"At first, we received all the lead time anyone could ask," he remembers. "But later on, the staff around the President became increasingly secretive about trip plans, and cooperation wasn't what it should have been. It got so that all of us on the crew lived in mortal fear that one day the helicopter would arrive from the White House with the President and *Air Force One* wouldn't be ready."

The readiness of the two primary presidential planes, SAM 27000 and SAM 26000, holds a lesser priority than that of the big Boeing 747s that function as the national airborne command post—the Doomsday assignment—in event of a nuclear emergency. A command post aircraft is literally ready to fly on a moment's notice, with a crew on board or standing by on an around-the-clock basis, whenever the President may need it.

But the pilots and crew members of SAM 27000 and SAM 26000 are always on call, even when off duty at Andrews Air Force Base. Most reside on the base or close by; their homes are linked to the White House switchboard or to the presidential pilot's office—sometimes both. It's not unusual, even at a social function, a theater, or a supermarket, for a crew member's belt-worn "page boy" to beep an urgent summons.

The primary aircraft are maintained in ready-to-go status at the mammoth hangar at Andrews. "Normally we keep about 56,000 pounds of fuel on board at all times, which is sufficient for about three hours' flying," McClelland says. SAM 27000 waits in its hangar with tractor equipment already attached so that it can instantly be pulled out to the boarding ramp. Sufficient food for at least one in-flight meal is kept in the freezers of *Air Force One*'s kitchen, part of the hangar complex.

Routine domestic flights, such as Carter's trip to Missouri, Nixon's frequent hops to Key Biscayne, and Johnson's dashes to the LBJ ranch, require little advance preparation or notice. Quick trips sometimes can be kept secret until the White House decides to go public.

Pilot Albertazzie and co-pilot McClelland flew to LaGuardia Airport in New York on one occasion to pick up Mrs. Jacqueline Kennedy Onassis and her two children for a private dinner with the Nixons at the White House. The visit was not announced until the former First Family was back in New York later that night.

For the presidential pilot and crew, an advance trip is an opportunity to become familiar with the arrangements at every air-

112

field and to make certain that *Air Force One*'s needs will be adequately tended while on the ground, including the need to depart instantly if an emergency arises in the United States or in the country being visited.

There is scarcely a world capital that the President's pilots of the last few years have not visited at least once. But changes in local facilities that may have occurred since the last trip make it advisable to recheck things on the spot. And, of course, no matter how often *Air Force One* has touched down at Paris or London, each visit varies from the one before, including the weather.

Frequently, however, a presidential visit is a first-time occurrence. During the 1976 presidential campaign, for example, McClelland flew SAM 27000 on an advance trip to Keene, New Hampshire, to test out the airport facilities.

"Everything was fine on the advance flight," he said, "but the weather turned absolutely lousy on the February night of President Ford's trip here. We had no trouble with *Air Force One* because we had familiarized ourselves with the field. But the press plane missed its approach in the fog and had to go around for a second try at landing."

The unsung heroes of presidential travel are the Air Force advance agents, a cadre of about forty captains, majors, and lieutenant colonels who volunteer their time and talents to smooth the way for every *Air Force One* journey. Selected by the Air Force Project Office for presidential flight support and trained by the presidential pilots, these middle-level career men—mostly pilots—tend to the aircraft's needs at every stop: fuel and food replenishment, ground telephone lines, ramp space, boarding stairs of the proper height, arrangements for fire trucks, ambulances, and emergency equipment, and even the selection of the precise spot on the tarmac where the nosewheel of the huge plane will stop.

"They're invaluable," said McClelland. "A good Air Force advance agent means the difference between a lousy stop and a great one."

To perform his duties, the advance man needs sufficient advance notice of a trip so that he can arrange to leave his regular Air Force post and scurry out to the city where he is assigned

113

to work for *Air Force One*—at home or abroad. He wears civilian clothes for his special assignment.

"That works," said Albertazzie. "Civilian clothes give him the upper hand because local officials don't know if he's with the Secret Service, the White House staff, or some other federal agency."

So, whenever you see *Air Force One* taxiing toward its assigned stopping place at an airport, look around for a nonchalant fellow in civilian togs who probably will be standing in the path of the airplane. If you watch closely, you will see his hands rise in a slow, steady movement until they close together in front of his chest. When that happens, the President's plane will stop, the pilot will shut off the engines and the door will open. But before your eyes are diverted by the sight of the President, glance again at the chap in front of the aircraft. You will be looking at the man who is in charge of all ground arrangements for the arrival of *Air Force One* and its subsequent departure.

Once the President's travel schedule is released by the White House, the presidential pilot's office dispatches a precise "trip message" to every military and civilian agency involved in the journey and to those whose duties require constant knowledge of the whereabouts of the President's airplane. Among those receiving trip messages are the Joint Chiefs of Staff, and the individual military branches, the Strategic Air Command, Tactical Air Command, Central Intelligence Agency, National Security Council, National Security Agency, Federal Aviation Administration, and the American ambassadors in the countries to be visited, as well as their Defense Department attachés.

The message lists the estimated times of arrival and departure of the presidential aircraft for each stop, the intended route and altitude of the flight, the name of the aircraft commander, designation of the radio call sign as *Air Force One*, the type of aircraft, and its tail number. The message also sets forth the essential support requirements for each stop: boarding stairs, auxiliary ground power, air-conditioning equipment, and fuel replenishment needs. The message always announces that security for *Air Force One* will be governed by U.S. Air Force Regulation No. 207–13, which spells out exactly how the aircraft is to be guarded and what extraordinary measures will be required.

The Air Force advance agents then take care of executing the details, as well as arranging for crew housing close by or at the airport. The White House Communications Agency installs special telephone lines at every stop for the pilot, navigator, and key crew members so they will be in constant touch with each other, the guards at the aircraft, the Secret Service command post and White House assistants accompanying the President.

The President's personal plane, of course, is only one of several aircraft involved in White House trips. The backup craft, usually SAM 26000, always goes along on foreign journeys and is prepared to substitute for the primary *Air Force One* (SAM 27000) on domestic trips even though it may not always leave Andrews Air Force Base.

"We have the backup serviced and ready to go every time the President flies," said McClelland. "If a mechanical problem develops on *Air Force One* at the last minute or some other emergency occurs, the backup plane is our insurance policy."

Although it is expensive and time-consuming to keep a backup Boeing primed for takeoff, the system avoids the international embarrassment for an American President that befell Soviet boss Leonid Brezhnev during the summit meeting in Moscow in 1972.

Nixon and Brezhnev already were aboard the big Soviet jet that was to fly them to Kiev when the red-faced pilot came back with word that his plane wouldn't start. Nixon volunteered the services of his own backup plane, which was standing by. Brezhnev would have none of that. "We, too, have a backup plane," he boasted.

The trouble was that the Russian substitute wasn't ready to go. It had to be fueled, the engines had to be uncovered, and the interior cabins serviced for use by Brezhnev and Nixon. "They spent almost an hour preparing their backup plane," said Albertazzie, *Air Force One*'s pilot at the time. "We just couldn't believe what was happening."

The backup plane never flies empty. It carries extra members of the President's staff, Secret Service men and State Department officials for whom there is no space aboard the President's airplane. On foreign trips, there is never an effort to conceal the presence of the backup aircraft. But White House sensitivity to

115

criticism sometimes leads to extraordinary efforts to "hide" the backup plane on domestic journeys.

A common tactic is to arrange for the backup to land at a destination well in advance of the President's arrival so that it can be parked in a hangar or a remote corner of the field out of sight of the press. Sometimes the backup's arrival is delayed until the President's motorcade has left the airport.

"During the Nixon years, if the staff feared there would be gripes about using two planes when one would do, we had an alternate way of keeping the backup plane from being noticed," Albertazzie said. "We'd have the backup circle overhead until *Air Force One* and the press planes had departed. Then we'd bring in the backup to pick up those staff people or Secret Service agents who needed transportation to the next stop or back to Washington."

The crews of the presidential primary and backup planes are interchangeable and customarily switch back and forth as the need arises—with the exception of the presidential pilot, who, whenever he flies, always commands the aircraft carrying the President. The commander of the backup plane usually flies as co-pilot on the advance trips that precede a presidential journey, thus gaining an opportunity to familiarize himself with the route and airport landing procedures at every stop.

In addition to the two presidential planes, a modified jet tanker aircraft, converted to VIP use and resembling a Boeing 707 without windows, is used to ferry White House staffers and protocol personnel needed to make final preparations for the President's arrival at each city on his itinerary. Two other aircraft usually fly out early, too—the "car" plane carrying the President's bullet-proof limousine and the Secret Service follow car, plus the "WHCA Bird" that transports the sophisticated communications equipment required to keep a Chief Executive in instant touch with the White House and every other place on the globe.

Sometimes other aircraft are required as well. For example, if the President needs helicopters at a certain destination abroad, they are put aboard a C-141 cargo plane and flown out ahead of his arrival. The choppers also are shipped within the United States whenever there is insufficient time for them to make the trip under their own power.

116

Thus, counting a press plane or two, the fleet for a major presidential journey comprises from five to eight big jet aircraft. And that total, of course, doesn't include the air-sea rescue planes keeping watch over *Air Force One* as it streaks across the ocean at 560 miles an hour.

On *Air Force One*, the crew doesn't bother with the pre-takeoff lecture about seat belts, oxygen masks, and emergency exits required on scheduled airline flights. For one thing, the interior is so compartmented that passengers couldn't readily see an instructor in the aisle. For another, most of those aboard are veterans of air travel; they know the drill by heart. Yet in-flight safety is a prime concern.

Each crew member, from the most junior steward to the pilot, has a specific assignment in event of an emergency aloft. Ditching and evacuating procedures are rehearsed constantly during proficiency training flights. And every passenger, on boarding, finds a small pamphlet at his seat with reminders of what to do "in the unlikely event of a mechanical malfunction."

A crash landing is so awful a thought that *Air Force One*'s passengers tend to skip over that section in the booklet. But the paragraphs on ditching at sea read as optimistically as a presidential speech, beginning with an assurance that the airplane "is provided with modern, practical emergency equipment for your safety and convenience."

After a command to "prepare for ditching," *Air Force One*'s passengers are advised to "calmly and efficiently loosen your tie and collar or remove necklaces, glasses, hats, shoes and to discard sharp objects which you may be carrying." After your assigned crew member has helped you out of an emergency exit and into the water, you may then inflate your life vest. "After the ditching is accomplished, you will board large modern rafts equipped with emergency supplies to ensure the maximum safety and comfort in these circumstances. . . ."

Nothing is said about "presidents and cabinet members first," but the President would get special attention in an emergency, as the nation would expect. While the pilot, as the last man out, is checking to make certain that everyone else has left the plane, an air-sea rescue plane would be not more than a few minutes away—bringing paramedics, divers, and rescue equipment. *Air Force One* is tracked so intently by other aircraft and ships at sea

117

that it is possible to believe that a presidential ditching at sea would occasion a dramatic rescue rather than a national tragedy.

Presidential air crews pride themselves on punctuality. They know how to get the plane to run on time. A President might be tardy in getting aboard *Air Force One*, or weather might cause a delay, but late departures and arrivals are not a result of crew inefficiency.

Airport authorities are cooperative, too. On both military and civilian fields, flight controllers customarily give *Air Force One* a clear priority over other craft. The President's plane ordinarily does not have to wait its turn for takeoff. Nor, on nearing an airport, is it put into a holding pattern or stacked upstairs, as frequently happens with commercial airliners.

Contrary to popular belief, presidential pilots do not request preferential treatment. Ground authorities provide it because it makes common sense. It simplifies safety and security procedures for the President of the United States. And, of course, it's good politics. Very few airport officials or employees want to be known as the s.o.b. who gave the President a problem.

Takeoff and landing proficiency, however, does not come about accidentally. Albertazzie's crew practiced and polished their techniques at every opportunity between presidential trips. It got so that Albertazzie could fine-tune a departure or a landing right down to the split second.

Landings were especially rehearsed, since Presidents like to arrive on the dot. Most presidential arrivals, moreover, are complicated procedures. If the White House and Air Force advance teams have done their work properly, there will be a crowd on hand, perhaps a band or two, an official greeting party of local dignitaries, reporters, and television crews, a caravan of cars to form the presidential motorcade, and, of course, the required police escort and Secret Service protection. So it is vitally important that *Air Force One* perform its proper role in the ceremonies, reaching the designated spot on the field, the engines being shut down and the door opened at the precise moment on the schedule. Presidents don't try to be late, although they can make a reasonable excuse when they are. But to be early, even by five minutes, is embarrassing all around.

As a result of constant practice, *Air Force One* crews have worked out an intricate system to deliver the President to the exact "parking" position required for each occasion. Long before the wheels of the big jet touch the ground, the cockpit crew concentrates on making the preplanned "block time." Simply put, it is the moment when the nosewheel of the President's airplane stops at a predesignated spot on every airfield at home or abroad, a spot usually marked by a white-taped "X" on the ramp. Getting to that tiny piece of real estate on a precise second of time after thousands of miles of flying may seem a mystifying feat, but presidential pilots have it down to an exact science. Block time counting actually begins about 200 miles away, when *Air Force One*'s navigator announces the plane's position and speed. Thanks to its advance trip, the crew knows exactly where the plane should be at that point, and at 100 miles out, at 80 miles, 10 miles, and the very moment of landing.

"We know precisely the taxiing route we have to take and the time it takes, since we have rehearsed it," said McClelland, President Carter's pilot.

Once on the ground, the navigator begins the final countdown to the spot the "X" marks: "Four minutes . . . three minutes . . . two . . . one . . . thirty seconds . . . twenty seconds . . . ten . . . nine . . . eight . . . seven . . . six . . . five . . . four . . . three . . . two . . . NOW."

During the last twenty feet of *Air Force One*'s approach to the "X", the pilot keeps his eye on an Air Force advance man who is watching the nosewheel as it slowly moves toward the spot.

"All the while, he is carefully bringing up both hands, closer, ever closer together," said Albertazzie. "When his hands join, the pilot knows the plane is on the mark. The plane stops. A ground mechanic quickly puts blocks under the wheels. And the time will be exactly as called for on the President's schedule."

Albertazzie's prowess at split-second arrivals, no matter how long the flight, amazed the time-conscious members of the Nixon staff. They kept waiting for him to goof. In mid-1969, on the long trip from Honolulu to Midway Island during Nixon's round-the-world trip, Press Secretary Ronald Ziegler bet five dollars against Col. James Hughes, the Air Force aide, that Albertazzie would not be able to have the door open at exactly 7:17 P.M., the scheduled time for Nixon to leave the plane at Midway. The second hand on the clock, Ziegler insisted, had to be "straight up." Ziegler lost his bet. Thereafter he needled Albertazzie about not only controlling the plane, but its clocks as well.

Ziegler, of course, was jesting. But others on Nixon's staff were not altogether happy with such constant punctuality. One was H. R. "Bob" Haldeman, the dour chief of the Nixon staff.

One day, shortly before departing Washington on a presidential trip, Albertazzie received a telephone call from Colonel Hughes. "Haldeman wants you to be ten minutes late on your arrival tonight," Hughes said. Albertazzie, puzzled, asked why.

"He doesn't want you to be arriving on time all the time," Hughes explained. "He told me he would like to have you bust an ETA [Estimated Time of Arrival] every now and then."

"That doesn't make sense," Albertazzie protested. "There ought to be a reason."

"I guess," said Hughes, "that Haldeman doesn't want anyone else to be right all the time."

"Well," Albertazzie retorted, "you tell Mr. Haldeman that if he wants the flying done that way, he better get the President another pilot." Albertazzie never heard another word about it.

Air Force One's crew has fashioned a popular game out of block time—"nosewheel roulette." The valve stem on the left nose tire serves as the marker. Before landing, each player picks a number from one to twelve, as on the face of a clock, and puts up a dollar. With the pilot serving as judge, the cash pot goes to the player who most accurately picks the wheel's ground-zero point on the block "X." If it results in a tie, say 7:30 rather than 7 or 8, the holders of both numbers split the money. Sometimes members of the White House staff or the Secret Service join in the fun.

"It's a game you can't fix," observed Albertazzie. "The nosewheel is spinning at about 120 miles an hour when it touches the ground."

Timing errors in *Air Force One*'s schedule began cropping up as Nixon's White House staff, jealously guarding its turf, took over most of the operational planning for presidential trips. Some of the bloopers were colossal.

En route from Manila to Jakarta during Nixon's global journey in 1969, Albertazzie discovered that Dwight Chapin's office

120

had factored in the wrong time zone changes. The result was that *Air Force One* had to "kill" a full two hours by zig-zagging across the Pacific skies in order to avoid putting the President into Indonesia two hours ahead of his scheduled arrival.

Thereafter, Albertazzie and Lt. Col. Don McKeown, the navigator, quietly took to double-checking every trip sequence for themselves—whenever they could get their hands on the tentative master schedule. "Frequently we spotted errors of five to sixty minutes in the White House's mathematics—fortunately, in most cases, in time to get the corrections made before the trip actually commenced," Albertazzie said.

Sometimes the mistakes were even more costly to the taxpayers.

"I remember one trip on which we flew the President to Walla Walla, Washington," Albertazzie said, "and he then took a helicopter to go to the airport at Pasco. If the White House staff had only told us in advance that Pasco was his destination, why, we could have flown *Air Force One* directly there—the field was big enough. Instead, helicopters from Washington were flown across the country to Walla Walla to airlift the President to Pasco and back again." The helicopters, of course, one for the President and two more for Secret Service and staff members, then had to chopper their way back across the continent to Washington.

The best-laid plans go awry if the President himself is late getting to the airplane or, as more frequently happens, stays too long on the ramp talking to local bigwigs or decides on the spur of the moment that he wants to "work the crowd" along the fence before taking his departure.

Every President, at home or abroad, seems to need a crowd "fix" before he boards *Air Force One*. The habit is hard to kick, even when he knows he is running late and may have difficulty getting to the next stop on time. Moreover, pressing the flesh seems to be a sacred presidential duty—at least presidents tend to look on it that way—no matter how exasperated or frustrated their staffs become as the minutes go by.

Nixon was usually a punctual man and, even while pumping hands of the clamoring spectators, would sometimes glance at his wristwatch and squint down the fence to see how far the crowd extended. Or he would glance up at the cockpit window to see if Albertazzie was ready to go. Albertazzie, in turn, would try to catch the eye of Ron Ziegler or the chief Secret Service agent by elaborately tapping his wristwatch with a finger. "That usually worked," Albertazzie said. "After a few more handshakes, the President would start moving toward the stairs to the plane."

Major Robert Barrett, President Ford's military aide, sometimes would call down from the plane's doorway when the President dallied too long on the ground. "Get the hook!" Barrett would shout to no one in particular but in a voice intended for the presidential ear. "Get the hook!" Ford, grinning, invariably got the message. "Whaddya mean—get the hook?" he would josh as he climbed aboard. "What hook?"

Although *Air Force One*'s pilots do not demand priority clearance for arrivals and departures at airports, they do attempt to arrange special flight paths or air corridors between a President's most frequently used airports. For President Johnson, that meant a secure air route between Andrews Air Force Base and Bergstrom Air Force Base near Austin, Texas, and the LBJ Ranch. During President Nixon's days, special flight paths ran from Andrews to Homestead Air Force Base in Florida, handy to his Key Biscayne home, and from Andrews to El Toro Marine Air Station in California, a short helicopter hop from his residence at San Clemente. For Jimmy Carter, a presidential air corridor connects Andrews with Robins Air Force Base in Georgia, the installation closest to Plains.

Special flight paths serve several purposes. They are the shortest and therefore the fastest routes between Washington and a President's frequent destinations. At the same time, they permit *Air Force One* to avoid the air traffic on commercial lanes serving airports nearby and also allow the plane to ascend and descend at faster speeds than are standard under FAA rules for commercial flights.

On overseas journeys, an official of the U.S. Customs Service always accompanies the presidential party in order to assist with clearance procedures. His primary function, on the return flight to the United States, is to eliminate the necessity of having the

122

President and his entourage, including the press, go through customs checking of baggage and personal effects upon landing on American soil. This "courtesy of the port" began during the Eisenhower administration and is a much-prized fringe benefit of traveling with a President. Every person on the trip signs a customs declaration to cover purchases abroad, and if he or she is over the permissible limit, a bill may come later from the Customs Service. But that hardly ever happens, and only when someone is suspected of flagrantly abusing the privilege.

Most often, the abuse involves not valuable treasure but outlandish gewgaws that passengers want to bring home. Exotic statuary and large wood carvings are commonplace on return flights to the United States. A flight steward recalls a VIP junket to the Far East that touched down in Hong Kong for the required shopping spree. On the day of departure, an admiral showed up at the plane with a full-sized rickshaw.

"I told him what he could do with his rickshaw," said the steward. "He didn't appreciate my advice one bit, but the damn thing stayed behind."

The steward, however, was relieved of his assignment on the spot. He was sent back to Washington on a commercial plane and given another job. Talking back to the brass is no way to win Brownie points in the military service.

Chapter Four
In the Beginning . . .

Howard M. Cone was in Manhattan on January 7, 1943, when the call came from transatlantic operations officer A. E. LaPorte of Pan American World Airways. Cone had been expecting it for almost a week. Get out to Bowery Bay, he was ordered, and fly the *Dixie Clipper* to Miami that evening in preparation for an unannounced mission.

Cone telephoned his wife at home and asked her to meet him at planeside with his Navy Reserve officer's uniform and travel gear. When he reached the *Dixie*, he noticed an old friend, Pan Am pilot Richard Vinal, making similar final preparations for the *Atlantic Clipper*, a sister Flying Boat. Both planes were under orders to fly together to Miami; both pilots knew something important was in the wind—but little else.

Pan Am's transatlantic manager John C. Leslie had received a little more notice than the two pilots, but he had not become overly curious. The directions he had gotten from Washington after New Year's Day were quite familiar. The Navy Department wanted two Boeing 314s, then under wartime contract, to be in Miami on January 11, equipped for a special mission.

To Leslie, such messages were an old story. For more than a

year, the Flying Boats had been ferrying important passengers for the government. Pan Am's Clippers had been used on similar missions by Prime Minister Winston Churchill of Britain, Queen Wilhelmina of the Netherlands, Greece's King George, the U.S. Navy's Admiral Chester P. Nimitz and the U.S. Army's General George C. Marshall. About the only unusual request for this trip was that one of the two Clippers be provided with a double mattress. Indeed, the orders Leslie sent out to the Pan Am hangar at LaGuardia Field, N.Y., were less elaborate than for some previous trips.

To command the two Flying Boats on this mission, Pan Am routinely assigned the two Masters of Ocean Flying (highest commercial pilot rating in the world) who were scheduled to take out the next flights: Cone and Vinal. Each plane would have a standard crew of ten men.

Late on the 7th, Cone and Vinal gunned the two huge, camouflaged Flying Boats across the murky waters of Bowery Bay, slowly gained altitude over the Atlantic, and set course for Miami, 1,000 miles and 7½ hours away. They weathered a heavy snowstorm off Cape Hatteras that gave them a few anxious moments, but landed safely early on January 8 at Dinner Key, Pan American's marine base in Miami. The day following, the two pilots received their next flying orders: Proceed across the Caribbean to Port of Spain, Trinidad, with the passengers who would arrive at Dinner Key in the early hours of January 11.

Cone and his crew were aboard the *Dixie Clipper* long before dawn. He was handed a curt note saying only that he would be carrying nine passengers. No names were given, which Cone considered unusual. But then this was wartime. The Navy seemed to be getting more secretive with each passing day.

Twenty minutes before scheduled departure, another passenger list arrived. It was headed by a "Mr. Jones," followed by such names as Harry Hopkins, Admiral William D. Leahy, Admiral Ross T. McIntyre, and five others.

Cone blinked, gulped, and turned to the dispatcher. "No—not really!"

The dispatcher solemnly nodded. Moments later a swift Navy launch loomed out of the cool predawn mists, cut its motor, and slid quietly alongside the *Dixie Clipper*. Passenger No. 1 was

126

helped aboard the plane, Naval Reserve Lt. Cone snapped a salute, and somehow found the right words to say: "Mr. President! I'm glad to have you aboard, sir." The first presidential flight in history was under way.

Franklin Delano Roosevelt loved to travel, but not by air. A gregarious man who relished the company of other people, he preferred to go by rail or ship, savoring the leisure and comfort those familiar modes of transportation afforded a President of the United States. His physical handicap, moreover, made flying difficult; the aircraft of the Thirties and early Forties were not designed to accommodate persons in wheelchairs. And the airplane's speed took the fun out of traveling for FDR. "I'm in no hurry," he once explained. "The sooner I get where I'm going, the sooner people will be wanting something from me." So while Roosevelt served in the White House longer than any President, he made only three trips by air during his entire time in office.

Still, he made history.

Roosevelt was the first Chief Executive to travel by air, the first to fly abroad, the first to visit a battle theater since Abraham Lincoln, and the first to set foot on the continent of Africa. He achieved these distinctions in January 1943 when he flew the *Dixie Clipper* from Miami to Casablanca in North Africa to meet with Prime Minister Churchill and Allied military leaders to plan the invasion of southern Europe.

That trip accomplished one other thing of importance to the presidency and the future of aviation. It gave birth to the idea that there ought to be at least one airplane with the specific and primary mission of transporting a President of the United States.

Back in 1942 and early 1943, the concept of a "Flying White House" was hotly debatable. Indeed, there was considerable consternation over the prospect of flying the President to Casablanca. Some of his advisers felt it was a risky wartime undertaking, especially for the leader of the free world. Apart from the physical discomfort that Roosevelt would have to endure, there was the very real danger that the plane might be attacked by enemy aircraft. Hitler's Luftwaffe would have relished nothing better than an opportunity to shoot down a lumbering American airplane bearing the President himself. But the trip had to be made, Roosevelt had said, so risks had to be taken. The Secret

127

Service already had ruled out travel by ship, informing the President that the menace of German submarines was too great to sanction.

Much later, when public announcement of the historic flight was made, Americans everywhere were just as divided as Roosevelt's advisers had been. Some thought it was a foolish, unnecessary trip. Others admired FDR's audacity. Psychologically, it proved to be a tremendous boost for the Allied cause. It testified to friend and foe alike that the momentum of the war, at long last, was running against the Axis powers in Europe and the Mediterranean.

Wartime censorship and the extraordinary need for secrecy and security, unfortunately, have obscured many of the details and much of the drama of that first air trip by a President in office. Still, sufficient data is available to underscore the difficulties and the significance of transporting a President by airplane thirty-five years ago.

With Roosevelt safely strapped in his seat, Howard Cone taxied the *Dixie Clipper* away from Dinner Key in the Florida darkness, and lifted the big sea bird on a long slow climb to 7,000 feet. Over the Great Bahama Bank he turned to co-pilot Frank Crawford. "Let's not forget that this is just a normal operation," Cone said, trying to hide the excitement within.

Crawford grinned. "That's right," he replied, "but this one *will* be something to tell our grandchildren."

An hour later, with the rising sun glinting into the cockpit, Cone turned the controls over to Crawford and went back to check on Passenger No. 1. He found the President clad in baggy slacks, a loose sweater, and an open-collar shirt happily poring over navigation charts. Peering out the window, FDR spotted an area where once he had gone deep sea fishing. A bit later, over Haiti, he inquired if their route would take them over the old citadel built by Henri Christophe, the second-largest masonry structure in the western hemisphere. With Cone relaying the directions to the cockpit, Roosevelt guided the *Dixie Clipper* by the land features he recognized below, "just the way you would give directions to a cab driver."

Flying closely behind the *Dixie Clipper* was the *Atlantic Clipper* under pilot Vinal. Aboard were military and diplomatic offi-

128

cers, some of Roosevelt's aides, and additional Secret Service agents who would be needed at the Casablanca conference.

Ten hours and 1,633 miles after leaving Miami, the improvised "Flying White House" and the backup Clipper landed on the bay at Port of Spain, Trinidad. Everybody went ashore to spend the night in quarters arranged by the U.S. Navy. Cone and the *Dixie Clipper* crew worked late to arrange a surprise for Roosevelt. When he came back aboard the next morning, the plane was decked from wing to tail with Navy signal pennants spelling out HAIL TO THE CHIEF. The President, an old Navy man, was delighted. But Admiral Leahy was not present to compliment the crew. His cold had worsened during the night. Admiral McIntyre, the President's physician, felt it wise that Leahy stay behind to recuperate.

From Trinidad, the two Clippers soared southeast on the next leg of the journey, a 1,227-mile flight along the eastern coast of South America to Belém, Brazil, at the mouth of the Amazon River. During the eight-hour jaunt, Roosevelt whiled away the time by reading, lunching, napping, and playing solitaire. As Cone later recounted for Pan Am's publication *New Horizons*, purser Albert Tuinman and steward Edward Garcia made it appear that FDR's cold lunch had been planned all along. But the fact was they had no choice. The exhaust-heated Prestone system that provided cooking heat for the galley had failed during flight. It would have to be repaired—if repairs were possible—during the three-hour layover at Belém for fuel and servicing.

Roosevelt and the rest of the passengers went ashore at Belém. As Cone discovered shortly thereafter, so had Tuinman. The time for departure was almost at hand and FDR already was aboard before the purser reappeared in the bow of a steel Navy scow, bearing an ample supply of food for the *Dixie Clipper*'s passengers and crew. "Tuinman was the hero of the trip," Cone said. "He somehow had discovered a U.S. Coast Guard cutter in port and had scrounged the food in a desperate, but successful attempt to feed the President in a proper manner."

For one stomach-gripping moment, however, Cone thought the presidential flight might end right there in the harbor at Belém. In pulling alongside, the bulky scow almost rammed a hole in the thin-skinned hull of the *Dixie Clipper*.

Once more airborne, the two Flying Boats set out across the South Atlantic toward West Africa, specifically the port of Bathurst in British Gambia, not far from Dakar. All that evening, that night, and during most of the next day, the *Dixie Clipper* droned steadily eastward on its 2,500-mile ocean hop, the longest leg of the trip. To relieve the monotony, Harry Hopkins and Cone persuaded Roosevelt to become a member of the Short Snorters Club, the latest craze among members of the U.S. armed forces overseas. It had become the custom, especially on transoceanic flights, for servicemen to exchange autographed dollar bills (or the equivalent in scrip or local currency) that could be cashed in at a service club for a snort of whiskey.

Roosevelt readily agreed, presenting an autographed dollar bill to six of the seven Short Snorters present. Cone, a new initiate himself, dearly coveted one of the FDR bills as a memento of the historic trip. But he happened to note that the President had only six dollars in his possession. So Cone quietly withheld his own claim as FDR handed out the prized souvenirs.

The big Clippers landed in midafternoon at Bathurst, where their share of FDR's journey to Casablanca ended. Roosevelt and his accompanying war planners boarded two land-based C-54 airplanes, owned by Trans World Airlines but operating under wartime contract with the U.S. Army Air Corps.

To enable the crippled President to enter or leave the tall C-54, it had been necessary to contruct large and bulky ramps for his wheelchair. Such ramps were not necessary for getting Roosevelt on and off the Boeing 314 Flying Boat, which was why the Secret Service had chosen it. But now that the President was on the continent of Africa, bound for Casablanca and a few interior trips, he would have to forgo the seaplane.

While the *Dixie Clipper* waited at Bathurst for his return, the President and his military chiefs flew off in a four-engine TWA transport piloted by Otis F. Bryan, a company vice president on active duty as a reserve major. The overland route from Bathurst to Casablanca covered 1,500 miles. For Bryan, the chance to fly the President on the final leg of his secret journey to Casablanca was unforgettable. He recalled FDR's jaunty air and good nature, despite the fact that he had been flying steadily for almost three days since leaving the United States.

"He was an excellent passenger," Bryan said. "He was much interested in the territory over which we flew and always asked many questions. But he didn't ask for special privileges. In fact, we removed several seats to make him a bed, but he preferred to sit up and stay awake because the others in the plane didn't have similar conveniences."

If Roosevelt suffered fatigue from his long journey, he refused to show it. Within a few hours after arriving at Casablanca on January 14, he and Churchill and their Allied commanders began the first session of the conference. It lasted until 3 A.M. the following morning.

Following ten days of meetings there, Roosevelt next flew 2,000 miles aboard Bryan's C-54 to Liberia, America's oldest ally in Africa, for a session with President Edwin James Barclay. A day later, he arrived back at Bathurst and boarded the waiting *Dixie Clipper* for a flight west across the South Atlantic to Natal, Brazil. There he conferred with an old friend, President Getulio Dornelles Vargas of Brazil, and reviewed American troops at the Natal air base.

From Natal, Roosevelt once more boarded Bryan's C-54 for the trip to Port of Spain in Trinidad, where he inspected the new U.S. Navy base and retrieved Admiral Leahy, his personal chief of staff. It was a good thing Leahy had remained behind. His cold had turned into a sharp bout of influenza, which would have been aggravated had he continued to Casablanca with the President.

For the final homeward flight to Miami, FDR once again boarded the *Dixie Clipper*. It was Roosevelt's sixty-first birthday, and pilot Cone and the crew were determined to make it a festive occasion. Purser Tuinman and steward Garcia prepared a special birthday dinner for the President, which took him by surprise—or so he pretended, at any rate.

Cone committed an unpardonable act; he was late to the party. The plane was cruising over Haiti and the Dominican Republic, flying through an unusually heavy buildup of cumulus nimbus clouds that threatened rough weather and, at minimum, a great deal of turbulence. "We had climbed to an altitude higher than I liked," Cone explained. While oxygen bottles had been placed aboard for Roosevelt's comfort at high altitudes, Cone

131

wanted to avoid their use if he could. "I felt I should not leave the controls while confronted with the problem of clouds, high mountains, and the altitude."

Finally as the *Dixie Clipper* cleared Port-au-Prince, the weather eased. Cone turned over the controls to co-pilot Crawford and belatedly joined the dinner group in Roosevelt's compartment. "I didn't say anything about the reasons for my tardiness because I didn't want to cause any concern," he said. After dining on caviar, turkey, peas, potatoes, and coffee, Roosevelt was presented with a big birthday cake baked especially for him and smuggled aboard at Trinidad. Amid an off-key rendition of "Happy Birthday, Dear President," Roosevelt cut the cake with a flourish and served up large portions to everyone aboard, including members of the crew.

Then the President's companions (except Cone, who regretfully had to abide by regulations) drank a champagne toast to the Chief Executive and surprised him with presents: a portfolio of rare Trinidad prints and a carved cigarette box.

Cone handed the President two letters, one from each of the crews of the two Flying Boats, containing contributions to the President's Birthday Ball Fund, his favorite charity for youngsters suffering the effects of polio, like himself. Roosevelt termed it "the happiest moment of my trip" and promised to mention the contributions to reporters who would be on hand for his news conference in Miami the next day. But there were so many questions concerning the Casablanca meeting with Churchill and the next phase of the war that FDR never got around to it. The President made up for his oversight, however. A few weeks later, Cone's mailman delivered a letter on White House stationery. It was a personally penned note from FDR, thanking him and the Clipper crews for their contribution to the polio foundation.

There could be no mistaking the historic significance of the Casablanca journey, easily eclipsing the previous "first" FDR had established in 1932 by flying to Chicago from Albany, New York, to accept the Democratic party's presidential nomination. That trip, aboard an American Airways Ford Trimotor, had been the first flight by a party nominee; this trip was the first airplane voyage by a sitting President. Moreover, it had occurred in wartime, through skies in which Axis planes roamed and over waters infested with German submarines. And in great secrecy. Not until unwitting war correspondents were flown to Casablanca on the final day of the conference did the world learn that the President of the United States, the Prime Minister of Great Britain, and their highest military commanders had been meeting there for ten days.

The contrast between air travel 35 years ago and now, even for a President, is instructive. The straight-line distance from Washington to Casablanca is 3,875 miles. A modern jet transport could have made the trip comfortably, and without stopovers, in seven hours. But in 1943, the limited range, slower speeds, and lack of sophisticated navigational aids in the Boeing 314 and Douglas C-54 had required four legs of flying, three stopovers, a change of planes, and more than three days' travel time for the President—in each direction. The circuitous route required the President to touch three continents, cross the Equator four times, and spend approximately ninety hours in the air. When his train travel between Washington and Miami was included, Roosevelt had covered more than 17,000 miles before he was once more back home in the White House.

The success of Roosevelt's flight to Casablanca had a dynamic effect on the conduct of American diplomacy, on presidential politics, and on aviation generally. No longer was it necessary that the President travel by rail or ship to reach a distant city or a foreign capital. Now, quite obviously, he was liberated. He had been given wings.

That realization was a happy circumstance for the Army Air Corps, as it was then called, the fastest-growing branch of all the armed services. The high command had been preparing for the day when it could persuade the President and Congress to cut its apron strings to the U.S. Army and allow the flying service to become an independent "Department of the Air Force," equal in status to the Army and the Navy.

Until Roosevelt's air trip to Casablanca, it had been the Navy's pleasure and responsibility to provide a ship for the Commander-in-Chief's overseas travel, on business or vacation. Now the Air Corps had an opportunity to prove its indispensability to him and the nation—and grasped it instantly.

133

A few weeks after the Roosevelt journey, the Air Corps reached a decision that would make it unnecessary for a President, if he wanted to fly, to charter a commercial airliner. The Air Corps would provide a custom-tailored airplane, with the special mission of transporting the President of the United States.

What the brass could not foresee, however, was that the aircraft it designated specifically as the "President's airplane" would never be used by him. This first of a kind, the predecessor of today's *Air Force One*, was *Guess Where II*, a scarcely-remembered adaptation of the famed B-24 Liberator bomber.

It proved to be a remarkable airplane, used by Mrs. Eleanor Roosevelt and high government officials on trips all over the globe. It set many speed and nonstop distance records in 1943 and 1944 during its service with the White House, always waiting for the day when the President himself would board his special airplane.

What marred its place in presidential history was that when it came time for Roosevelt to fly in it, approval was denied by the Secret Service on suspicion of a technical flaw. Still, it went everywhere he went, a backup aircraft flown by his own specially designated pilot, a sort of bridesmaid but never a bride. For these reasons, *Guess Where II* fully deserves a sentimental asterisk on the roster of "presidential aircraft."

Guess Where II was a businesslike, four-engine C-87A built by Consolidated Aircraft Corp. And while it was really a transport version of the B-24 bomber, utilizing the same airframe, it had features with special appeal to Roosevelt's staff. The cabin floor was low to the ground, allowing easy access for FDR's wheelchair, and its long-range capability meant that fueling stops could be held to a minimum, an especially important feature for long overseas flights. Earlier C-87As with the Air Transport Command already had established a reputation for easy maintenance, respectable performance, and speed.

From a large order of C-87 cargo planes then under construction at Consolidated's plant in Fort Worth, Texas, three airframes were selected on May 4, 1943, moved to a remote corner of the factory, and placed under heavy security. All three were earmarked for conversion into C-87A passenger planes and assignment to Washington's National Airport in the "Brass Hat Squadron," as the VIP flying unit was dubbed. Although it was obvious to the aircraft engineers and workers that something unusual was afoot, none was aware that Airplane No. 159 was destined to become "the President's airplane."

When it arrived at Washington on June 6, the prospective first *Air Force One* looked just like any other of its olive-drab sisters. Serial No. 124159, painted in standard yellow numerals on its twin tails, was its only distinctive identification. Only a few officers in the squadron and some FDR assistants knew that this one's primary mission was to fly the President.

Its interior, however, had been specially designed to provide the latest in passenger comfort. Along the right side of the roomy fuselage were four "Pullman" compartments, each with facing double seats and a removable table that could be converted into upper and lower berths. Across the aisle and opposite the center compartment was a large sofa that accommodated three persons. It and an adjoining lavatory could be incorporated into the center suite by means of curtains, thus providing an executive cabin for the President. The commodious tail section contained a Tappan aircraft galley with an electric range and oven, plus a large walk-in closet and linen storage area. The plane could seat twenty passengers or sleep nine.

While they outfitted an airplane especially for the President, the generals were busy with another historic task, the selection of the first "presidential pilot." Lt. Gen. Harold George, the three-star boss of the Air Transport Command, personally made the choice. He assigned his own pilot, Maj. Henry Tift Myers, to the new position.

"Hank" Myers was never much on military spit and polish. A native of Tifton, Georgia, a town founded by his grandfather, Myers coupled a soft drawl with flashing dark eyes and an infectious grin—the epitome of the dashing World War II "flyboys" who flew like demons and broke women's hearts across the globe. Myers had won his Army Air Corps wings in 1931 at Kelly Field in Texas. He stayed in the service a few years and then went to work for American Airlines. He had logged over 10,000 flying hours when he was called back into the Army Air Corps in May 1942 to become aide and personal pilot to General George.

Since his most recent flying experience had been in DC-3s, Myers was sent to Fort Worth for transition training in the B-24 bomber in preparation for piloting the new presidential aircraft.

There was no celebration of the plane's arrival at Washington's National Airport that day in early June, nor any recognition of its presence beyond the assignment of guards to the hangar area. The term "presidential airplane" had hardly been coined. At the time, nobody could foresee the glamour and the prestige that someday would embrace a Commander-in-Chief's personal aircraft and its pilot.

Myers fell in love with the spanking new C-87A Liberator, an emotional attachment that was to last long after the plane was retired. It was popular for wartime pilots to invent descriptive nicknames for their assigned aircraft. But what to call this one? The special mission of the plane was to carry the President, but it would not do to pick a nickname that would reveal its identity. Myers, ever resourceful, came up with one he thought was a natural, nicely in keeping with the mystery of the plane's likely travels: *Guess Where II*. He had the name painted in flowing script above the door.

Within six weeks, Myers and the new plane were off on their first extensive trip, a round-the-world fact-finding mission by five senators and top military brass. One of the passengers, Senator Albert "Happy" Chandler, of Kentucky, was intensely nervous about flying. Whenever the plane encountered air turbulence, Chandler would burst forth with loud singing of gospel hymns. "I guess he thought he was on the *Titanic*," Myers later quipped.

Among other things, *Guess Where II* set an incredible record on that journey, flying nonstop from Ceylon to Australia, a distance of 3,200 miles, over Japanese-controlled waters, past Japanese-held Sumatra and Java—fully loaded, unarmed, and without military escort.

But the primary role of *Guess Where II* was to fly the President, and Myers and his hand-picked crew kept waiting for that first all-important call. It came in November 1943, as Roosevelt made plans for his participation in the upcoming secret conferences with Russia's Josef Stalin and Britain's Winston Churchill at Teheran and Cairo. Although the transatlantic crossing was to

136

be made aboard the USS *Iowa*, Roosevelt preferring the more comfortable quarters of a ship, the use of aircraft would be mandatory for the final legs of the journey in the Mediterranean region. All airlift requirements were centered around *Guess Where II* as the logical plane.

Then, a few days before departure time, word filtered down to Myers that the President again would use TWA's contract C-54 Skymasters as he had done on part of his first air trip in January that year. The news was a distinct blow, not only to the crew, but to the Air Transport Command, which had carefully organized the trip and controlled the aircraft involved. Transporting the Commander-in-Chief during wartime was rightfully a task for the military. Myers, perhaps showing his old loyalty to American Airlines, suspected that Trans World Airlines "had got into the White House by the back door." But unexpected circumstances had developed that made it justifiable to switch the aircraft the President was about to use.

The Secret Service, ever fretful about presidential security, had been gathering reports of unexplained tail buffeting and oscillation problems involving other C-87s. One incident concerned a C-87 that had just taken off from Florida. Unable to bring the plane under control, the crew had parachuted to safety, leaving the plane to fly unattended into Mexico, where it crashed.

News accounts of the mysterious problem greatly disturbed the Secret Service. The Army Air Corps and the plane's manufacturer, Consolidated Aircraft Corporation, ordered extensive tests to find out what was going on. Investigations traced the problem to separate sets of electrical toggle switches in the cockpit that controlled the operation of the plane's propellers and the engine's cowl flaps. The switches were located close together and were similar in appearance. By inadvertently activating the wrong set of switches, C-87 co-pilots were opening the cowl flaps during flight, creating considerable buffeting and "fish-tailing" of the aircraft.

Although the solution came in time to lift the restrictions on the use of *Guess Where II*, the White House and the Secret Service decided that trip preparations were too far along to cancel TWA's C-54. But the trip planners did see a possibility that FDR

137

might be able to use *Guess Where II* if he visited other places not equipped with the loading ramps required for Roosevelt's entry into the high cabin door of the C-54. So Myers was instructed to fly *Guess Where II* out to the Mediterranean as a spare aircraft.

Roosevelt stuck to his advance schedule for Teheran and Cairo, so there was no opportunity for him to use *Guess Where II*—nor any reason to publicly identify the plane as the official presidential aircraft. Once again, TWA's Otis F. Bryan was FDR's pilot on his air hops in North Africa and the Middle East aboard TWA's C-54 executive transport No. 232950.

Bryan encountered one scary moment during a landing approach to Malta. The Skymaster's hydraulic pump gave out, making it impossible to lower the flaps. "I told the President," Bryan said, "but he simply instructed us to do the best we could and chuckled, 'Sounds like we'll have a good time.' " While FDR and his aides cinched up their seat belts and braced for the inevitable, Bryan took the plane in faster than normal, whizzed past the bomb craters along the runway, and carefully braked to a stop. As Bryan recalled, "We didn't even have a blowout."

One of Bryan's most unnerving experiences occurred when Roosevelt dispatched the plane to Turkey under tight secrecy to bring the Turkish president to a meeting at Cairo. Enemy fighter planes were in the area, so Bryan took the Skymaster in at night and without a military escort so as to make it appear a routine flight. But German intelligence was not deceived by that ploy. Moments after arriving at Ankara, Bryan heard Nazi propagandist Lord Haw-Haw announce on Radio Berlin that the plane had just landed.

Bryan's fondest memory of the Cairo conference is the sight of Winston Churchill, with bathrobe flying, dashing across the runway at Cairo to say goodbye to Roosevelt. "It was early in the morning and Churchill hadn't had time to dress, so he wore only pajamas and a robe. FDR was so amused that he asked a photographer to take a picture, much to the chagrin of the prime minister."

Meanwhile, Hank Myers and *Guess Where II* had managed to share some of the excitement of the Cairo Conference after all. The Russians had double-crossed the Americans by releasing publicity about the meetings while the conference was still in

138

session. American correspondents, furious about being scooped, were demanding that Steve Early, FDR's press secretary, find a way to get their stories and pictures to the United States. Early called Myers at his Cairo hotel.

"The President would like to know whether you can fly to Washington in thirty-six hours," Early said.

Myers thought a moment. The usual trip from Cairo to Washington, by way of a refueling stop in Brazil, required two days.

"No reason why we can't," he told Early, "provided we can fly on a route through the Azores. You get that cleared for us and we'll do better than thirty-six hours."

Early went in to see the President and came back on the phone almost immediately. "You can fly any way you want," he told Myers. "You're the only one who can get the news back in some sort of time."

The Azores, of course, were a Portugese possession in the mid-Atlantic. But the British were operating the air base at Lajes for antisubmarine patrols. The British government had given permission for *Guess Where II* to land there, but it became evident as the plane approached at daybreak that British units on the island had not gotten the word. For Myers and co-pilot Elmer F. Smith it promised to be a hairy occasion.

British practice was to challenge unexpected aircraft and shoot at them simultaneously, a procedure that threatened to make an enemy out of the best of allies. Moreover, *Guess Where II* was running low on fuel. Anxious not to provoke the antiaircraft batteries on the ground, Myers contacted the British authorities by radio, first to convince them that the approaching *Guess Where II* was indeed a friendly craft, and second, to assure them that landing authorization had been granted at Cairo. Smith, a man of few words, summed up the outcome. "After a brief discussion," he said later, "we were given permission to land. We made one pass over the field, circled, and landed." As an afterthought, he added laconically, "Although the discussion did not touch on the matter of fuel, it is true that we did not have enough to take us to any other airfield."

Guess Where II was only the second American plane to land at Lajes during the war. After a hearty welcome by the British ground forces, the plane roared off with refilled tanks on the final

139

leg to the United States. When the flight ended, the plane and the exhausted crew had shortened the record from Cairo to Washington by a full day. In fact, they had made the trip in twenty-four hours, half the usual flying time and twelve hours less than Roosevelt's request. The next morning, over their breakfast tables, Americans read the firsthand accounts of the momentous events taking place halfway around the world.

Although Roosevelt himself never boarded *Guess Where II*, it fulfilled at least part of its "presidential" mission by taking First Lady Eleanor Roosevelt on a month-long tour of American bases in the Caribbean and South America in March 1944. The President personally prepared the itinerary for his wife—a 13,000 mile journey to prove to American boys in those areas that while they were not in the frontlines of Europe and the Pacific, they were doing a vital job and were not forgotten. Mrs. Roosevelt, traveling under the code name "Rover," was an appreciative passenger.

"She worked in her compartment with her secretary most of the time and never wanted any of us to bother about her," Myers recounted. "She also traveled light and so we had no baggage problems with her. On the ground, we tried to follow her when she visited with the GIs, but she wore us out, as she did the generals who were guiding her."

When the trip ended, the First Lady gave the crew members three dozen orchids that she had accumulated in South America—and followed that up later with individual gifts of a handsome salad bowl bearing a silver plate commemorating the flight. Said Myers: "She figured the gifts would help us out with our wives at home."

Despite the fact that *Guess Where II* never experienced the tail buffeting that had plagued some other C-87s, White House confidence in the plane had been shaken. Consequently, plans for another aircraft were quietly begun in the fall of 1943. Since the Douglas C-54 had already proved itself a plane worthy of the President, the Army Air Corps decided the new plane for Roosevelt should be a superspecial version of the reliable Skymaster. *Guess Where II* retained its White House status until the arrival of the new presidential plane. Then it was shunted aside to more obscure duties with the VIP transport squadron at Washington and, finally, to other bases in the country.

140

On October 30, 1945, the plane made its final flight, landing at Walnut Ridge, Arkansas, where it was handed over to the Reconstruction Finance Corporation for eventual disposal. As Major Robert C. Mikesh later recounted in *Air Force* magazine, "there it stood in the midst of row upon row of silent, war-weary bombers and transports. *Guess Where II* showed no strain of war, and received no recognition for its once-esteemed position. While air museums proudly possess other presidential planes, *Guess Where II*, the first of the special breed, was eventually reduced to scrap."

Its replacement was conceived in a bundle of classified documents dispatched from AAF headquarters to Douglas Aircraft Company at Santa Monica, California, and bearing the code name "Project 51."

Under Contract No. 20284, Douglas was instructed to build a passenger aircraft worthy of the President of the United States. The Air Corps and the company selected fuselage No. 78 from the assembly line and moved it to a secluded area of the Douglas plant. Workmen assigned to the job were only aware that their efforts were being constantly surveyed by an unusual number of inspectors, both civilian and military, whose purposes were shrouded in secrecy.

They were, in fact, attending the birth of a four-engine plane that was to gain world renown as the *Sacred Cow*, the name bequeathed by admiring and irreverent White House correspondents.

Not only was the *Sacred Cow* to be custom-tailored to please the President of the United States, it was to be outfitted for a very special one. Although Roosevelt already was midway into his unprecedented third term, with no hint that he would seek—or be elected to—a fourth term, a decision had been made to equip this plane in ways that would cater to his fancies as well as accommodate his physical handicap.

Just behind the main passenger cabin, Douglas engineers skillfully concealed a battery-operated elevator that could lift Roosevelt and his wheelchair directly from the ground to the cabin floor. So neatly was it done that Air Corps generals regularly used to bet VIP visitors that they couldn't find it during flight.

The Secret Service wanted the elevator for security reasons as

141

well as for Roosevelt's convenience. On his first two flights—the historic one to Casablanca and the second in November 1943 as part of his trip to Teheran to meet with Josef Stalin—it had been necessary to construct special ramps to enable the President to enter or leave an airplane. The ramps were long, bulky, and impossible to conceal. Moreover, their presence on any airfield was a sure sign that the President of the United States was about to arrive. The elevator in the *Sacred Cow* would make such ramps unnecessary.

Roosevelt's personal staff also relayed a special request to E. Gilbert Mason, the chief interior design engineer for Douglas Aircraft who planned the *Sacred Cow's* layout. The President, Mason was told, didn't like being "cooped up" for long periods, whether aboard ship or an airplane. During his first two air trips, Roosevelt had managed, with difficulty, to visit with the pilots who were flying his airplane. He was fascinated with their techniques and experiences, exhibiting a little boy's curiosity about everything to do with the aircraft. Was there anything Mason could do to enable FDR to enjoy the new presidential toy?

Mason could and did. He had already designed a special, collapsible wheelchair of chromium steel and leather that could be rolled into the elevator at ground level and hoisted to the corridor in the passenger section. From there, the chair could be wheeled to almost every place on the plane that Roosevelt might wish to go. So Mason designed a removable set of steel rails on which FDR's wheelchair could be rolled up to the cockpit floor level. There he could take up a choice position between the two pilots' seats, with the wheelchair locked as securely in place as any stationary seat back in the passenger compartment. Roosevelt was delighted.

The presidential suite on the *Sacred Cow* was a commodious stateroom measuring $7\frac{1}{2} \times 12$ feet, laid out in a manner that enabled FDR's wheelchair to move about with ease. Among the special furnishings was an upholstered swivel chair, fastened to the floor, but within easy reach of an oxygen mask, reading lights, and a telephone connecting with the cockpit and three other staterooms. A conference table occupied the middle of the presidential compartment.

On one side wall were four large maps on rollers, plus four enlarged flying instruments to satisfy Roosevelt's curiosity—an air speed indicator, an altimeter, a compass, and a clock. Atop a small storage cabinet was an electric fan to keep the breezes stirring in hot weather. At one end of the suite was a sofa that could be converted into a bed. Another side of the room contained two chairs that could be folded when not in use. In all, the presidential suite had a seating capacity of seven.

One unusual feature was a large picture window near the swivel chair so that Roosevelt could enjoy the view. The window was constructed of bulletproof glass to thwart any would-be assassin's bullet. But, as Major Mikesh observed, "the surrounding skin of the aircraft would hardly have stopped an icepick!" The Secret Service, as usual, fretted because the big window instantly separated this C-54 Skymaster from the garden variety, making it easier to identify and more difficult to provide security on the ground and in the air. So an aluminum template was ordered that could be placed over the picture window whenever necessary. Cut within the center of the template was a standard C-54 window aperture. Thus, to any casual onlooker, the plane would have the appearance of an ordinary C-54 (or DC-4 as it was known in civilian aviation).

The unusual interior, the elevator, and the picture window were not the only features that distinguished the *Sacred Cow* from the 1,163 other DC-4 type cargo and personnel carriers used by the military services during World War II and the immediate postwar era. It was really one of a kind, a meld of the basic C-54A model with B-model wings, special ailerons that fitted no other craft, specially stressed landing-gear doors to protect the wheels and help ensure safe landings, plus the latest in radio and navigational equipment. But to preserve anonymity, the airplane carried only the customary external markings of the Army Air Corps, including its routine serial No. 42-107451.

Douglas Aircraft completed Project 51 in June 1944. Major Myers, FDR's pilot, took delivery on June 12 and flew the airplane from Santa Monica to Washington's National Airport. There it was assigned to the 503rd Wing of the Air Transport Command, which handled transportation for top government officials. But President Roosevelt was not the first to enjoy its comforts.

143

The first official mission of Myers and the other six crew members of the *Sacred Cow* was to fly Secretary of War Henry L. Stimson and other senior military leaders from New York to Naples, via Casablanca, to check on the progress of the Allied campaign against Hitler's war machine in southern Europe. The trip began on July 1, just three weeks after the D-Day invasion of France. Although the *Sacred Cow*'s route skirted the zones of heaviest fighting, no chances were taken with the VIPs aboard. American fighter planes, based in North Africa, provided protective cover for the hop from Casablanca into Naples. On the return flight to the United States seventeen days later, the *Sacred Cow* neatly demonstrated its capabilities by making the first nonstop flight from London to Washington—3,800 miles—in seventeen hours and fifty minutes.

Another record was set soon afterward, when Roosevelt dispatched Myers and the *Sacred Cow* to Rio de Janeiro to bring China's Madame Chiang Kai-shek to Washington. The 5,300-mile trip was made with only two stops and in twenty-two hours and fifty-five minutes—the first time a plane had flown more than 5,000 miles in one day.

Late in 1944, Roosevelt assigned his personal aircraft to yet another high-level mission, transporting three generals and three admirals on a tour of American fighting units in the European and Pacific theaters as part of a fact-finding operation aimed at the reorganization of the Army and Navy. Taking off for the Far East, Myers pushed the *Cow* on a 25,000-mile journey, with flights averaging nearly ten hours a day between Honolulu and Kwajalein, Saipan, Guam, Peleliu, Leyte, and back.

It was at Leyte, en route to a conference with General Douglas MacArthur, that the *Sacred Cow* nearly ended up as a casualty—and on the ground, at that.

Only one airstrip, at Tacloban, was available to the Allies and, given the active air war with the Japanese, it was considerably overworked. Myers came in swiftly, called the tower, and was told by the harried air controller that he could have just fifteen minutes on the ground. If the plane wasn't gone by then, it would be shoved into the sea.

As Myers recounted in an interview later, "The operations officer told me that the field would only hold 200 airplanes, that it had 230 on it already, and fifteen more were coming in. 'Okay,' I said, 'just give me some gas and I'll take off—I don't much like it here anyway.'

"I gassed and pulled up at the end of the runway for a takeoff just as they had a red alert and the pursuit planes started to scramble for the sky. A bunch of fighters started taking off from one end of the field and, at the same time, a bunch of troop carrier C-47s were coming in for landings at the other end. The fighters would head right for the incoming transports and then zoom up over them, missing them by inches. It was a hectic few minutes.

"I could not get off the runway, with the pursuits taking off right over us and the transports heading for us from the other direction. I could not decide whether to tell my passengers to jump and run for safety or to stay in the airplane. I finally spotted a place to park and ran the *Cow* off the strip. But they told me to get it out of there, too, or they would push it into the ocean. I tried to explain to them that we had a lot of generals and admirals on board to see General MacArthur, but they said they didn't give a damn, they were fighting a war.

"I finally got things straightened out—after the alert was over. We found a place to park the plane for a day and a half until the conference was finished."

President Roosevelt used the new presidential aircraft for the first time in February 1945 to travel to Yalta, in the Crimean region of Russia, for another top-secret conference with Churchill and Stalin. Although Hitler's forces were retreating everywhere in Europe, guns still blazed on many fronts. Transporting the President of the United States to the Soviet Union was thus a project of utmost secrecy and security.

The arrangements, as finally approved, called for Roosevelt to travel by ship, the USS *Quincy*, to the Mediterranean isle of Malta. From there, the *Sacred Cow* would fly him to the Yalta conference. With loving care, pilot Myers and the hand-picked crew prepared the *Sacred Cow* for its inaugural flight with the President, testing and retesting the special elevator and making sure the engines and navigational equipment were in perfect condition.

Nobody, obviously, could have known that Roosevelt's first flight in the *Sacred Cow* would be his only one.

A graphic account of the *Sacred Cow*'s role in carrying FDR

145

to Yalta is contained in the official records of the ceremonies at Andrews Air Force Base that marked the presentation of the historic plane to the Smithsonian Institution upon its final retirement from flying duties on December 4, 1961:

The contention of the men who flew the *Sacred Cow*, that all its flights were "strictly routine," is not entirely borne out by other historians, as witness some of the details of Trip No. 15:

Classification: TOP SECRET.

Code Name: "ARGONAUT."

Destination: YALTA, USSR.

The *Sacred Cow* left Washington at sunset on January 21, 1945. A very sharp eye might have noted that a different serial number had been substituted for 42–107451. Pilot was Colonel Myers and co-pilot was Otis A. Bryan, a TWA executive and a reserve officer called to active duty—with great secrecy—for the occasion.

With only the crew aboard, the President's airplane arrived at Naples on January 24 and at 7:05 the next morning, took off on a dry run into Saki, the Russian airfield some 60 miles from Yalta.

Colonel Myers and the *Cow* neared Saki ahead of their estimated arrival time and in very thick weather. They made a straight-in letdown, the approach so fast the Russian ground defenders never had a chance to train their weapons on the airplane.

After completing his manners to the Soviet officers, Myers returned to Malta to emplane his ranking passenger, traveling under the sheltering code name "Sawbuck" but better known as Franklin D. Roosevelt. . . . On February 3, 1945, President Roosevelt made his first flight in the *Sacred Cow*, departing Malta (where he had arrived in the USS *Quincy*) in the still dark of 2:30 A.M. and arriving at Saki at 9:10 A.M.

While waiting for the outcome of the Big Three conference, Colonel Myers flew another dry run, this time from Saki to Deversior (near Cairo), where FDR would be returned to the custody of the Navy, meeting Arabia's Ibn Saud on the *Quincy*.

The day before the *Sacred Cow* was to airlift the President to Cairo, she broke a connecting rod in her number 2 engine. The crew landed safely, located another C-54 and promptly commandeered a sound engine, which they installed overnight. Mr. Roosevelt was delivered to the Navy on the dot of 1:15 P.M., February 12, 1945.

The official account ignored tense moments for President Roosevelt on the hop across the Black Sea from Malta to the Saki field that served as the airport for the Yalta Conference. A Soviet plane suddenly crossed into the *Sacred Cow*'s flight path and seemed on the way to a tragic collision over the sea. This time, the presidential plane had a P-51 fighter escort. Its leader immediately ordered an attack to remove the threat to Roosevelt's safety. Sensing instinctively that an aerial dogfight between American and Russian planes would cast a pall over the crucial Yalta meeting, Myers countermanded the attack order and quickly dropped the *Cow* down 1,000 feet to get out of the way. The lone Russian never changed course, possibly unaware of his close brush with history.

Also ignored in the official account of the Yalta flight was Pilot Myers' unhappiness with the FDR staff over the naming of Bryan as his co-pilot for the *Sacred Cow*. He thought it was a "political" move. Myers, a former American Airlines flyer, disliked giving anyone from TWA a choice spot on his crew. Furthermore, he felt it was his perogative as pilot to choose his co-pilot—in this case, Elmer F. Smith, with whom he had always shared the cockpit.

"So while Bryan had to be taken along, Hank treated him only as a passenger," said Smith. "Hank insisted that I occupy the right hand seat and share in all the flying duties. As I recall, Myers never let Bryan get near the controls."

During the conference, Myers and the crew were billeted in a Saki resort building ordinarily used as a vacation site for Russian workers. Myers, Smith, and navigator Ted Boselli quickly discovered a microphone crudely concealed in their quarters. To while away the long evenings, the trio concocted wild yarns to tantalize the Russian secret police.

One of the most curious of the Russians was General N. V. Yermachenkov, head of the Soviet naval air forces, who could not see enough of the *Sacred Cow*. The ubiquitous NKVD agents never let Yermachenkov out of their sight. On one tour of the plane, Myers showed the Soviet general a new and secret altimeter. Yermachenkov nodded impassively to indicate he knew all about it. Myers next showed Yermachenkov the plane's loran navigational equipment, a device so new that only a handful of U.S. Air Corps officers were aware of its existence. Again, the Russian general insisted he knew all about loran. Myers finally tumbled to the reason. Yermachenkov was determined not to admit ignorance in front of the accompanying Soviet secret police; to do so would have reflected adversely on the Russian air force and might have cost Yermachenkov his job. The NKVD kept such close watch over the general that when Myers lent him some popular American magazines from the *Sacred Cow*, they were returned a few hours later by a messenger who said Yermachenkov did not need them.

The *Sacred Cow*'s very next trip after the Yalta Conference was to have been a routine "milk run" to England and France, carrying presidential adviser Bernard Baruch on a special economic mission for Roosevelt. It ended in shock and sadness on April 12, 1945, with the news of FDR's death at Warm Springs, Georgia. The remainder of the trip was immediately canceled, as the *Sacred Cow* sped back to Washington for Roosevelt's funeral.

"Those stories you may have read about people stopping you in the streets to say they were sorry were true," Myers said on his return from Europe. "FDR truly was a beloved man in Europe, and when he was on our plane we had a kind of feeling of greatness. Even though he joked and talked to you easily, you always had the idea that this would be part of some history book."

Some time later, asked to compare Roosevelt and Harry Truman from his unique vantage point as presidential pilot for both, Myers judged them to be "as different as night from day." Truman, Myers said, "is like the man around the corner, a friend of yours, who made good in the biggest way possible. He's plainspoken and friendly . . . home-folks—good American home-folks."

Chapter Five
The Wild Blue Yonder

Franklin Roosevelt did more than set a record as the first President to fly while in office. He legitimized air travel for all who followed him, and thereby imparted a valuable psychological boost to America's commercial airlines. If flying is safe enough for a President, people reasoned, it is probably safe for us, too.

The man who stepped into Roosevelt's shoes shared that faith with enthusiasm. FDR opened the era of presidential flight; Harry Truman established it.

President Truman made his first flight in the *Sacred Cow* on May 5, 1945, barely three weeks after taking office, following the death of Roosevelt. It was a one-day round trip between Washington and Kansas City, Missouri, to visit his home in nearby Independence. It was also the first domestic presidential flight in history.

Truman liked flying and kept the presidential plane busy. On June 26, the *Sacred Cow* lifted him across the Rockies to San Francisco where the victorious Allies of World War II had gathered to adopt the charter of the United Nations. The next month, the *Cow* sped Truman to Germany for the Potsdam conference with "Uncle Joe" Stalin and Winston Churchill—the

149

summit meeting that sealed the division of Germany and shaped the boundaries of postwar Europe.

To reach Potsdam, Truman reluctantly heeded the advice of his counselors that he make the Atlantic crossing by ship. It was a long voyage aboard the USS *Augusta*. Truman, no sailor, made clear his distaste for "this boat." At Brussels, he found the *Sacred Cow* and Hank Myers' crew waiting for him, with a gentle ribbing about his being such a slowpoke.

The Potsdam conference brought to public light the unmistakable signs of strain between the Soviets and the West. It was Truman's first summit conference. Josef Stalin's behavior led him to observe that "force is the only thing these Russians understand." He came away convinced that the Kremlin leadership was planning world conquest.

In that grumpy mood, Truman was less than enthusiastic about returning to America via another slow sea voyage. He asked Myers for a flight schedule from Berlin to Washington aboard the *Sacred Cow*.

"We can leave Berlin at 5 P.M.," Myers told the President, "and have you back at National Airport by 9 A.M. Washington time."

"I've got a good mind to do it," Truman told Myers.

The crew immediately set about preparing for the flight. But the President's advisers were set against it. He needed the rest that the sea voyage would give him. Moreover, they insisted, it would be safer.

Truman resisted—until he got a long-distance call from First Lady Bess Truman at the White House, a call arranged by the staff. Truman sighed, agreed to stick to his original travel plan, and instructed Myers to scratch the plane trip home.

Although the *Sacred Cow* was, in fact, the "Flying White House," Harry Truman did not reserve it for his exclusive use. It was his to fly whenever he wanted, but the plane kept busy— on his orders—between presidential trips.

After Congress adopted the Marshall Plan for rebuilding war-stricken Europe, the *Sacred Cow* took General Marshall and Secretary of State James F. Byrnes on an inspection trip of the Continent, establishing the first nonstop New York–Paris flight since Lindbergh and the *Spirit of St. Louis* in 1927. Among its

150

notable passengers at various times—all transported in the presidential plane on Truman's orders—were Churchill, China's Mme. Chiang Kai-shek, Poland's General Sikorski, and most of America's ranking military leaders and cabinet members. Former President Herbert Hoover made a trip in the *Sacred Cow*. At Truman's insistence, General Dwight Eisenhower, the Supreme Allied Commander in Europe, flew in the plane when he made his triumphal return to the United States in June 1945.

The *Sacred Cow*'s most controversial trip was the flight from Washington to Independence, Missouri, on Christmas Day in 1945. Truman wanted to go back home for Christmas dinner. Before the day was over, the President was roundly denounced in the nation's press for needlessly jeopardizing his life. Colonel Myers, the pilot, was accused in one news magazine of being so wildly irresponsible as to "risk flying in a blizzard just for the hell of it."

Interestingly, nobody aboard the *Sacred Cow*, least of all the President, was aware of any danger or difficulty until the papers came out.

Here is an Air Force version of what happened, as contained in a news release issued several years later to explain the value of weather-avoidance radar then being installed on the next presidential plane, the *Independence*:

At 5 A.M. Christmas Day, Col. Myers went to the airport to check the weather. He left the *Sacred Cow* in the warm hangar. But a similar plane, which was to take the usual contingent of President-covering newsmen to Missouri, was towed out of its hangar and put on the line, ready for a possible takeoff.

When it commenced to sleet, which indicated desirable warm air aloft, Col. Myers needed to know how far he'd have to climb to reach that warm air—a plane can ice dangerously in a few moments.

Precise altitude-temperature reports are secured from ROAB, balloons equipped with instruments and automatic radios. They reported at 10 A.M., and Col. Myers called the White House to stand by. The reports showed safe, flyable layers of warm air to Kansas City over two routes, via St. Louis or Nashville. Myers notified the White House and a few minutes later they took off.

The trip was routine. But the press [plane] had trouble. After

151

standing in the sleet for several hours, its wings were thickly covered with ice and it couldn't leave with the *Cow*. It had to be towed back into the warm hangar until the ice melted.

By then, the weather may have changed. At any rate, the pilot didn't fly in a convenient strata of warm air and the newsmen had a rough and frightening trip. When they arrived over the snow–covered Kansas City Airport, the pilot, unacquainted with the field, had to make three passes at it before he could get lined up with the glaring white, snow-blanketed runway. By this time, nervous newsmen were convinced that what happened to them had also happened to President Truman. It simply wasn't so.

"I got calls from everybody, top to bottom, when the newspaper stories about the 'hazardous, perilous' flight appeared," Myers said.

The first call came about 8 P.M. on Christmas Day, just after a weary Myers had turned in at his hotel in Kansas City. It was from Gen. H. H. "Hap" Arnold, in Washington, demanding to know "what the hell was going on." When Myers sleepily professed ignorance, Arnold commanded, "Go down to the lobby and get a paper and when you've read it, call me back."

Headlines screamed that the President had risked his life flying through pea soup fog and ice, and head winds so violent that no commercial plane would have attempted the trip.

"Was I surprised!" Myers said later. "I felt like General Eisenhower when he got back from France after VE–Day and was asked if he had been worried during the Battle of the Bulge. 'You bet,' Ike replied. 'Three weeks later when I got the American papers. And then it scared the hell out of me.' Well, I hadn't worried about the flight from Washington to Kansas City either—until I saw the papers."

For days thereafter, the nation's press lambasted Truman for risking his life. "Careful, there," admonished *Time* magazine on January 7, 1946. Felix Belair of the *New York Times* labeled it "one of the most hazardous 'sentimental journeys' ever undertaken by an American chief of state." *Newsweek* magazine opined that Truman seemed determined "to make news by risking his neck." Added the *New York Herald Tribune*, "While we all like and admire high officials who do not think that their own

152

necks are the most important things in the world, the hard fact remains that those necks very often are.''

Truman shrugged off the critical stories. As he told Myers on his return trip to Washington a few days later, ''Actually, I'm safer up here than on those icy Kansas City streets.'' He was right, too. On its way back from the airport, the car that brought Truman out to the plane had skidded crazily and careened into a truck.

Although the *Sacred Cow* had several close brushes with disaster, one of the oddest occurred on the ground at Paducah, Kentucky, the home town of Senator Alben Barkley, who later became Truman's Vice President. Truman and Barkley had flown there for a political appearance. Nobody anticipated the great crowds that lined both sides of the runway to watch the *Sacred Cow* take off.

As the plane taxied down the runway, gaining speed, a woman with five children started across the strip. In the center, suddenly aware of the danger, she froze in panic. The youngsters screamed and clung to her skirts. It was too late for Myers to stop the plane, but as he flashed into an intersection with a cross runway, he jammed on the brakes, spun the nosewheel, and with tires screeching, swung the *Cow* into a sharp turn. As Myers told Dickson Hartwell in a *Collier's* magazine interview in 1949, it was ''like taking a corner in an automobile at 40 miles an hour.''

Later Myers chided Barkley about the incident, suggesting that some of his Kentucky constituents were less than bright. ''Why, man,'' replied Barkley indignantly, ''my people aren't dumb. They just aren't afraid to die.''

Truman's delight in doing the unexpected found full range aboard the *Sacred Cow*. Sometimes he would invite so many persons to fly with him that they would have to be turned away at the airfield for lack of space. On other occasions, he would deliberately keep the passenger list to a bare minimum so he could enjoy his solitude aloft, or spend the flight in the cockpit chatting with Myers, Smith, and the crew.

On his frequent air trips home to Independence, as Myers confided to close friends, Truman had issued standing orders that he was to be notified whenever the plane was over Ohio, the

153

home state of Republican Robert A. Taft. The two had been political foes in the Senate; their clashes became more frequent during Truman's White House days.

Duly alerted by Myers that the *Sacred Cow* was flying over Ohio, Truman would walk aft to his lavatory. Moments later, after the President had returned to his seat, Myers would get a presidential command over the intercom to activate the waste disposal system. That happened to be a fairly routine procedure aboard many aircraft built during the war, and, Myers explained, it was a capability retained by the *Sacred Cow*. The discharged liquids, of course, evaporated quickly in the cold, dry air outside. But it was Truman's way of having a private joke at Taft's expense.

The incident illustrates the unusual rapport that existed between Truman and Myers. Perhaps it was because both were products of small town life, essentially earthy and unstuffy men, eager to shed the trappings of office at every private opportunity. Myers relished nothing more than the chance to fly the *Sacred Cow* with the President aboard. For his part, Truman found the presidential plane a sanctuary away from the White House, one place where he could, when he wished, get away from it all for a few hours.

Truman was addicted to practical jokes and Myers delighted in assisting him whenever the opportunity arose. A memorable occasion came on Sunday, May 19, 1946, a day the President, on the spur of the moment, decided to fly home to visit his elderly mother at Independence.

It also happened to be a festive day in Washington. America had just entered the age of jet aircraft. Thousands of people were in the parks and on the rooftops to watch a dazzling air show by new P-80 fighter planes in the skies over the city. Truman, having given the press the slip, boarded the *Sacred Cow* at Bolling Air Field, across the Potomac from National Airport. With him were only two Secret Service agents. Myers took off quickly.

Moments after lift-off, the President came into the cockpit and looked out admiringly at the jet fighters swooping around Washington. As Myers related later to writer Seth Kantor in *Male* magazine, Truman said, "You know, Hank, those boys are putting on a fine show. They've given me—an idea. Mrs. Truman and Margaret are over there on top of our [White] House, and do you suppose we could . . . could we dive on them? . . . like a jet fighter? I've always wanted to try something like that."

"Well, there's no harm in it," Myers said to the President. "But somebody's sure gonna catch hell for it and I'm gonna blame you."

"I've got broad shoulders," Truman said. "How about it?"

Myers turned the *Sacred Cow* toward Washington, leveled off at 3,000 feet, and nosed the plane over the Washington Monument—already a violation of air security regulations. He had entered the zone encompassing the Capitol and the White House, which is out of bounds for air traffic.

"They can ground you for flying over it; they can take away your license; for all I know, they can send you to the electric chair for it," Myers observed. "But so what? Even the President has to live a little. . . ."

He throttled up to full power and turned to Truman, strapped securely in a seat behind himself and co-pilot Elmer F. "Smitty" Smith.

"Now?" Truman asked excitedly.

"Now," replied Myers.

He set the *Sacred Cow* on a dive run straight for the White House, the four engines screaming like buzzsaws.

"We shot past 2,000 feet and I could see the handful of people on the Truman's roof watching us stiffly. Down at 1,500 feet our angle was still steep and our noise was deafening. Past 1,000 feet—the flat, white target looked big, filling our whole world.

"At 500 feet, I had the *Cow* leveled and we roared over the White House roof wide open. I caught a split-second glimpse. Everyone there was frozen with fear and wonder.

"No one, least of all the Truman ladies, saw the President. But his face was pressed against the window; he was waving and laughing. They must have recognized the plane, though. Since it had been built in wartime, it didn't have any special markings or a presidential seal, but its tail number was clear to them—2107451.

"We climbed up to 3,000 feet again, swooped, circled, and fell into another dive. Everybody was watching us. But this time,

Margaret and her mother were jumping and waving. We shot past them at a little below 500 feet and roared back upstairs once more. Then we went on, as fast as we could, toward Missouri. We'd buzzed the White House."

Myers recalls Truman as being "awfully happy" at giving his wife and daughter a special show. But on the ground all hell had broken loose. Washington police, Air Force security units, and Secret Service headquarters (unaware that Truman had slipped out of the White House with just two bodyguards) thought a maniac had commandeered the President's airplane. Washington's newspapers, radio stations, and the Civil Aeronautics Administration were deluged with phone calls from anxious and curious spectators.

Finally, Bolling Field headquarters reached the *Sacred Cow* by radio and put out the news: Yes, it had been the President's plane that had been diving on the White House. And, yes, the President himself was aboard and had, in fact, ordered the dive. As Myers said, "That was the last we heard about it." Officially, at any rate. But in the press, Truman once again was scolded for childish grandstanding and for risking his life.

Although Myers was a gutsy pilot with a daredevil streak, he also was considered extremely competent and unflappable in emergency situations. Gen. "Hap" Arnold once described him as the "Paderewski of our profession," a pilot always in command of his instrument and capable of drawing out its best. Such skill stood him and the *Sacred Cow* in good stead on many occasions, especially the time he was returning from Paris with a load of furloughed GIs after the war.

Two hours out of Ireland, Myers encountered the most violent updrafts in his experience. One of them pushed the plane up to 14,000 feet in a matter of seconds, although Myers had instantly reduced engine power. Moments later, a violent downdraft sent the *Cow* plummeting toward earth, with Myers fighting desperately to retain control. At 3,500 feet, with all of the engines wide open, the plane continued to fall toward the sea. At 2,000 feet, Myers put the propellers into takeoff pitch, the equivalent of low gear in an automobile, but nothing seemed to halt their plunge. For the first time, as Myers subsequently recounted in *Collier's* magazine, he had an apprehension of death—and failure.

"There had been a series of airline crashes killing 83 people.

Mr. Truman had made a statement confirming his confidence in aviation and here was I, his own pilot, letting him down by disappearing in mid-Atlantic. Most clearly of all, I remember thinking of the devastating blow the loss of the *Sacred Cow* would be to aviation."

Even as his mind raced with such thoughts, the plane dropped to 1,000 feet, still unable to escape the downdraft that imprisoned it. Suddenly there was a blinding explosion. The *Cow*'s nose lighted up in a ball of white and blue fire. Myers was stunned; his eyes glazed by the flash. He could not see the instrument panel. His trousers were pushed up around his knees. He had a dazed recollection that the co-pilot seat was empty. Engineer Fred Willard, who had been sitting there while co-pilot Smith was napping in a rear bunk, was no longer beside him.

Myers, reacting now by instinct, pulled on the controls. Strangely, this time the plane responded. The altimeter began to climb. The buffeting ceased. The plane was out of danger.

From somewhere behind him Myers heard the voice of Willard asking, "Can I get you something?" The concussion had tossed the engineer to the flight deck. Myers instructed the crew to check on the passengers. They were badly shaken, but all right otherwise.

Myers feared the *Sacred Cow* was in no condition to continue across the Atlantic. He headed instead to Iceland and the U.S. air base there, so the plane could be inspected and repaired. On landing, the crew decided the plane had been hit by a bolt of lightning. They counted more than two dozen small scorched holes, about the diameter of a pencil, in the *Cow*'s fuselage. But the luck of the *Sacred Cow* held. No serious damage was uncovered. After detailed inspection and testing of the controls, engines, flaps, rudder, and landing gear, the plane was able to resume its journey to the States.

Flying in rough weather seldom daunted Harry Truman, but it occasionally unnerved visiting dignitaries, including Winston Churchill. In March 1946, Myers recalled, Churchill was scheduled to fly back to Washington with Truman following his famous "Iron Curtain" speech at Fulton, Missouri. The local weather was "a little bad," Myers said, and Truman asked him, "How about it, Hank?"

"The weather reports are okay, sir," Myers responded.

"All right," Truman said. "I'll fly."

Churchill looked out the window, saw the lowering clouds, and decided to go to Washington by train.

"We had a pleasant flight of one and a half hours," said Myers. "Mr. Churchill arrived the next day."

Truman trusted Myers' judgment on weather more than he trusted anyone else's. Taking the President to Waco, Texas, for an honorary degree at Baylor University, Myers warned that a threatened rainstorm might turn into sleet, grounding them there unless the program was kept to a tight schedule. Myers stayed at the airport, keeping a watch on the thermometer, while the President and his party were in the university auditorium.

When the temperature dropped to thirty-three degrees, Myers put in an urgent call to the hall and asked that Truman be advised. As the incident is recalled in Waco, Truman arose in the middle of someone's speech, apologized to the faculty and the audience, and said: "Hank Myers says if I'm not at the airfield in fifteen minutes, he won't be able to take me to Washington." They abbreviated the ceremony and Truman got back to the plane in time.

With the end of the war, the *Sacred Cow* had become a highly visible symbol of the power and authority of the President of the United States. There was no longer any reason to hide the handsome plane behind the sterile anonymity of other Air Force Skymasters.

In a spirit of celebration, letters began pouring into the White House and U.S. Army Air Forces headquarters urging that a special insignia be affixed to the presidential plane. Walt Disney designed one version—the face of a smiling cow with a halo over one horn and an Uncle Sam top hat over the other. Myers and the crew preferred another design that came in the mails. It showed a bemedaled and haloed cow flying over a globe. But dignity and decorum prevailed. The White House decreed that the *Sacred Cow* was too important to carry a comic insignia on its bosom.

Colonel Myers came up with the idea of painting on the left side of the nose of the plane the flags of the countries the *Cow* had visited. That seemed fitting. So forty-four flags went on the fuselage shortly after the end of hostilities. Seven more flags

158

were added before the plane was retired from presidential service in July 1947 and assigned to the VIP transport fleet.

Seven years later, in 1955, the *Sacred Cow* was transferred again, this time to the Headquarters Command at Bolling Air Force Base outside Washington, where it was used primarily for military administrative flights. While at Bolling, the venerable *Cow* got a facelift; the addition of weather avoidance radar considerably changed the contour of its nose.

On October 17, 1961, Major Gen. Brooke E. Allen, commander of the Air Force Headquarters Command, took the *Sacred Cow* up for its last flight—a short hop to Andrews Air Force Base. At impressive ceremonies on December 4, 1961, the *Sacred Cow* was decommissioned and placed in the custody of the Smithsonian Institution.

The first official presidential airplane was thus retired from active service after having flown 1,500,000 miles, totaling 12,135 hours and 25 minutes in the air. But of that, only 43,000 miles—less than 3 percent—represented actual travel by Presidents Roosevelt and Truman during the *Sacred Cow*'s four-year assignment to the White House. Presidential flight was still in its infancy.

The *Sacred Cow* was not shunted aside in 1947 because it was unreliable or inadequate to the task of transporting the President. It was simply a matter of keeping abreast of the times.

With the war over, the pace of development in the air transport industry was breathtaking. New technology in engines, metals, navigational instrumentation, and airframe construction warranted White House attention. In some ways, the *Sacred Cow* was like an aging hoofer who knew all the steps in the routine, but younger dancers had more agility and fewer wrinkles.

In the late Forties, the Douglas DC-6 was the latest and newest long-range airliner in commercial service. Air Force officials and Truman's staff decided it would be just the thing for presidential use. And, naturally, they wanted one as soon as possible. So Douglas Aircraft and Air Force executives approached American Airlines, which had a large order of DC-6s on the production lines in California. Would American agree to surrender one of its ordered planes to accommodate the White House? American would—and did.

Fuselage No. 29 was selected to become the country's second

presidential aircraft. The Air Force gave it serial number 46–505 under a contract signed with Douglas on November 2, 1946. Externally, there was little difference between the fuselage of the presidential DC-6 and its sister aircraft being completed for American Airlines on the same production line. About the only feature that an observer might note was the installation of three closely grouped windows on the right rear side. The windows marked the location of the President's stateroom.

The interior, of course, was a far cry from both the commercial DC-6 airliner and the Air Force's regular transports. E. Gilbert Mason, the Douglas designer who had conceived the arrangements aboard the *Sacred Cow*, came up with a handsome and functional layout for the President's new plane.

The presidential suite, one of the four main sections within the 67-foot cabin, occupied the entire rear part of the fuselage. On the bleached mahogany door to the stateroom, Mason placed a replica of the Great Seal of the United States, inlaid in natural wood colors. The door opened into a spacious compartment decorated in chocolate brown, dark blue, and light gray, with tan accents.

Focal point of the suite was a large swivel chair, a reclining model upholstered in two-tone blue barkweave cloth. It was fixed beside a window on the left side of the stateroom. In front of the chair was a conference table-desk of bleached mahogany, also inlaid with the Great Seal. For dining, the table could be extended to seat eight. Opposite the table was a built-in double seat covered in natural elkhide. On the right side of the suite, beneath the three-section window, was a long elkhide sofa that converted at night into a full-sized bed. The room also contained a mahogany filing cabinet, a built-in wardrobe for clothes, bedding, and linen, and a curtained storage cabinet. Just to the left of the presidential chair was a telephone intercom and controls for a concealed radio. On the front wall, on either side of the entry door, were instruments indicating the plane's speed, altitude, and compass direction. Roll maps could be drawn down from a case recessed in the ceiling. For efficiency, comfort, and elegance, this presidential suite clearly surpassed the one Mason had designed for the *Sacred Cow*.

The Air Force, meanwhile, was wrestling internally with

The Dixie Clipper, the first plane in history to be used by a President in office.

Returning to Washington in 1943 from Casablanca on the first presidential flight, FDR celebrated his 61st birthday aboard the *Dixie Clipper Flying Boat* with Fleet Admiral W. D. Leahy (left), Presidential Adviser Harry Hopkins and pilot Howard M. Cone (right). U.S. NAVY PHOTO

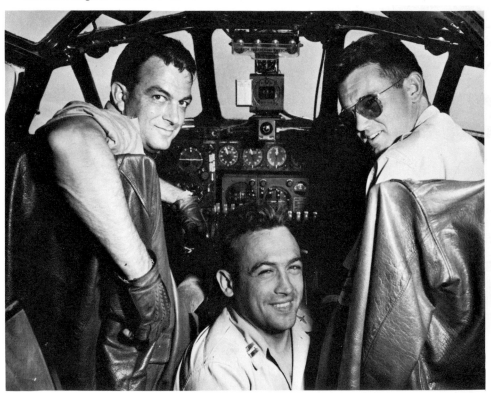

Lt. Col. Henry "Hank" Myers (left), the first presidential pilot, with two of the elite crew members of the Roosevelt and Truman years: Lt. Elmer F. Smith, (right) co-pilot; and Captain Ted J. Boselli, (center) navigator. SMITHSONIAN INSTITUTION

The Sacred Cow, a Douglas DC4 Skymaster, the first plane specifically built for presidential service, 1944. U.S. AIR FORCE PHOTO

The Sacred Cow was fitted with an ingenious electrically operated elevator to lift Franklin Roosevelt's wheelchair.
DOUGLAS AIRCRAFT PHOTO

Jaunty Harry Truman, holding his hat and a cane, leaves *Air Force One* upon returning to the capital from a Florida vacation. He loved flying and did more than any
other President to assure the public that the airplane was a safe and speedy means of
travel for Presidents. WIDE WORLD PHOTOS

President Truman's plane, the *Independence,* was gaudily painted to resemble a giant American eagle. The three windows toward the rear mark the President's suite. This Douglas DC6 flew Truman to Wake Island in 1950 for his historic meeting with General Douglas MacArthur. U.S. AIR FORCE PHOTO

Snow falls on Washington National Airport as President Truman waves good-bye on his way to Independence, Missouri, for the 1950 Christmas holiday. Truman ignored his advisers' pleas that he postpone his trip because of the inclement weather. WIDE WORLD PHOTOS

Dwight Eisenhower began using the first of his three Lockheed Constellations when he was Supreme Commander of Allied Forces in Europe. He continued to use them during his presidency, naming each one *Columbine* after the blue Colorado flower of Mamie Eisenhower's home state. U.S. AIR FORCE PHOTO

A rare moment aboard *Air Force One*—a war-weary President Johnson confers with former President Eisenhower about American policy in Vietnam. Ike had cautioned LBJ against a land war in Asia. Y. R. OKAMATO, LBJ LIBRARY

Crowds jam National Airport to welcome President and Mrs. Eisenhower back to Washington in 1955, following his convalescence in Denver from a heart attack. Among those waiting at the foot of the stairs of *Columbine II* are, left to right: Eisenhower's son, John, and his wife; Chief Justice Earl Warren; and Vice President Richard Nixon. HANK WALKER, LIFE MAGAZINE, © 1955 TIME, INC.

President and Mrs. John F. Kennedy board *Air Force One* after a 1961 state visit to Canada. LEONARD MC COMBE, LIFE MAGAZINE, © 1961 TIME, INC.

President John F. Kennedy leaves his plane at Nassau in the Bahamas, December, 1962. WIDE WORLD PHOTOS

The most famous, most published photograph ever taken aboard a presidential airplane was the swearing in of Lyndon B. Johnson at Dallas' Love Field, November 22, 1963. The President is flanked by Lady Bird Johnson and the just widowed Jacqueline Kennedy. CECIL STOUGHTON, LBJ LIBRARY

The casket containing the body of slain President John F. Kennedy arrives from Dallas and is moved from *Air Force One* to a Navy ambulance at Andrews Air Force Base, Maryland, November 22, 1963. WIDE WORLD PHOTOS

Lyndon Johnson, a restless passenger, often took over the observer's seat in *Air Force One's* cockpit to chat with the crew. FRANCIS MILLER, LIFE MAGAZINE, © 1968 TIME, INC.

Lyndon Johnson doing what he liked best—holding court over lunch around his mammoth, kidney-shaped desk—during a 1966 campaign trip. The switch below the telephone panel permitted LBJ to lower the desk to coffee table height. BILL EPPERIDGE, LIFE MAGAZINE, © 1966 TIME, INC.

President Nixon, flanked by Press Secretary Ron Ziegler in shirt sleeves, briefs *Air Force One's* pool of correspondents during a 1971 trip to Europe. Author J. F. terHorst of *The Detroit News* stands behind the plaid upholstered seat.

WHITE HOUSE PHOTO

President Nixon flew aboard Chinese Premier Chou En-lai's personal plane, a Soviet II-18, en route from Peking to Hangchow in 1972. At left are Secretary of State William Rogers and National Security Adviser Henry Kissinger.

Items used by the President and passengers of *The Spirit of '76* include (top to bottom) the President's flight jacket, a cigar humidor, a program of stereo music selections, a Bible, a napkin, personalized stationery, and a matchbook. U.S. AIR FORCE PHOTO

Chou En-lai leads a delegation of top Chinese officials in greeting President and Mrs. Nixon on their arrival in Peking in 1972. UNITED PRESS INTERNATIONAL PHOTO

Richard Nixon makes his first speech as former President at El Toro Marine Station, near San Clemente, where *Air Force One* landed after his resignation on August 9, 1974. With him are son-in-law Edward Cox, daughter Tricia and wife Pat.

Richard Nixon, no longer President, says farewell to Col. Ralph Albertazzie, his *Air Force One* pilot, after landing in California to begin his San Clemente exile.

First Lady Betty Ford grabs the railing while President Gerald Ford stumbles on the rain-slicked stairs as he leaves *Air Force One* in 1975 at Salzburg, Austria. This mishap, more than any other, created the impression that Ford was clumsy, an image that dogged him for the remainder of his presidency.

WIDE WORLD PHOTOS

First Lady Rosalynn Carter snoozes on the President's knee during a news conference aboard *Air Force One* on the way home from Europe early in 1978. National Security Adviser Zbigniew Brzezinski is at far right. WHITE HOUSE PHOTO

Lt. Col. Henry Myers, pilot of the *Sacred Cow* and the *Independence,* 1944–1948. SMITHSONIAN INSTITUTION

Col. Francis Williams, pilot of the *Independence,* 1948–1953. SMITHSONIAN INSTITUTION

Col. William Draper, pilot of the *Columbine III,* 1953–1961. SMITHSONIAN INSTITUTION

Col. James Swindal, pilot for John F. Kennedy and Lyndon B. Johnson, 1961–1965. SMITHSONIAN INSTITUTION

Col. James Cross, pilot for Lyndon B. Johnson, 1965–1968. SMITHSONIAN INSTITUTION

Lt. Col. Paul Thornhill, pilot for Lyndon B. Johnson, 1968–1969. SMITHSONIAN INSTITUTION

Lt. Col. Ralph Albertazzie, pilot for Richard M. Nixon, 1969–1974. SMITHSONIAN INSTITUTION

Col. Lester McClelland, pilot for Gerald Ford and Jimmy Carter, 1974–present. WHITE HOUSE PHOTO

another problem concerning the new presidential aircraft: What should it be called?

Pentagon officials never had liked the name an irreverent press corps had bestowed upon the first presidential plane. The brass thought it frivolous for a President of the Unites States to arrive anywhere, especially a foreign capital, aboard an airplane dubbed the *Sacred Cow*.

Indeed, as the Associated Press noted in a Washington dispatch on May 17, 1947, "so many church people have written in to complain that Charles G. Ross, presidential press secretary, prepared a special letter explaining that the *Sacred Cow* was a nickname for which the White House had no responsibility." So the search for a suitable name for the new presidential plane became a project of urgent priority, especially when one leading aviation magazine began referring to the new aircraft as *Sacred Cow II* while it was still in production.

Some military men thought it should have no popular name at all, simply its Air Force number. But more practical heads argued that the press and the public would never settle for that. There was too much romanticizing about a President's plane.

Senior Air Force officials wanted to call it the "Flying White House," the name originally intended for the *Sacred Cow*. At least it was a dignified name and it expressed the purpose of the craft. But that too ran into resistance from the pragmatists. The "Flying White House" had not caught on with the first presidential airplane; what reason was there to believe it would be acceptable this time?

In the end, Air Force brass deferred to the suggestion of presidential pilot Hank Myers. He proposed the plane be named the *Independence*. It captured the historic spirit of the United States, and it had the virtue of being the name of Truman's home town in Missouri. Moreover, Myers said, the Commander-in-Chief liked it. That settled the argument.

Being a substantially larger aircraft than the *Sacred Cow*, the *Independence* offered considerably more space for presidential staff and accompanying guests. The main passenger cabin, located immediately forward of the entrance area, accommodated twenty-four passengers for daytime flights. For overnight flights, the seats could be opened out, in semi-Pullman fashion,

161

to provide sleeping space for twelve persons in upper and lower berths.

While the facilities for passenger comfort were impressive to laymen, the technical equipment and navigational aids aboard the *Independence* testified to tremendous advances in aeronautical science since Roosevelt's first flight in the *Dixie Clipper* back in January 1943. Powered by four 2,100-horsepower Pratt & Whitney engines, the *Independence* had a cruising speed of 315 miles an hour and a maximum speed of 358 miles an hour! It featured Curtiss electric propellers of the three-bladed, full-feathering, constant-speed type. Extra gasoline tanks gave it an absolute range of 4,400 miles without refueling.

The *Independence* was the first Air Force transport to use water injection, an inexpensive "shot in the arm" that gave each engine 300 additional horsepower on takeoff and thus enabled it to easily lift off the ground with only three engines operating, if necessary. The *Independence* also was equipped with an experimental radar nose capable of detecting areas of heavy precipitation and turbulence for thirty miles ahead, thus aiding the pilot in avoiding heavy weather. This was one of the important advances in transport aviation in the 1940's; the *Independence* was the first DC-6 to have it.

The cockpit instrumentation was impressive, too: a radio altimeter that gave the actual height over terrain or water, a double radio compass, an electronic autopilot, and an instrument landing system that included a glide path receiver, marker beacon receiver and localizer, plus the latest in radio transmitting and receiving equipment. The *Independence* boasted the most advanced air-conditioning system available, including automatic pressurization to keep cabin pressures at comfortable levels at high or low altitudes. It was a far cry from the oxygen bottles that had been put aboard the *Dixie Clipper* for FDR's first presidential air trip just three years before.

And for the first time on a presidential aircraft, it became possible not only for a Chief Executive to work comfortably aboard on White House business, but to keep in constant touch with subordinates back in Washington. The *Independence* featured a radio teletype transmission system capable of sending or receiving printed messages over a distance of 3,000 miles—automatically coded and uncoded so that presidential communications could not be intercepted by eavesdroppers.

With the war over, it was no longer considered politically hazardous for a President to have a luxurious airplane at taxpayer's expense. Any airplane so obviously constructed with one passenger in mind seemed entitled to an exterior paint job worthy of its exalted status. The *Independence* thus became the first presidential plane to look the part. Indeed, it blatantly advertised itself as the aircraft that carried the President of the United States.

The Douglas designers had been trying to develop a distinctive insignia for the fleet of DC-6s being built for American Airlines on the same production line as the *Independence*. Since the airline's motif was the American eagle, the stylists had crafted a distinctive version of an American Airlines eagle that actually enveloped the entire airplane. As it turned out, American didn't like the Douglas proposal, so it was abandoned.

But Air Force planners had seen the early drawings and were seized with the notion of employing the eagle as a symbol for the *Independence*. It was, after all, the national bird.

With hardly any encouragement at all, the designers at Douglas happily went back to their sketchpads to adapt American's discarded design into something suitable for the President's airplane. To make sure it wouldn't be rejected this time, Douglas Aircraft offered the government a bonus—the company would foot the $1,500 bill for painting the *Independence*.

Thus when the *Independence* was unveiled at commissioning ceremonies in Washington on Independence Day 1947, the public saw an airplane that could only be described as spectacular. It looked like a gigantic bird.

The nose of the *Independence* had been transformed into the head of an eagle. In deep navy blue! Stylized feathers, in two shades of blue, swept back along both sides of the fuselage. On the tail section, three blue feathers outlined in yellow, fanned up on the vertical stablizer. The words THE INDEPENDENCE were boldly inscribed on the fuselage just behind the pilot's window.

But spectator's eyes were inexorably drawn back to the nose of the aircraft. The cockpit windows looked for all the world like the eyes of this man-made eagle. They peered over a broad beak

163

and a mouth, also outlined in pin stripes. Originally, the beak was painted brown, but when somebody nervously opined that the press corps might dub the plane the "Brown Nose," the beak was hurriedly repainted a golden yellow. Later the beak was painted a light gray and, eventually, white.

Whatever else might be said about the *Independence*, it was a gaudy airplane, more likely to be mistaken for a flying circus than a "Flying White House." Its saving grace was the feisty nature of the man it served. Harry Truman saw it—and liked it. Nothing else really mattered.

Since the Douglas DC-6 was a newcomer in the transport field, Colonel Myers had planned to fly it about the country to build up approximately a hundred hours of "shakedown" time. Much to his chagrin, the White House had other plans for the presidential plane, starting immediately after its delivery to the 503rd Base Unit at Washington's National Airport.

The Greek ambassador to the United States had died, and suitable transportation was required to carry the body back to his native land. Until this time, the traditional procedure was to return the bodies of dignitaries by ship. But since World War II was over and Greece was a sensitive issue in the increasingly tense dialogue between Washington and Moscow, the Truman administration wanted to avoid using a warship for this mission. The obvious alternative was to employ a VIP plane.

The *Sacred Cow* was still available, but its entry door was too narrow to accommodate the heavy box containing the ambassador's coffin. There was no choice but to use the *Independence*. Unfortunately, the coffin could not be turned once it cleared the doorway, the entry passage being too confining. Colonel Myers decided to leave the coffin in the entry way.

It proved to be a considerable obstacle to members of the crew and the official escorting party attempting to go from one part of the plane to another. "We had to climb over the darn thing in rather undignified fashion—but there was little else we could do," one passenger recalled.

What they did was make the best of an awkward situation, accomplishing it several hours after leaving Washington. A pad and a linen tablecloth were discreetly placed atop the massive box, transforming it into a bar for serving drinks to the passengers! The *Independence*'s first official flight thus was something of a Grecian wake.

Another early flight of the *Independence* provided an embarrassing surprise for other units of the Air Force. While returning Treasury Secretary John Snyder to Washington from a conference in Rio de Janeiro, the plane's No. 1 engine conked out between Lima, Peru, and Albrook Air Force Base in the Panama Canal Zone.

Alarmed Air Force officials at Albrook immediately dispatched a B-17 bomber and an escort of P-47 fighters to intercept the *Independence* and keep watch over the limping craft. Shortly thereafter, Colonel Myers spotted the rescue planes cruising far below him, heading in the wrong direction. They were searching for the *Independence*, assuming it was skimming the waves in the crippled fashion of an older, unpressurized wartime transport.

Myers calmly radioed that he was cruising at 20,000 feet, the cabin pressures were good, and that he would meet them back at Albrook. In fact, the *Independence*, with three engines operating, reached the Canal Zone base before its "rescuers" did.

President Truman's first flight on the *Independence* occurred two months after its commissioning—a trip to Rio de Janeiro for the Inter-American Defense Conference in September 1947. Pilot Myers remembered it as the occasion for one of Truman's deadpan pranks on his wife. Mrs. Truman and daughter Margaret had gone along as special guests of Brazil, the host country.

"Margaret is like her father," Myers said. "She loves flying. Nothing worries her in the air. Mrs. Truman has never shared their flying confidence, but I'd mark her down as one of the bravest passengers I ever took along. She went out of her way to 'appear' relaxed, to spare my apprehensive feelings, and to be a good sport. But flying was unpleasant to her. We all knew it.

"On this particular journey, I scheduled a stop in Belém, Brazil—a place that had runways built to wartime specifications. A ship as big as the *Independence* would never have been able to come in there except for its equipped reversible propeller action, then brand new, which would allow slower, shorter landings.

"I informed Mr. Truman that we would be able to try the reversible props at Belém and I warned him, since he had never

165

experienced the effects before, that there would be a lot of gunning motor roar attached to it. I reminded him especially to warn Mrs. Truman in advance. I knew it would worry her otherwise.

" 'Nuts,' he said. 'I'm not going to tell her that at all. She wouldn't understand it in the first place. She'll take it all right.'

"It was a smooth flight. At Belém, I circled and came in for the reversible prop demonstration. Mrs. Truman girded herself for the landing, which she did normally. Her husband and daughter were calm as usual. And then there was the sudden shaking, a booming of the reversible action.

" 'Oh, my!' the First Lady gasped. She was extremely uneasy. 'What's happening to us?'

"The President, savoring his obvious chance, took full advantage of it. He glanced quickly out of the window. He staged his face with worried wrinkles and said in a hurried shout: 'The plane is falling apart!'

" 'Whew!' Mrs. Truman uttered a long sigh of relief and leaned her head back to relax. 'If that's all that happens when this thing falls apart,' she said pleasantly, 'then it's not as bad as I've expected.' "

Myers had one landing with the *Independence* that autumn which nearly claimed Margaret Truman's life—along with his own and the crew's. As he related in *Collier's* magazine, Truman sent the plane out to Detroit to pick up Margaret, who had been taken ill with laryngitis during a vocal appearance there. Myers was about to commence his landing approach into National Airport in thick weather when the automatic pilot failed at 1,500 feet. The plane suddenly nosed down. At the airport, where the *Independence* was being watched on ground control radar, it appeared to dive off the bottom of the screen. Working fast, Myers gained control of the big craft, pulled it up to about 5,000 feet, and came in again, this time with a perfect landing.

As Margaret stepped out of the plane, she asked Myers what the sudden descent and fast climb were all about. "Oh, that wasn't anything," Myers assured her with a smile. "Just checking procedures."

During its five years as the President's airplane, the *Independence* underwent major equipment modifications, partly to incorporate the latest in aeronautic improvements and partly to correct deficiencies that plagued the early DC-6s.

166

One of the latter was a nasty habit of developing cabin fires from the aircraft's heating system. It seems that the overflow from transferring fuel was being picked up in the air scoop going to the cabin's air-heat exchanger. After one fatal accident, the government ordered all DC-6s grounded for inspection and correction of the deficient system. So the *Independence* returned to the Douglas factory in California on November 11, 1947, where it remained until the heating system was operating perfectly. So concerned were officials of Douglas and the Air Force about the safety of the President and other VIPs that the *Independence* did not resume White House service until May 6, 1948, nearly six months later.

A six-month absence of the primary presidential plane would be unthinkable in today's scheme of things at the White House, particularly during a presidential election campaign. It did not seem so extraordinary in the winter of 1947 and the spring of 1948, however.

Truman could still call upon the *Sacred Cow* as a backup aircraft during the factory layover of the *Independence*. And bad-weather flying was not then so prevalent as now. Many airfields still lacked the sophisticated navigational instrumentation essential for bringing in planes during periods of heavy fog, sleet, and snowstorms. Pilot Myers, in fact, advised the White House against counting on a presidential plane as the basic transportation during the months of late fall, winter, and early spring.

"From October to May, I can't guarantee we can keep a schedule," he had said. "But from May to October, I can take the President anywhere in the States he wants to go."

Then, too, Harry Truman in 1948 was in love with the idea of the campaign train, as it had been used in the past by Roosevelt and other favorite candidates. Roosevelt had made profitable use of a special presidential railroad car, dubbed the "Ferdinand Magellan," on stumping tours camouflaged as nonpolitical visits to various federal projects and installations. On any train trip he could classify as nonpartisan, Truman could travel at government expense, even though there might be political stops along the way. Thus, as a matter of political convenience, the "Ferdinand Magellan" took precedence over the presidential plane in 1948.

There had been another important change for the *Indepen-*

167

dence during its long layover in California. Colonel Myers resigned from the Air Force in January 1948, choosing to resume his civilian career as a pilot for American Airlines.

Ever the free spirit, Myers plainly could not abide the creeping bureaucracy that gradually spread over the peacetime armed forces. He missed the easygoing flying days of the war and the immediate years that followed. Truman offered to make him a White House aide, which might have meant a general's star for Myers. But it also would have cut down on his flying time. After six years in uniform, the country's first presidential pilot told Associated Press why he had stepped out. "The military fuss-budgets were about to corner me. If I'd stayed in another day, I would have had to fill out a form."

But there were other reasons, too, as Myers explained during a radio interview after rejoining American Airlines. His job as presidential pilot kept him away from his wife and young son for too long periods of time. At thirty-nine, Myers was beginning to appreciate the regularity of hours that commercial flying offered—"making a trip to and from a point, then three days off and the chance to relax and work around my house and the boat I have on Eagle Mountain Lake, just outside Fort Worth." But he admitted he would miss the excitement of world travel, and the pleasure of rubbing elbows with presidents and the world figures who had been his passengers as presidential pilot. And Myers, an inveterate storyteller, would miss the chance to restock his inventory of presidential yarns. Even on that radio broadcast, he couldn't resist the opportunity to spin a final one.

" . . . Then there was the time when Jimmy Byrnes, then secretary of state, flew to Paris. He took with him two watermelons from his South Carolina farm—one for himself and one for the crew. The watermelon he gave us finally became probably the most traveled watermelon in the world. It flew with us for about 13,000 miles before being eaten. From the U.S. to Paris, back to the U.S. again, and from Washington to Kansas City. Well, President Truman finally helped us eat it on the return flight from Kansas City because the food department hadn't placed any dessert aboard the plane. It was so good—even after all this travel—the President came back for a second helping."

Hank Myers' successor as presidential pilot was Lt. Col.

Francis W. "Frenchie" Williams, who had served as co-pilot on the *Independence*. Like Myers, Williams was an alumnus of American Airlines. "I saw in him the kind of take-charge guy the job required," Myers said. For Truman and the *Independence*'s crew, the selection of Williams made for an easy and comfortable transition.

Just how long Williams and the *Independence* would continue to serve Harry Truman was a matter of great uncertainty during 1948. Truman's popularity was plummeting everywhere—in the opinion polls, among Democratic leaders, and especially in the halls of Congress, where the Republican majority made life miserable for him. The political experts were predicting the election of a Republican president in November. No one of any stature thought Harry Truman, with Kentucky's Alben Barkley as his running mate, could possibly defeat the Republican ticket of Thomas E. Dewey of New York and Earl Warren of California.

Officials high in the Air Force evidently agreed with that notion. And thereby hangs the tale of a handsome airplane. Along with Tom Dewey, it also lost the presidential election of November 2, 1948.

The Air Force, it seems, had ten Lockheed Constellations (C-121As) on order from the factory in California. What an impression it would make on incoming President Dewey, the high command reasoned, if there were a new presidential airplane ready and waiting for him when he took office in January 1949!

Lockheed records show that the first of these new triple-tail, four-engine beauties was modified while on the production line and given a special executive configuration worthy of a Commander-in-Chief. Receiving Air Force serial No. 48–608 and designated VC-121B, the only such aircraft built, the sleek plane was accepted by the government on November 12 and flown to National Airport in the capital on November 24, 1948. By that time, of course, the surprising election results were in. Harry Truman was set for four more years in the White House.

Unofficially, the plane had been dubbed the *Dewdrop*, an apt monicker for the aircraft destined to carry Dewey. Fortunately, the name had not been painted on the aircraft ahead of election day. Since the "8608" was new and more advanced than the *In-*

169

dependence, it was offered to Truman as his presidential aircraft. By then, the President had heard of the Air Force *faux pas* through the White House grapevine. He thought it hugely funny and replied in the words of a popular song: "I don't want it—you can have it—it's too big for me!"

After the election, a Truman fan presented the President with a mustache cup as a souvenir of his upset victory over the mustachioed Tom Dewey. Only partly in jest, Truman sent the cup to the Air Force with instructions that it be put aboard Constellation "8608." For several years thereafter—except for occasional and mysterious disappearances—the mustache cup was prominently displayed in a cabinet in the plane's "presidential" cabin.

Although rejected by Truman, the plane was employed as a backup aircraft for the *Independence* on frequent occasions. Principally it was used by the Secretary of the Air Force, whose seal it bore, and by Secretaries of State George Marshall and, after 1952, John Foster Dulles. During assignment to Defense Secretary Charles E. Wilson in the Eisenhower years, the name *Dewdrop* finally appeared on the plane's nose. During the Kennedy administration, the *Dewdrop* became the primary aircraft for Air Force Secretary Donald Quarles. He removed the name and replaced it with replicas of the flags of the thirty countries it had visited.

Pentagon records disclose that "8608" managed to make one notable contribution to aviation history. During the Christmas holidays of 1948, shortly after Truman's victory, it established a speed record from Washington to Burtonwood, England, of twelve hours, eight minutes flying time. Aboard were Secretary of the Air Force Stuart Symington and Vice President Alben Barkley. When the plane returned to Washington, crew members discovered something that hadn't been there previously. Barkley's initials had been carved into the table in the main cabin of the plane intended for "President" Dewey.

It was shortly after dawn on Sunday, October 15, 1950, when the *Independence*, with Frenchie Williams at the controls, circled Wake Island and began its long, slow glide to the landing strip. Harry Truman was nearing his rendezvous with General of

170

the Army Douglas MacArthur, the hero of the Pacific war, on a barren dot of sand and coral midway between Hawaii and Japan.

The President had flown 7,000 miles from Washington for his meeting with the Supreme Commander for Allied Powers. Mac-Arthur had served since the end of World War II as the American "emperor" of Japan and, since the outbreak of hostilities in Korea, as the commander of United Nations military forces arrayed against North Korea.

On the way to Wake, the *Independence* stopped briefly for refueling in St. Louis, Missouri, and overnight at Fairfield-Suisan Air Force Base in California. At Honolulu, Admiral Arthur Radford's wife greeted Truman with a kiss and the customary garland of flowers. While the President took time to tour the U.S. military installations in Hawaii, Frenchie Williams and the crew replenished the *Independence* with food and fuel, and tidied up Truman's cabin and the rest of the interior in preparation for the nighttime hop to Wake Island, 2,300 miles away. This would be the longest air journey of the Truman presidency. Williams affectionately patted the plane's sleek aluminum skin. The three-year-old *Independence* was performing magnificently.

Seven hours later, Williams set the wheels down on Wake Island's slender runway, taxied past the rusting skeletons of Japanese tanks and planes, swung around MacArthur's personal aircraft, a gleaming new Constellation, and eased gently to a stop. Air guards pushed open the door of the *Independence*. Harry Truman stepped out briskly to greet MacArthur at the foot of the landing ramp.

It is odd, in retrospect, how sensational this meeting became in 1973 with the publication of Merle Miller's oral biography of Truman, *Plain Speaking*. As if baring a top secret twenty-three years after the event, Harry Truman and his longtime personal physician, Dr. Wallace Graham, described for Miller a moment of high drama in the skies over Wake Island—the *Independence* and MacArthur's plane circling each other warily while the two principals argued by radio as to which of them would land first in order to greet the other on the ground.

"I was with the President when he was going to meet MacArthur on Wake Island," Dr. Graham related to Miller, "and MacArthur was always a showman type. He deliberately tried to

171

hold up his landing so that we would go in and land ahead of them. Harry caught it right away, and he told MacArthur, 'You go ahead and land first. We've got plenty of gas. We'll wait for you.' And that's what happened. That's what we did."

Added Truman: "MacArthur was always play-acting, and he wasn't any damn good at it. I knew what he was trying to pull with all that stuff about whose plane was going to land first, and I wasn't going to let him get away with it. . . . I made it quite clear that he was to go in first, and he did."

Truman then embellished the story for Miller by declaring that when he landed in the *Independence* and looked out at the welcoming party, "MacArthur wasn't there. Even after we stopped the engines and they opened up the door of the plane, the bastard still didn't show up. So I just sat there. I just waited. I'd have waited until hell froze over if I'd of had to. I wasn't going to have one of my generals embarrass the President of the United States. Finally the son of a bitch walked out of one of the buildings near the runway there. He was wearing those damn sunglasses of his and a shirt that was unbuttoned and a cap that had a lot of hardware. . . ."

It made a great yarn, naturally, and Miller's book would seem to have scooped the scores of Washington correspondents who had accompanied Truman to Wake Island for the historic meeting with MacArthur.

The trouble was that there wasn't a word of truth to the Truman-Graham account!

Miller had tape-recorded his interviews with Truman in the early 1960s, already a decade after the Wake Island meeting, and Truman's memory clearly was faulty. The former President, then seventy-seven, and his elderly physician had merely concocted the story out of their imaginations.

None of the reporters on the trip had witnessed any jockeying in the skies over Wake, nor did they report at the time that MacArthur had kept Truman waiting at planeside.

"It was all baloney," says Robert Donovan, who covered the Wake Island meeting for the *New York Herald Tribune*, and whose definitive series about the Truman presidency started with *Conflict and Crisis*. "Nothing like that happened at all at Wake."

172

Truman himself, in his *Memoirs* published in 1956, devotes but a brief paragraph to the actual landing at Wake Island, with no hint of contretemps with MacArthur about who would land first. And Truman wrote: "General MacArthur was at the ramp of the plane as I came down."

MacArthur had arrived twelve hours earlier from Tokyo and had spent the night on Wake Island. His suntan khakis were immaculate, devoid of all decorations except the cluster of five small stars that adorned his open collar. He wore the battered gold-encrusted cap that was the MacArthur trademark. Pilot Williams thought it looked a little more rakish than usual. President Truman noticed a sweat line, and remarked later that MacArthur's cap had "evidently seen a good deal of use."

The two had never met before. MacArthur had spent the last thirteen years in the Pacific. There was a great deal of speculation about why Truman had decided to fly halfway around the earth to a lonely outpost in the middle of the Pacific, which normally served as a navigation station manned by six Coast Guardsmen. The President had several reasons.

With the war going well in Korea for the UN forces, Truman wanted to hear from MacArthur, in person, that his military strategy in Korea would not alarm the new Communist Chinese regime in Peking and provoke its intervention on the side of the retreating North Koreans.

MacArthur had come to Wake with a different explanation for Truman's visit. Brig. Gen. Courtney Whitney, MacArthur's confidant and political adviser in Tokyo, saw a connection with the midterm congressional elections two weeks hence. He had suggested to MacArthur that the President wanted to rub elbows with the legendary general in hopes of convincing voters back home that the Democratic administration deserved credit for the progress of the war.

MacArthur didn't bother to salute his Commander-in-Chief, an omission carefully noted by the *Independence* crew and long remembered by Truman. *Time* magazine later described their first encounter as comparable to "sovereign rulers of separate states approaching a neutral field." After a prolonged and ostentatious hand-shaking session for the benefit of the accompanying photographers and reporters, the two men drove off to a Quonset hut just beyond the airstrip. They talked privately for an hour and then reconvened for a second session in Wake Island's tiny Administration Building, this time with advisers present.

By ten o'clock in the morning, the meetings were concluded. MacArthur told waiting reporters that no wartime general had ever had "more complete and admirable support" than he had been given during the Korean operation, a conflict he had assured Truman would be over by Thanksgiving Day. The President termed it a "most satisfactory conference," hailed MacArthur as one of the country's "greatest soldier-statesmen," and pinned a fifth oak leaf cluster on the general's shirt.

Truman boarded the *Independence* amid the cheers of onlookers. Pilot Williams gunned the engines and sped the plane down the bumpy runway. At 11:25 A.M., five hours after arriving, the *Independence* was airborne for Hawaii. On the flight back to the States, Truman worked on the speech he would give at San Francisco's Opera House immediately upon his return.

En route to Washington aboard the *Independence*, Truman reflected happily on the sanguine press accounts of the Wake Island meeting, his address in San Francisco, and the private assurances MacArthur had given to the effect that the Red Chinese army would not risk a Korean war with the United States. Truman penned a personal letter to MacArthur that read, in part: "Our meeting has had a splendid reaction here in the United States, and I think it was well worthwhile if for no other reason than that we became personally acquainted."

Two weeks later, in the early hours of November 1, the American Eighth Cavalry Regiment was savagely mauled by a surprise infantry assault from two Chinese divisions numbering 20,000 men, about forty-five miles south of the border between China and Korea. China had indeed entered the war.

As intelligence sources later pieced together the evidence, the Chinese had begun infiltrating across the Yalu River into Korea the day after the *Independence* flew Truman home from Wake Island.

Chapter Six

From Prop Wash to Fan Jet

Having entered the White House in 1953 as the new Republican broom that would sweep away the political vestiges of twenty years of Democratic rule, Dwight D. Eisenhower needed a presidential airplane to match his image. The *Independence* simply would not do.

Fortunately, an airplane that suited Ike's fancy already was on hand with Special Air Missions (SAM) at Washington's National Airport. It was a Lockheed Constellation, virtually identical to the C-121 he had used as Supreme Commander of Allied Forces in Europe in 1950 and 1951.

The new presidential "Connie," Air Force No. 48–610, was personally selected from the SAM inventory by Major William G. Draper, the new presidential pilot. Draper had flown Eisenhower during his time with SHAEF and the two men had become good friends. Ike requested the Air Force to assign Draper as presidential pilot. Draper, in fact, doubled as the Air Force aide to the new President, a prestigious post he retained throughout Eisenhower's eight years in the White House.

But what to do with Truman's airplane and Truman's pilot?

Colonel Williams was assigned to a new job as a group commander after January 20, 1953, Truman's last day in office. The *Independence* was stripped of its distinctive markings, its honored name disappearing from the fuselage. Although it continued to be used by SAM to fly high-ranking dignitaries around the country and abroad, to the casual observer it no longer looked different from any other DC-6 in the VIP transport squadron—unless one noticed the three closely grouped windows on the right side marking the location of the presidential cabin.

Eight years later and quite by coincidence, the former *Independence* gained a brief, final fling in the presidential spotlight. With his own airplane undergoing modifications, President John F. Kennedy flew Truman's favorite from Washington to New York on April 27, 1961. Not until he came aboard did Kennedy realize whose aircraft he was flying. Although its interior had been greatly modernized, the young President was fascinated to find in the executive cabin the same wall instruments—compass, altimeter, and speedometer—that Harry Truman loved to watch.

In 1963, the aging craft was transferred to the Tactical Air Command for use as a staff plane. In August 1965, after eighteen years of service, Harry Truman's airplane was decommissioned and placed in the Air Force Museum at Wright-Patterson Air Force Base in Dayton, Ohio. It is still on display there.

Eisenhower decided to call his new presidential airplane *Columbine II*, carrying on the name he had given his original "Connie" in Europe. The name was painted across the plane's nose in a flowing script, together with a painting of a blue columbine, the official flower of Mamie Eisenhower's home state, Colorado.

Draper chose this particular Lockheed Constellation because of its fine record during the four years it had served the Air Force since delivery from the factory on January 7, 1949. Initially, 48–610 had been one of a special fleet of "civilianized" government planes contracted out to Lockheed Air Service to support American military bases in Iceland. For nearly a year, 48–610 had flown nine round trips each month from Islip, New York, to Keflavik. Its performance had been flawless in all kinds of weather. When Eisenhower acquired the plane as his presidential aircraft, it already had logged 650,000 miles in 3,000 hours aloft—no minor feat. But there was a sentimental reason, too, for selecting this particular Constellation. It was the airplane in which Draper had flown President-elect Eisenhower to South Korea in November 1952 in fulfillment of his campaign promise to seek a speedy settlement of the Korean War.

Columbine II immediately underwent modernization to meet Eisenhower's requirements. A twenty-foot compartment in the waist section was converted into a private suite for the new President. Two specially constructed chairs for Ike and Mamie were installed. Two long couches, convertible into a pair of three-quarter-size beds, were placed along the walls of the suite. A handsome conference table occupied the center. Two telephones were installed beside Eisenhower's chair, one serving as an intercom with the cockpit and presidential aides, the other to be hooked to a land telephone line whenever the aircraft was on the ground. The suite also featured a small bar for entertaining guests, a framed color photograph of columbine blossoms, and a display panel of navigational instruments for Ike's information during flight. To the rear of the presidential suite was the plane's main entry door. Further back was the lavatory, tastefully appointed and roomy enough to double as a dressing room. *Columbine II* carried a crew of eleven and seating space for twenty-four passengers.

Eisenhower preferred flying to all other modes of travel and, in fact, was the first President to have been a pilot in his own right. During his early Army years in the Philippines, Ike learned to fly the old Stearman PT-13, a light "grasshopper" craft. He acquired nearly one hundred hours of flying time under instructor William "Jerry" Lee, the colorful aviator who later became an Army general. But Ike's fondness for airplanes was not shared by the First Lady. Mamie was deathly afraid of flying and made no secret of it. She fretted over Ike's air trips even more than she worried about her own. Indeed, she told friends, the fear of flying was one of her prime concerns about becoming the wife of a President. She knew that Ike, as well as herself, would be expected to fly far and frequently in the conduct of presidential business.

It became Bill Draper's special ambition to convince Mrs. Eisenhower that air travel was safer than any other form of transportation, in spite of news accounts of airliner crashes and rough flying weather. He began his missionary work by extolling the *Columbine II*'s remarkable safety record, the skills of its hand-picked crew, and the technological strides being made to ensure smoother, trouble-free flight. Colleagues say Draper's pet safety lecture for Mamie went like this:

"I firmly believe that an airplane is so much safer than an automobile that I can't even compare the two. I'd rather fly any time than drive on these highways today, never knowing when you will come up against a driver who can't tell the difference between red and green, or who can't judge the difference between fifty and a hundred feet, or who is drunk. The most dangerous part about an airplane trip, Mrs. Eisenhower, is the ride to and from the airport."

That approach, plus scrupulous attention to seat belts and takeoff and landing procedures in Mamie's presence, apparently had its desired effect. After nine months and 22,000 miles of flying with him, Mamie became relaxed enough to needle Draper about air safety. She also began wearing a pair of pilot's wings, engraved with the word *Columbine*, which Draper presented to her. It was a sign that she considered herself a special member of the crew. Mrs. John S. Doud, Mamie's seventy-five-year-old mother, became such an airplane buff that she sometimes turned up at the Washington airport to ride with the crew on practice flights.

Columbine II boasted the latest in instrumentation, including loran, the long-range navigational system, and weather surveillance radar. Draper had a pilot radarscope right at his knee. It gave him a continuing check on approaching aircraft or obstacles within 200 miles of the presidential plane. To avoid thunderstorms or rough flying weather, Draper frequently detoured several hundred miles to obtain a smooth flight path.

To prepare for an emergency aloft, *Columbine II*'s crew regularly put itself through bail-out procedures aimed at getting one person, the President, into a parachute and out of the aircraft in a matter of seconds. At Draper's insistence, the plane carried thirty parachutes, a ratio of six for every five passengers. The extra chutes, he reasoned, would be handy in case a nervous passenger might unintentionally pop open a chute inside the cabin while putting it on.

178

Eisenhower was an ideal passenger, meticulously heeding safety instructions and keeping his seat belt fastened even while working in his executive cabin. Unlike Harry Truman and some later presidents, Ike was not in the habit of wandering up and down the aisle or popping into the cockpit. He kept a favorite tweed jacket on the *Columbine* at all times. As soon as he got aboard he would shed his business coat and slip on the jacket. Knowing Eisenhower's penchant for western novels, Draper and the crew kept a generous supply on hand and regularly updated it with the latest ones. The crew could tell that all was well with Ike whenever they saw him engrossed in a book instead of his stack of official papers.

Feeding Eisenhower was easy. He preferred light meals aboard and would just as soon have cold cuts as a steak—although the *Columbine II*'s galley was well stocked with food and always contained a bottle of prepared martinis in the refrigerator.

On long flights crossing several time zones, Draper had to "push the boss around a little" in order to work out a schedule for eating and sleeping that would make a reasonable compromise between flight time and body time. When Eisenhower broke off his vacation in Colorado in September 1953 to return to Washington for the funeral of Chief Justice Fred Vinson, Draper ordered the President to bed right after the 9 P.M. takeoff from Denver. It was already midnight in Washington. On such occasions, Draper instructed the stewards to make up the bed even if it was still daylight. Then he would personally go back to the President's compartment and say, "It's time to relax, Mr. President." Eisenhower's response was usually an obedient "Okay, Bill."

Draper customarily flew the *Columbine II* at altitudes of 12,000 to 13,000 feet in order to achieve a comfortable cabin pressure equivalent to 2,000 to 3,000 feet. Although 18,000 feet was the normal cruising altitude for a plane like the Constellation, the internal pressure would have been equivalent to about 8,000 feet altitude, Draper noted. "At the end of six or eight hours at a cabin altitude of 8,000, the President would feel like he had put in a hard day's work even though he had just sat and read."

179

Like presidential pilots Hank Myers and Frenchie Williams before him, Draper had come into military service from the commercial airlines. And, like them, flying had been an ambition ever since boyhood days—in Draper's case, in the small town of Stow Corners, Ohio. He was a pilot for Pan American Airways when the Japanese bombed Pearl Harbor in December 1941. He was offered a commission in the Army Air Corps and flew B-24 and C-54 transports across the Atlantic and in the Burma-Indochina theater during the war. After the war, he elected to remain in the military.

Draper already was a pilot with the "brass hat" transport squadron when he first flew General Eisenhower on a special survey of NATO bases in Europe for President Truman in 1950. Eisenhower, then serving as president of Columbia University, was tapped in December that year to return to Europe as supreme Allied commander. And Draper was tapped to go with him as his personal pilot and aide. It was a role Draper retained for the next decade, remaining as Ike's pilot until Eisenhower relinquished the presidency to John Kennedy on January 20, 1961.

By November 1953, Mamie felt comfortable enough aboard *Columbine II* to accompany the President on a three-day visit to Ottawa, Canada. It was Eisenhower's second presidential trip out of the country, the first having been a quick flight earlier in the month for a half-day visit with Mexico's new President Ruiz Cortines to dedicate the Falcon Dam on the Rio Grande at Nuevo Guerrero.

Columbine II got a heavy workout in 1954, as Eisenhower strove to duplicate the Republican congressional victories that had brought the party to control in Capitol Hill with his own election to the White House two years before.

On August 30, for example, he left Denver in the middle of the night on a flight that put him in Washington at 6:45 A.M. After breakfast at the White House with Governor Walter Kohler of Wisconsin and Gen. Lucius Clay, Ike visited with Governor John Lodge of Connecticut, signed the Atomic Energy Act, addressed the national convention of the American Legion at noon, got a haircut in his office, and flew out to Des Moines in *Columbine II* with former President Herbert Hoover aboard. Arriving at 5:20 P.M., he motored to the Iowa fairgrounds for a speech at 6:30. At 7:15 he was airborne once more for Denver. Two hours later, the President was back at the home of Mamie's mother, Mrs. John S. Doud, 570 Lafayette Street. As he left the airplane, Ike thanked pilot Draper and the air crew, saying they now could "take a day off."

But *Columbine II* was never destined for a long career as the President's plane. Draper, the Air Force, and the White House staff had their eyes on an advanced version that Lockheed had developed for the commercial airlines. It was the Super-Constellation, eighteen feet longer, with increased fuel capacity for greater range, and powerful new engines for greater speed. Draper took delivery at Burbank, California, on September 10, 1954, and flew it to National Airport.

There, in elaborate ceremonies on November 24, Mamie Eisenhower christened Air Force No. 53–7885 as *Columbine III*—with a flask of water flown in from Colorado instead of the usual bottle of champagne. The new presidential airplane was to spend more than six years serving the White House, a stint unmatched by any other propeller craft.

Immediately after the ceremonies, Ike and Mamie flew off to Augusta, Georgia, for a five-day golfing vacation over the Thanksgiving holidays. On board *Columbine III* for its first presidential flight was Eisenhower's British comrade of World War II, the colorful Field Marshal "Monty" Montgomery. Monty spent much of the trip examining the new airplane and spinning wartime yarns in the cockpit with Draper and the crew.

Although *Columbine III* bore the seal of the President and was his official airplane, it was customary during the Eisenhower administration to make it available on important occasions to key government officials. Secretary of State John Foster Dulles used it frequently on diplomatic missions. Eisenhower often dispatched it abroad to bring royalty and foreign heads of government to Washington for White House meetings and to convey them on trips around the United States.

In July 1955, *Columbine III* took Eisenhower and Dulles to Geneva, Switzerland, for the first peacetime summit meeting between Western leaders and the post-Stalin leadership of the Soviet Union—Marshal Bulganin, Nikita Khrushchev, and Foreign

181

Minister Molotov. Ike came away with an impression that Khrushchev, while lacking the title and deferring publicly to Bulganin, "was the real boss of the Soviet delegation." It was a shrewd judgment.

Columbine III's crew found Eisenhower to be much more reserved than Harry Truman. For one thing, he was practically a teetotaler and, while he enjoyed humorous stories, he disliked off-color yarns and usually cut short the tale spinner with an icy glare or a curt remark. Still, Chief Master Sgt. Dwight Snider, a senior steward with both Truman and Eisenhower, rated Ike "a regular sort of fellow" who sometimes drank his soup directly from the bowl. "Other guests would look at him and then at each other and take up their bowls and do the same thing. It was funny to watch it happen."

Eisenhower logged an average of 30,000 miles and one hundred hours a year aboard *Columbine III*, most of it on domestic trips. The comfortable Connie would have been used even more by Ike if it had not been for the advent of the first jet transports in the summer of 1959. From then on, the fast, smooth-riding Boeing 707 became the favorite conveyance of presidents for long journeys. *Columbine III* remained Eisenhower's official aircraft until January 20, 1961, his final day in office. Then it was decommissioned and integrated into SAM's regular fleet of VIP transports where it joined two other ex-presidential airplanes, *Columbine II* and the *Independence*. *Columbine II* eventually was consigned to the scrap heap at Davis-Monthan Air Force Base in Arizona, the service's "graveyard." *Columbine III* was spared a similar fate. In 1966, it joined the *Independence* on display at the Air Museum at Wright-Patterson Air Base.

Not generally known is the fact that Eisenhower had several other "presidential" aircraft—each of them a speedy, twin-propeller L-26 Aero Commander, manufactured by the Aero Design and Engineering Company of Bethany, Oklahoma. The light little planes already were popular for short-distance flights by military brass. When Ike acquired his farm near Gettysburg, Pennsylvania, it took very few trips from Washington by car to convince him that something speedier was needed. So he asked Draper to look into the possibility of acquiring a small airplane suitable for a shuttle service. The Pentagon was only too happy to cooperate. It took some argument, however, to bring the Secret Service around to the President's point of view.

The Secret Service worried about the safety of small aircraft for presidential use because they lacked the high altitude capabilities, the instrumentation, and the stability of large planes. Until the spring of 1955, they would not permit a President to fly in any aircraft with less than four engines. (Not until 1957 were helicopters judged safe enough for presidential travel.) But Ike was insistent. There had to be a faster way to move him back and forth between Washington and Gettysburg than by a motorcade on a busy highway, a procedure that took four hours round trip. And the *Columbine III* was too big to land at Gettysburg's modest airport.

"I know there are small aircraft that can do the trick," the President told James J. Rowley, chief of the White House Secret Service detail. "I know you have reservations about the idea. So find a model that suits both of us."

After months of test flying and study, the Secret Service and officials of the Federal Aviation Administration selected the Aero Commander as the most suitable for Eisenhower's needs. The Air Force promptly placed an order on May 23, 1955, for fifteen Aero Commanders, but it did not disclose at the time that at least one was destined for the use of the President.

Meanwhile, to ease Ike's impatience, the factory offered the loan of a sales demonstrator, plane No. N2724B. Draper and the Secret Service jumped at it. And so, on June 3, 1955, a President of the United States flew for the first time in a light aircraft. With two pilots and accompanied by Rowley, Ike made the seventy-three-mile trip in thirty-two minutes. The Aero Commander landed on the sod runway at Gettysburg Airport. Following close behind was an Aero Commander carrying three more Secret Service agents, plus several Beechcraft L-23 Twin Bonanzas with a delegation of White House reporters to record the historic airlift. After a brief automobile tour of his nearby farm, Eisenhower returned to Washington. The return flight to National Airport took twenty-two minutes. In ten minutes more, Ike once again was back in the White House.

"Do you realize how much time we saved?" Ike happily asked Rowley. "Don't you agree that it was a safe trip?"

"Yes, sir," Rowley replied.

From then until Ike left office, an Aero Commander was kept handy for his use. The demonstrator went back to the company upon delivery of the first of the purchased Aero Commanders, and was later sold to a dealer in San Antonio, Texas. Ike's new Aero Commander, No. 55–4634, was flown to Washington on August 2 and officially designated as a presidential aircraft. During its first year, it flew ten round trips to Gettysburg with the President aboard and Bill Draper at the controls. When Ike went on vacation to Denver, Colorado, the Aero Commander was flown out as a standby for short local trips. Another time it carried Chancellor Konrad Adenauer of West Germany from New York to Gettysburg to meet with Eisenhower. Then they flew on together to Washington to continue their talks. In March 1956, the Aero Commander served as the "Greenbrier Airlift," ferrying the President of Mexico and top U.S. officials to White Sulphur Springs, West Virginia, for a diplomatic conference with Eisenhower.

In 1956, SAM acquired two Aero Commanders with improved engines and greater speed. The President's third little plane bore tail No. 55–4647; the other, No 55–4648, was used to carry additional Secret Service agents. The craft amply demonstrated their reliability and usefulness in the fall of 1955, after Eisenhower suffered his heart attack.

For six weeks, while Ike recuperated at his Gettysburg farm, the Aero Commanders mounted a shuttle service for government officials and White House aides. In July 1956, just as the presidential campaign was heating up, Eisenhower underwent major abdominal surgery following an attack of ileitis. So the "Gettysburg Airlift" resumed once more. Ike's Aero Commander was fitted with a bed to carry the President from Washington to Gettysburg, where he spent several weeks convalescing at his farm. By early August, Eisenhower had sufficiently recovered to assure the nation, not to mention worried Republican leaders, that he indeed would run for reelection in November.

Although eventually they were replaced with helicopters that offered portal-to-portal service from the White House itself, the Aero Commanders may have contributed to the history of presidential aircraft in ways that go beyond their own special niche. When they arrived on the presidential scene in 1955, their blue-and-white trademark was in bright contrast to the olive drab and dull silver tones then preferred for military aircraft. Air Force historian Robert C. Mikesh suggests that the Aero Commanders' color scheme influenced the Army and the Air Force to adapt the theme for other light, twin-engined passenger craft. It is entirely possible that the Aero Commanders introduced the blue-white-silver color scheme used today for VIP transport aircraft of the SAM command. To go only a small step further, it is conceivable that they also inspired the elegant Raymond Loewy–designed motif that has been the exclusive hallmark of *Air Force One* since the days of President Kennedy.

It was inevitable, given the state of the art, that SAM would acquire jet aircraft in the late Fifties to transport the government's high-ranking officials. Commercial airlines already had turned to the Boeing four-engine jet plane for long range flights. The planes of the 1254th Air Transport Wing (SAM) were aging propeller craft, in marked contrast to the sleek jet fighters, bombers, and tankers already in service within the air force. The East–West "cold war," America's international prestige, and growing soviet competition played roles, too.

No one in the upper levels of government was more aware of such matters than Dulles, the much-traveled diplomat of the Eisenhower cabinet. On more than one occasion, according to White House reports, Dulles had impressed upon President Eisenhower the importance of providing himself and the nation's other senior officials with the latest and best in air transportation.

The Soviet Union already had stolen a march on the United States with the launching of the first orbital satellite in 1957, a feat the U.S. would not match until the following year. The British had inaugurated the world's first international jetliner service as far back as 1952, with a flight from London to Johannesburg, South Africa. As Dulles was wont to point out to the President, the prestige of the United States suffered every time he arrived at an international conference aboard a propeller-driven airplane, while the Russian diplomats were coming in with Soviet

185

turbo-jets. In the global tug-of-war for the hearts and minds of other nations, Dulles argued, it was essential to establish in every way possible that America was technologically superior to the Soviet Union.

That reasoning suited the Air Force, too, but in the budget battle for post-Korea dollars, it had concentrated its spending on the development of the Strategic Air Command (SAC) bomber fleet, the latest in fighter aircraft, and the growing arsenal of nuclear-tipped weapons, including the new field of short- and long-range ballistic missiles. Jet service for VIPs had low priority.

Additionally, a high-level dispute raged within the Air Force over the control of jet transports. General Curtis LeMay felt that the only persons who should fly jet transports were the pilots of his KC-135 jet tanker fleet with SAC. Inasmuch as they already possessed the skills to handle big jet craft, he proposed that a whole unit of tanker pilots be transferred into the Military Air Transport Service (MATS) to take over the jet transport operation.

That power grab, naturally, was resisted by the commander of MATS, General William Tunner, who had run the Berlin Airlift in 1948–49. Tunner had no desire to see his operations swallowed up by LeMay's SAC–dominated group. General Thomas White, then Air Force chief of staff, took Tunner's side. SAC's tanker pilots, of course, had jet flying proficiency. But that skill could be acquired by the SAM pilots within MATS, White felt, without losing their expertise in dealing with the government's VIP air passengers.

Albertazzie, a member of White's personal air crew, couldn't have been more pleased. "I had begun to think I would never get to fly a jet airplane," he recalls.

The original schedule called for completion of training within sixty days, a reasonable time for pilots already skilled in propeller-driven transports. Then, suddenly, the rules were changed. General LeMay, a powerful personality within the Air Force high command, used his status as vice chief of staff to decree that the training period should be cut in half, to thirty days. Consternation over the new deadline struck trainees as well as General Tunner and James Gannett, then Boeing's chief pilot.

186

Tunner, Gannett, and Boeing's instructors looked over the group and decided there was only one trainee who had progressed far enough to meet LeMay's time limit—Ralph Albertazzie. As a result, he became the first qualified 707 pilot in the Air Force.

The first Boeing 707 was delivered on May 12, 1959. Exactly one month later, Albertazzie took it up on its first official trip. He flew General White and a delegation of Air Force brass to Colorado Springs, Colorado, for the commencement exercises of the first class to be graduated from the Air Force Academy. To celebrate the Air Force's first Boeing 707 flight, Albertazzie and his crew issued commemorative cards to the passengers as souvenirs of the event.

The three newly acquired 707 jets were like new toys to the government's VIPs. The Air Force's top generals were anxious to be among the first to travel in the luxurious craft. One of them was General LeMay, who commandeered a 707 for Albertazzie's second official trip—a flight from Andrews to Kelly Air Force Base in Texas.

Tough, cigar-smoking LeMay was the dominant—some would say the domineering—figure in the Air Force. His World War II exploits, his development of SAC's fleet of long-range nuclear bombers, and his colorful personality had made him something of a living legend.

LeMay had been one of the Pentagon's prime pushers for the acquisition of 707 jet transports for the VIP fleet. Although he had lost the skirmish to have SAC jet pilots take over the jet transport flying operation, he had successfully inserted three SAC aviators into the program as "instructors" for training of other SAM pilots.

As it turned out, only two of his protégés successfully made the transition from flying cumbersome jet bombers to piloting the faster, more maneuverable, and infinitely more sophisticated swept-wing 707s. But LeMay never lost faith in his SAC men, and remained dubious about the ability of the regular SAM aviators to make the switch from propeller craft to the Boeing 707.

LeMay, moreover, had a habit of taking over the controls on

187

every plane on which he flew. He said it helped him retain his proficiency. It also furthered his reputation as a general who would rather be in the cockpit than behind a desk.

So from the moment LeMay requested a Boeing 707 to fly him to Texas, SAM headquarters went into a tizzy. General Tunner wanted to show LeMay that his retrained crews were as capable as any SAC crew in handling big jets. But what if LeMay came aboard and said he wanted to fly the 707 himself? In fact, was he skilled enough to do it?

"My recommendation was that we not wait to be asked, but put the question directly to him," Albertazzie said. "If he said yes, I would just slide over to the right-hand seat as the instructor—copilot and let him take the controls."

Albertazzie was standing at the foot of the ramp when LeMay's limousine swept up to the shiny new Boeing 707. "I threw him a snappy salute and asked, 'Sir, would you like to fly her today?'"

LeMay squinted at the plane and fixed Albertazzie with an impersonal stare. "Thanks, Captain, but I wouldn't want to interfere with your training program."

Albertazzie stiffened. "Sir," he said, "this crew is trained."

"Good, Captain. Then I'll take 'er up."

Albertazzie gave the crusty general a brief familiarization checkout on the 707's instrumentation and flight procedures. That called for climbing first to about 400 feet and leveling off long enough to "burn off" the water used to assist the jet's takeoff, bringing up the flaps, setting the plane on its assigned course heading, and then climbing again to cruising altitude. The brief period from actual takeoff to 400 feet is a very busy time in the cockpit.

"We got LeMay airborne and I was performing all the takeoff procedures as fast as I could, including getting clearance from the tower, when I happened to look over to LeMay," Albertazzie recalls. "He had stopped climbing and was flying level at 400 feet on a course straight for the U.S. Capitol—at about 300 miles an hour!"

"I quickly gave him the proper instructions, he took it up to 7,000 feet, and we got out of there. I heaved a sigh of relief."

LeMay did a creditable job of piloting the plane to Kelly in

Texas, and, on the return flight to Washington the next day, flew the 707 again. "He was a good student," Albertazzie said, "peppering me with questions and noting the differences between flying a SAC bomber and a Boeing transport."

A couple of days later, Albertazzie got a telephone call from General LeMay's aide at the Pentagon. "You must've done a pretty good job with the old man," the aide remarked. "He thought you were one of his SAC guys."

The arrival of the Boeing 707 jet transports brought about a major change in SAM's operations. With the slower propeller-driven craft, it had been customary to assign a plane and a crew to a specific VIP trip until the mission was completed, even if the itinerary was lengthy and the plane might be on the ground for days at a time. Under that system, the aircraft commander was left undisturbed by SAM headquarters until the trip was over and the plane was back at home base at Washington.

Not so with the jets. For one thing, they were enormously expensive. It did not seem right to let a $6,500,000 aircraft (the price tag in 1959) sit on the ground for more than a day. Second, their speed and range made it unnecessary to leave them out on an assignment on which they might be unused for several days at a stretch. Last but far from least, the jets were a prestige item. Every military and civilian official in the upper echelons of government wanted to travel aboard a 707 executive jet.

The result was that Albertazzie and the other 707 aircraft commanders soon found themselves flying one VIP mission after another. "For example, we could take somebody to a London conference, then fly home in eight hours and perform two or three other short missions in the United States before returning to London to pick up the first VIP." That style of operation, in effect, transferred command and control of the aircraft from the pilot to SAM headquarters, which handled the scheduling of VIP flights.

That system, of course, didn't apply to the plane that might be used by the President. It was his to have and to hold as long as he was away from Washington. But it applied to all other government VIPs, who were the most frequent users of the first three Boeing 707s acquired by SAM in 1959.

Sometimes, the system didn't make much sense, as, for exam-

189

ple, the time Albertazzie flew a group of senior military commanders to a NATO conference in Athens, Greece. "I had just checked into my hotel room after the long flight when the telephone rang. It was SAM headquarters back in Washington. They ordered us back to Washington immediately to run another trip.

"When we returned, we found that Deputy Defense Secretary Roswell Gilpatric and an aide wanted to be flown out for a defense speech on the West Coast. Originally they had planned to travel by commercial airliner, but, at the last minute, decided to go out on an Air Force jet. Gilpatric simply exercised his seniority right to commandeer the plane. So we flew him out to the coast and then returned to Athens to pick up the military group. All in all, it was a little hard on my crew and darned costly for the taxpayers."

In 1959, Eisenhower became the first Chief Executive to travel by jet. Using one of the three Boeing 707s just added to the SAM fleet—specifically SAM 970—Ike left Washington on August 26, before the first rays of dawn streaked the eastern sky. With Draper at the controls, the VC-137A sped Eisenhower to Germany for a meeting with Chancellor Konrad Adenauer and whisked him to London to see Prime Minister Harold Macmillan and to pay a call on Queen Elizabeth. Then Ike flew to Paris to confer with President de Gaulle and shuttled over to Scotland for a bit of golf and relaxation at Culzean Castle in Ayreshire, Scotland, before returning to Washington on September 7.

The departure from London was not without its embarassment for pilot Draper. Anxious to impress the British onlookers with the new Boeing, Draper simultaneously depressed the starter controls for all four jet engines. Suddenly the engines erupted with billowing smoke and shooting flames. It was nothing serious; the ever-present fire-truck crews quickly extinguished the blaze, and inspection disclosed no damage that would impair the flight. But Draper had learned a lesson the hard way. While he could start the four piston engines on *Columbine III* in such rapid sequence that it appeared to be simultaneous, it was best to start the Boeing 707's jet engines in pairs.

The silver Boeing 707 made a tremendous impression on Eisenhower. Before he left Washington, he had brought Mamie out to Andrews Air Force Base to show her around "the mammoth machine," as he called it in his memoirs of the White House years, *Waging Peace.* "Both in size and speed, the new airplane completely dwarfed the *Columbine*, the Super Constellation that we had long considered the last word in luxurious transportation. However, no airplane ever looked attractive to Mamie. Afterward, I settled back in my compartment with the Secretary of State and underwent an exhilarating experience, that of my first jet flight, with its silent, effortless acceleration and its rapid rate of climb. . . ."

Flying a jet was a new experience for Draper, too. He and the presidential air crew had just completed jet training at Castle Air Force Base in California and specialized training on the Boeing 707 at the company's plant at Seattle, Washington.

Just as impressive as the comfort of the new airplane was the ease with which it could move a President about. On this first jet flight by a Chief Executive, the Boeing covered 8,711 air miles in 19 hours, 27 minutes of flying time. Major Mikesh noted something else in his 1963 monograph for the American Aviation Historical Society. Using conventional piston-driven airplanes, Eisenhower had averaged approximately 120 hours of flying time a year, covering about 30,000 air miles. But with the use of jet aircraft in his last year in office—1960—Ike's air time increased by 62 percent (193 hours) and his air mileage rose by 262 percent (78,677 miles)!

The newly acquired Boeing inspired Eisenhower to think boldly about something he had not been able to do in the first six years of his presidency. He had always yearned to travel beyond Europe to the Asian subcontinent and perhaps to North Africa, where he had not set foot since the hectic days of World War II as Allied commander. Now, in the winter of 1959, with Congress in adjournment, with Soviet Premier Khrushchev having recently toured the United States, and with the world in a period of calm, the lure of jet travel made such a trip irresistible.

Ike summoned Draper to the White House to advise on the itinerary, especially on such matters as flight distances, time zone changes, and airports capable of handling a Boeing jet. It was a major undertaking; no President had ever before contemplated an official trip to eleven countries in eighteen days—and

191

mostly by air. Later presidents would go even further, and in less time, but Eisenhower would be the first to embark on such an extensive journey. That fact was not lost on him—nor on Draper, the press, and the American public.

The trip, starting December 4, would take the President to Rome (and the Vatican), Ankara, Karachi, Kabul, New Delhi, Teheran, Athens, Tunis, Paris, Madrid, Casablanca, and back to the White House. Draper had his hands full. He set out immediately on an advance trip to each of the prospective stops to check on airport facilities, fuel and food resupply, regional and local weather problems in the mountainous terrain of the Near East, and how to solve the problem of keeping the Boeing in constant communication with Washington.

The age of jet aircraft had not yet dawned in many of the places on Ike's list. Fuel for a Boeing 707 was not readily available, and had to be ordered in advance and stored for Ike's needs. In Turkey, for example, Draper discovered a source at the American base in Adana and arranged for it to be flown by tanker to Ankara. In Kabul, locked in the mountain fastness of Afghanistan, it was almost impossible to obtain the timely weather reports that were absolutely essential before Draper dared to land the President in a region of treacherous winds and sudden storms. King Zahir agreed to construct a portable weather tower to help monitor field conditions. And the American military attaché at Kabul backstopped Draper by flying his own C-47 up to intercept the President's airplane and radio plane-to-plane the latest weather data just before Draper began his descent.

At New Delhi, where Eisenhower's open limousine was engulfed in a sea of humanity estimated at nearly one million people, the President's pilot fretted about problems of a different nature. Prime Minister Nehru assured Draper that the Indian Army would keep the sacred cows from wandering onto the runway.

To fly from Ankara to Karachi, Draper had to pilot Ike's Boeing through a narrow Turkish-Iranian air corridor between the southernmost border of the Soviet Union and Iraq, an area in which a straying American C-130 recently had been shot down by the Russians. "The President wasn't nearly as worried as I was," Draper said later. Over the rugged mountains of Afghanistan, SAM 970 suddenly found itself bracketed by Soviet-built MIG fighters—part of the Afghan Air Force—an escort service that didn't much please Eisenhower or Draper, although for different reasons.

At Athens, Eisenhower and his entourage boarded the cruiser USS *Des Moines*, the flagship of the Sixth Fleet, and sailed thirty hours across the Mediterranean to Tunis. A day later, he sailed to the port of Toulon, France, where a special train was waiting to bring him to Paris for meetings with President de Gaulle. At Paris, Ike reboarded SAM 970 and flew off to Madrid to see Generalissimo Franco and then on to Casablanca. There, fierce Moroccan tribesmen greeted the arriving President and worried the Secret Service with a wild display of horsemanship and one-handed musket firing. That afternoon, Draper pointed the big Boeing northwesterly across the Atlantic toward Washington, landing at home shortly before midnight on December 22.

Washington was festooned with Yule lights and the White House tree never looked lovelier. It had been a wearying twenty-one-hour day for the sixty-nine-year-old President; he headed straight for bed. But in the family quarters on the second floor, as he recounted in his memoirs, Ike saw a startling scene. Four of his bridge-playing pals, including Gen. Al Gruenther and wisecracking George Allen, were seated around a table, playing cards as if nothing had happened.

"Hi," said Gruenther, barely looking up.

"Been away?" asked Allen. "What's new?"

Early in 1960, anxious to offset the rising tide of Castroism in Cuba, Eisenhower took off again on a ten-day tour of Latin America. On the flight from São Paulo to Rio de Janeiro on February 25, the radio operator handed the President a shocking message. Sixty-nine members of the U.S. Navy Band, touring the southern hemisphere and due to play at a presidential reception that evening in Rio, had been killed in a collision of their Navy transport with a Brazilian airliner. Sadly, Ike went to call on the three surviving bandsmen at a Rio hospital.

At Mar de Plata in Argentina two days later, President Arturo

193

Frondizi exclaimed repeatedly over the beauty and grace of Eisenhower's Boeing. "I knew, of course, about the Latin American tradition that whenever a guest admires an object, the host must give it to him," Eisenhower recounted later, apparently on the assumption that Frondizi was a guest of his. "Unhappily, however, the plane was not mine to give away. So I did the only thing possible: I invited President Frondizi to ride along to our next stop—the Andean resort city of San Carlos de Bariloche."

To make room for the Argentinian leader and some of his aides, Draper ordered the crew to remove the baggage of several White House staffers and consign it to another aircraft. Unfortunately, the luggage contained their tuxedos, without which they were unable to attend a formal dinner for Eisenhower that evening.

On the long flight from Montevideo to Puerto Rico on March 2, one of the four engines on the presidential plane conked out over the Amazon jungles, an incident that "enlivened" the trip, Ike said. Draper put SAM 970 down without mishap at Paramaribo, Surinam, where the President and his party transferred to a backup plane for the rest of the journey.

Ike's most important trip, however, never got off the ground. For months he had been looking forward to his visit to Moscow in the spring of 1960—the first such presidential trip in history and prompted, at least in part, by Nikita Khrushchev's flamboyant tour of the U.S. in September 1959. Eisenhower passed the word that he preferred to go to Russia aboard one of the spanking new jets. Khrushchev had come to America in a giant TU-114 turboprop, a spectacle that both impressed and embarrassed American officials. Now it would be Ike's turn at the game of aerial one-upmanship—and the CIA's.

As director of the Central Intelligence Agency, Allen Dulles was consumed by a need to penetrate the closed Communist empire directed from Moscow, which in the 1950s was thought to be pressing its Stalinist ambition of world domination. The Soviet Union, with its air fleet and a growing arsenal of atomic missiles, was capable of launching surprise attacks against an "open" United States. Moreover, from behind the Iron Curtain, the Kremlin possessed the capacity of mounting blackmail campaigns against the West by boasting of nuclear muscle that might be more fiction than fact.

194

Out of Dulles's innovative mind came the 1954 decision to build thirty high-altitude aircraft—the U-2 program—to conduct secret photo reconnaissance flights over the Soviet Union and its East European puppet states. Ike approved, although with reservations.

Then, out of Dulles's mind came another daring plan. The President's own aircraft was to be outfitted as a spy plane. There is no indication that Eisenhower approved this clandestine undertaking. Indeed, it is doubtful that he even knew about it.

Project Lida Rose was born inside the CIA late in 1959. The name was borrowed from a hit song in the Broadway show *Music Man*—a tune, ironically, that Ike liked.

The interior of one of the Boeings, SAM 970, had been specially configured to serve the President and other high officers of the government. With clearance from Defense Secretary Thomas S. Gates Jr. and top brass of the Air Force, SAM 970 soon became the object of attention by a CIA team that quietly attached itself to SAM at Andrews Air Force Base.

From Dulles's viewpoint, the plan made sense. For three years, commencing in 1956, U-2 reconnaissance flights had been bringing back marvelous photographs of the Soviet countryside, especially of Soviet missile launching sites, radar installations, secret airfields, railroad and shipping centers, shipyard activity, oil refineries and exploration, industrial plants, and troop and tank concentrations. Taken from altitudes in excess of 50,000 feet, where the U-2 was safe from Soviet fighter interception and antiaircraft, the pictures provided both corroboration and, sometimes, the refutation of intelligence reports supplied by agents inside and outside the Soviet Union.

Eisenhower himself exclaimed over the excellence of the photos. The U-2 cameras were of such high quality that test pictures taken 70,000 feet above American cities made it possible to count automobiles on the streets and spot the lines marking the parking areas for individual cars. Just as important as the positive information of what the Soviets did have by way of offensive military capability was the negative information of what they did not have. That robbed the Kremlin of a most powerful psychological weapon—the chance to exploit the ignorance and fears of the West.

But for all of their excellence, the U-2 photos remained pictures taken at very high altitudes. A plane like the President's could get much closer to the subject matter. Since Khrushchev had toured the United States, it was quite likely that Eisenhower not only would see Moscow but probably Leningrad, the Black Sea area, and perhaps even a point or two east of the Urals. It would be extremely valuable if the President's aircraft could photograph Soviet antimissile defense installations around the cities he would visit. Indeed, even aerial photos of bridges, road networks, rail lines, and the physical layout of Moscow and other cities would be valuable to the CIA and the Defense Department. Moreover, it was the intention of the Eisenhower administration to allow other high-ranking persons in the government—the secretaries of Defense and State, and top military officers—to use the new Boeing on overseas trips whenever Eisenhower didn't need it. Photographs acquired on such flights would be useful, too. So went the reasoning for surreptitiously turning SAM 970 into a spy plane.

Dulles had not necessarily set out to deceive the President. But sometimes, as he knew, it was a boon to political superiors if they were kept in the dark. It gave them a valuable commodity called "deniability" in event some outlandish piece of espionage was uncovered by the other side. Then they could, in all honesty, claim innocence of whatever had happened. Deniability was something Eisenhower didn't have—and could have used—on May 1, 1960, the day that U-2 pilot Francis Gary Powers was shot down over Russia.

The handsome Boeing was moved to a secluded hangar where, under tight security, the installation of high-resolution cameras and electronic control mechanisms was begun. With blowtorches and riveting guns, CIA's workmen fashioned a special compartment in the belly of the fuselage to house the components.

A special detachment was assigned to SAM to supervise Project Lida Rose. A special air crew was selected to operate the reconnaissance equipment. Even a special aviator was designated as the key man to employ the system aloft while Draper flew the airplane.

The controls were designed to be activated by the co-pilot from his seat in the cockpit. In the best tradition of the espionage trade, they were cleverly camouflaged to avoid detection by the unknowing, particularly by any foreign escort pilot or navigator who would be riding in the cockpit on flights into the Soviet Union or some other "closed" country.

Two instruments in the cockpit were modified to do the trick. One was the co-pilot's "fresh air valve"—very similar to the air inlets over passenger seats in any airplane. By rotating and adjusting the innocent-looking valve, the co-pilot could open and activate the big cameras hidden in the belly compartment below. To ensure proper camera performance, of course, the co-pilot needed to know that he was moving the fresh air valve in accordance with a prescribed sequence. So the CIA's electronic wizards performed a delicate surgical operation on SAM 970's magnetic compass.

On an airplane with modern navigational equipment, the magnetic compass is merely a standby gadget. It serves primarily as a reference for the direction of the flight, assuring the pilot and co-pilot that the aircraft's basic guidance system is functioning properly. (Theoretically, the magnetic compass should have alerted the crew of the ill-fated Korea Airline 707 that it had strayed off course into Soviet territory in 1978.) On a Boeing like SAM 970, the magnetic compass is swivel-mounted and, when not in use, it can be pushed out of the way into a recess in the cockpit ceiling.

For Project Lida Rose, tiny holes were drilled into the side of SAM 970's compass. Inside these apertures, the CIA surgeons implanted pinhead sequence lights that were visible only to the co-pilot—and only when he was seated in exactly the right position. By watching the sequence lights on the compass as he adjusted the fresh air valve, the co-pilot was able to determine—in one-two-three fashion—that the camera compartment doors were open, that the camera was in position, and that is was functioning. When the co-pilot decided he had shot sufficient film, he again adjusted the fresh air valve. This time, the pinhead lights on the compass would turn off in reverse sequence. When the last light winked out, he knew the compartment doors had closed, the cameras were safely hidden from view, and everything was back to normal once again.

Project Lida Rose performed remarkably during test flights.

197

Photographs taken from 30,000 feet were so sharp it was possible to read the license plate numbers on automobiles on the ground. Inside the Soviet Union, the high-resolution cameras were certain to pick up intelligence information that had been impossible for the U-2s to obtain. To test out the security of the camera installation, experienced but unaware mechanics and flight engineers were instructed to thoroughly inspect SAM 970 and the cockpit's instrumentation. None of them detected anything suspicious that might betray the secret. The project, estimated to have cost approximately $1,000,000, was pronounced a success. So tight was the security that only a handful of persons knew about it and they were sworn to secrecy.

Unfortunately for Dulles and the CIA, Eisenhower never made his planned trip to the Soviet Union. Khrushchev used the capture of Francis Gary Powers to accuse Eisenhower of "perfidy" in the Soviet skies. He stalked out of a Big Power summit meeting in Paris on May 15 when Ike refused to apologize for the U-2 spy flights. In the strained atmosphere that followed, Eisenhower's visit to Russia was scuttled too.

There was heavy irony in all of this. The CIA and Air Force intelligence officials were convinced that Soviet aircraft flying Russian dignitaries to the UN in New York were equipped with reconnaissance cameras. There was suspicion that similar equipment was aboard the TU-114 that brought Khrushchev to the U.S. in 1959. Indeed, this was advanced as a reason why Eisenhower's plane should be similarly outfitted.

In 1961, with President Kennedy in the White House, the reconnaissance cameras were removed from SAM 970. The camera team was disbanded. It never got the chance to photograph Soviet territory.

Dulles's U-2 program, it could be said, had shot down his Project Lida Rose.

With John F. Kennedy's arrival in the White House in 1961, a transport already in SAM service was selected as the official presidential aircraft. It was a Douglas DC-6, already seven years old and similar to the *Independence*. Unlike past presidential custom, Kennedy's piston-powered aircraft was left unnamed,

198

although there was some support within the White House for christening it *Caroline II* and thus carrying on the name of the Kennedy family's private airplane, a Convair 240 that the new President had used heavily during his campaign for office. Instead, the new presidential aircraft was known simply as SAM 3240, its tail number being 53–3240.

Externally, it resembled all the other DC-6 airplanes in the SAM inventory except for a presidential seal mounted on the fuselage just forward of the main cabin entrance. The interior was modernized to enhance its presidential status. Impressive new electronic and communications equipment was placed aboard to keep the President in touch with any part of the world. There was another change, too. In the past, presidential aircraft had been hangared at National Airport, a few minutes drive from the White House. This practice was changed in 1962, when SAM 3240 was moved to Andrews Air Force Base in nearby Maryland where SAM, the 1254th Air Transport Wing, had been transferred.

With Col. William Draper, Eisenhower's pilot, having been voluntarily reassigned to Alaska, President Kennedy had to select a new presidential pilot. He chose Col. James B. Swindal, a senior pilot within SAM who in 1959 had been placed in command of the detachment that operated the first three Boeing 707s acquired by the Air Force.

It was no secret that Kennedy much preferred to fly in the Boeings. He used SAM 3240 only on short trips to New York or Boston or destinations close to Washington that were not equipped for handling jet traffic. For most of its service under Kennedy, SAM 3240 functioned as a White House staff plane, either preceding or following Kennedy's plane. For a brief period, SAM had the habit of rotating the three Boeings, 970, 971 and 972, on a monthly basis for presidential use. Eventually the presidential air crew won its argument that SAM 970 be considered the primary Boeing so that they could concentrate their attention and care on it.

It was SAM 970 that flew Kennedy south to Key West in March 1961, scarcely two months after he had taken office. The purpose was to confer with Prime Minister Harold Macmillan of

199

Britain on a developing crisis halfway around the globe in a little country scarcely any Americans knew about—and whose name even the President mispronounced—Laos.

The British leader was flying up from the Caribbean in his own plane and arrived over Key West well before Kennedy.

"Hold and circle," came the orders from the Key West tower to the prime minister's plane.

"Impossible," replied the British pilot. "We have a Code Two [meaning Macmillan] aboard. Request permission to land."

"Sorry," came back the Key West air controller, "but we have a Code One [meaning Kennedy] ahead of you."

So Macmillan's plane circled until *Air Force One* touched down at Key West. Kennedy wanted to be on the ground to personally welcome the prime minister when he landed on American soil.

SAM 970 also served as *Air Force One* when Kennedy flew off to Vienna early in 1961 for a sobering encounter with Nikita Khrushchev. And it became the backup presidential plane when SAM 26000, a new Boeing intercontinental, came along late in 1962 to serve as the first officially designated "presidential aircraft" with jet engines.

The spanking new Boeing 707 arrived at Andrews Air Force Base outside Washington on October 10, 1962. It had a nonstop range of 7,000 miles, almost 2,500 more than SAM 970, and a top speed of 620 miles an hour. Powered by four Pratt & Whitney JT3D-3B turbo fan engines, the new star of the air fleet also could operate from shorter runways than those required by SAM 970 and the other two Boeing 707s that had been purchased in 1959 for airlifting top government officials.

Boeing built the new plane at its plant in Renton, Washington, at a cost to the taxpayers of $7,024,000. The sum, however, did not cover the necessary spare parts and ground support equipment. By the time it was turned over to the Air Force, the actual cost was approximately $8,600,000. Boeing absorbed the difference in honor of the occasion.

Physically, SAM 26000 was an impressive sight. Its gleaming, swept-back wings spanned almost 146 feet, fifteen more than the earlier Boeing 707s. It also was eight feet longer and weighed in, fully loaded, at 328,000 pounds—a good thirty-five tons more than its shorter sisters. Its effective payload exceeded thirteen tons of cargo and passengers. It could fly a President as high as eight miles above the earth.

In spite of its technical excellence and the latest in electronics, the new *Air Force One* left something to be desired. It had a faulty, old-fashioned floor plan.

Perhaps because executive jet aircraft of such size were a rarity due to their extremely high cost, interior designers lacked experience in fashioning an ideal layout. So the original configuration of the new Kennedy plane was patterned after the interiors of earlier propeller-driven models.

The presidential suite was located in the rear half of the fuselage. That meant the President would enter and leave the plane through the rear door, or what commonly is regarded today as the coach entrance on a commercial Boeing Stratoliner. The working and seating section for the White House staff and press pool were placed in the forward half of the airplane—in what today is considered to be the favored area for first-class travelers. That layout made sense in a propeller craft because the rear of the plane was farthest from the engines and thought to be quieter and more stable in flight. The layout didn't make sense in a jet aircraft, but Kennedy was too proud of his new acquisition to make any fuss over it.

Perhaps the most distinctive Kennedy stamp on the new presidential aircraft was its exterior appearance. Anxious to give the government's executive aircraft a more national character, Kennedy directed that the traditional military markings be scrapped. With the help of First Lady Jacqueline Kennedy, noted designer Raymond Loewy was persuaded to take over the project.

Loewy came up with a strikingly handsome blue-and-white color scheme. The insignia of the Military Air Transport Service was removed and so were the words UNITED STATES AIR FORCE that had appeared on previous aircraft of the SAM fleet. Instead, the words UNITED STATES OF AMERICA were emblazoned on both sides of the fuselage and the American flag was painted on the tail. On the new Boeing 707, large decals of the presidential seal were affixed on both sides of the nose.

Loewy's design was simple, elegant, and dignified. It spoke of the power of the nation and of the presidency as well, but did so with quiet grace. The design was an instant hit with everyone in government and with the public. And it has stood the test of time. The Loewy design has remained the *Air Force One* insignia from that day to this, accepted without question by four succeeding presidents.

Kennedy relished the privacy that *Air Force One* offered. But unlike Richard Nixon and Jimmy Carter, who used the privacy for working on staff papers and memoranda, Kennedy often chose to relax.

"He had a big bed back there," recalls Vernon "Red" Shell, his favorite flight steward. "On a short trip, say to Cape Cod, a one-hour flight, he'd skim through two or three newspapers real fast, maybe have a cup of fish chowder, then take a little nap. Whenever Jackie was along, she wouldn't take a nap. She'd just sit there and read. Kennedy enjoyed that plane more than anybody I ever saw."

"The Kennedy people drank more and ate less—I guess that's why I liked 'em," Shell chuckled. "Sometimes some of them would drink a little too much and the President would find out. He would shake his head at them and that would be enough to give 'em the message."

Shell, with his soft drawl, became one of Kennedy's favorite storytellers. He recalls it began with a bawdy joke that he told JFK aides Kenneth O'Donnell and Dave Powers during the advance trip to Europe in 1961. "Later, on the President's trip, I walked into his compartment and Dave said, 'Hey, Red, tell the President that story you told us.' Well, I was kind of embarrassed, but the President egged me on, so I told it. He slapped his leg and got a big kick out of it. After that he seemed more friendly to me than ever. We shared a lot of good stories, him and me."

The Kennedy good humor even extended to the press. On one flight back from Cape Cod, Kennedy was furious over a UPI story on the front page of *The Washington Post* that he had run his sailboat aground the previous day. Kennedy dispatched Press Secretary Pierre Salinger to protest to Alvin Spivak, the wire service's pool member on the trip.

"The President says the story is wrong," Salinger told Spivak. "We want a retraction."

"I can't do that," replied Spivak. "I've got the pictures right here of the *Victura* going aground with the President at the helm."

Salinger threw up his hands and reported back to the President. Kennedy telephoned UPI's Hyannis Port reporter who had witnessed the embarrassing moment. The President didn't deny the story, but asked plaintively: "Have you thought just what the Republicans will say about the Commander-In-Chief of the armed services running a little sailboat aground?"

Kennedy kept *Air Force One* busy during the last year of his life. In June he was off on a five-day trip to Hawaii, with stops along the way at the Air Force Academy in Colorado, the missile range in White Sands, New Mexico, a conference with Texas Democrats at El Paso, a tour of Navy bases in California, and a $500-a-plate dinner of Kennedy supporters in Los Angeles. Later that month, Kennedy embarked on his memorable journey to Berlin, where he delivered his famous "Ich bin ein Berliner" speech to a cheering, almost hysterical mass of West Berliners, nearly two-thirds of the population.

As he boarded *Air Force One* to leave Germany, Kennedy remarked to his aides, "We'll never have another day like this one."

From Berlin, *Air Force One* whisked Kennedy to Dublin, there to begin a blissful and sentimental journey among his kith and kin and thousands more Irishmen who proudly claimed they were. In Wexford, the county from which his great-grandfather had set off for America during the potato famine of 1848, Kennedy introduced to the happy crowd the "Irish Mafia" on his White House staff—Kenny O'Donnell, Dave Powers, and Larry O'Brien—and concluded with a grin, "And then I would like to introduce to you the pastor of the church which I go to, who comes from Cork—Monsignor O'Mahoney. He is the pastor of a poor, humble flock in Palm Beach, Florida."

August was a sad month for the Kennedys, but an active one for pilot Jim Swindal and the crew of the presidential plane. The

Kennedys' infant son, Patrick, died shortly after birth by emergency Caesarean section at Otia Air Base hospital in Massachusetts. The loss of Patrick affected the President and Jackie more deeply than all but their closest friends knew. While Jackie recuperated at Squaw Island, Kennedy shuttled regularly back and forth to Washington.

In September and October, the President was off again on a series of political trips to prepare for the 1964 campaign. He toured eleven western states (eight of which he had lost to Nixon in 1960), and wound up with a sunny weekend of relaxation at Bing Crosby's estate at Palm Springs, California, while longtime backer Frank Sinatra fumed and fussed. Sinatra had built a special helicopter landing pad beside his own Palm Springs mansion just to accommodate Kennedy.

The mixup was the fault of Kennedy's trusted right-hand man, Kenneth O'Donnell, who had accepted the Secret Service's recommendation without checking with Sinatra. O'Donnell took the blame and tried to soothe Sinatra, but to no avail. Word came back that the incensed Sinatra had taken a sledgehammer to the helicopter pad.

October found Kennedy winging aboard *Air Force One* to the University of Maine, Amherst College, Philadelphia, Boston, Delaware, and New York City. In November, the last weekend before his fateful trip to Texas, Kennedy flew to Florida for a spate of politicking and sunbathing. He took in the launching of a Polaris missile at Cape Canaveral, made speeches at Tampa and Miami, and relaxed beside the pool at his father's house in Palm Beach. Aboard *Air Force One* he picked Navy to beat Duke, giving pal Dave Powers ten points. When Roger Staubach passed Navy to victory, 38 to 25, he demanded Powers pay off immediately.

On Tuesday before he flew to Texas, the President informed O'Donnell that he and Jackie wanted to move up their departure on a planned trip to Japan, the Philippines, India, and Pakistan to a date early in January. And, as O'Donnell and Powers related in their memoir of the Kennedy years, *Johnny, We Hardly Knew Ye*, the President planned to see Ambassador Henry Cabot Lodge in Washington immediately after the Texas trip.

"Are you sure I'll be leaving Texas in time to have lunch here with Cabot Lodge on Sunday?" asked Kennedy. "He's coming all the way from Vietnam to see me, and I don't want to keep him waiting."

"Don't worry," O'Donnell said. "It's all set."

On Sunday, Lodge and O'Donnell were watching Kennedy's flag-draped coffin being carried up the steps of the U.S. Capitol.

Chapter Seven
November 22

It had been a good day. In fact, it could hardly have gone better. Texas-sized crowds had greeted the young President and his comely wife in San Antonio and Houston. Even the state's conservative establishment had been impressed by the unexpectedly large and friendly throngs. Now a light rain was falling as *Air Force One* swept onto the lighted runway at Carswell Air Force Base outside Fort Worth. The clock was pushing midnight, but neither the hour nor the drizzle could diminish the high spirits of everyone aboard.

Jacqueline Kennedy, making her first political trip as First Lady, sent word out to the clamoring reporters: "Texas friendliness is everything I'd heard it to be." Before going to sleep in the Kennedys' eighth-floor suite in the downtown Texas Hotel, she laid out the clothes she had selected for the next day in Dallas: navy blue blouse and matching purse, a raspberry-pink suit and matching pillbox hat. And, oh yes, a fresh pair of white gloves.

The flight from Fort Worth to its rival neighbor late the next morning took only thirteen minutes. It was scarcely long enough for Col. James Swindal to lift the handsome Boeing 707 above the clouds before beginning the long descent to Love Field in Dallas. As the plane slowly taxied toward the green and red terminal building, Swindal could see another large crowd waiting, jumping, waving. The sight from the cockpit persuaded him that not all of Dallas was anti-Kennedy, whatever the advance reports had been.

Air Force Two, a similar, older Boeing bearing Vice President and Mrs. Johnson, assorted Texas congressmen and LBJ aides, had already landed. Here in Dallas, as on the day previous in San Antonio, Houston, and Fort Worth, it was Johnson's duty as a native Texan to welcome the President and Mrs. Kennedy.

The crowd squealed with delight as the door on *Air Force One* opened and the Kennedys stepped into the dazzling sunlight. They moved quickly through a stodgy reception line of Dallas bigwigs and hurried over to touch hands with their cheering, straining admirers along the fence. Kennedy ignored the big Confederate flag someone held high in the rear of the swarm, but his appreciative eye caught the friendly signs HOWDY MR. PRESIDENT and WELCOME TO BIG D, JACK AND JACKIE.

Mrs. Kennedy, smiling radiantly and clutching a fresh bouquet of roses, stretched a dainty hand to the screeching teenagers and jostling grownups. The Kennedys spent nearly twenty minutes "working" the fence, far more than their schedule allowed but insufficient to satisfy their adoring fans. "I touched him, I *touched* him!" women shrieked. *Newsweek*'s Charles Roberts burrowed through the crush of photographers and Secret Service men to Mrs. Kennedy's side. "How do you like campaigning?" he asked.

"It's wonderful," she breathed. "Just wonderful!"

From the doorway of *Air Force One*, flight engineer Joe Chappell watched the motorcade form for the drive through downtown Dallas. Kennedy had ordered the "bubbletop" removed from his bulletproof Lincoln limousine so that people could see him and Jackie more easily. He also waved off the agents who usually rode on retractable footholds along the sides and rear of the car during its passage through crowded streets.

Kennedy wanted to show that he was not afraid to be in Dallas in spite of its hot-headed conservative climate. In 1960, a band of jeering housewives had spat on Lyndon and Lady Bird Johnson for running on the Kennedy ticket. Just a few weeks past, U.N. Ambassador Adlai Stevenson had been roughed up in Dallas. And this very morning, November 22, 1963, the *Dallas Morning News* had carried a full-page, black-bordered advertisement shrilly denouncing Kennedy as soft on Communism. Kennedy had read it disgustedly just before landing at Dallas.

Right behind the White House limousine came the "Queen Mary," a five-ton 1955 Cadillac security car, bristling with agents. Then followed the Vice President's convertible bearing visible evidence that the Kennedy trip was helping to patch the open rift between Texas Democrats: Senator Ralph Yarborough was riding with his old foe Lyndon Johnson.

Next came the automobiles for the White House press pool and photographers, more Texas VIPs and, finally, the chartered city buses for lesser politicians and Washington and Texas reporters. As the President's limousine started forward, there was a wild scramble for the buses by correspondents who had been following the Kennedys' hand-shaking tour of the airport fence. Roberts swung aboard the first press bus, seven vehicles behind the President.

The President's doctor, Admiral George Burkley, was not so lucky. Kenneth O'Donnell, Kennedy's chief aide, wanted to ride in the Queen Mary. So the doctor had to settle for the VIP bus near the end of the motorcade. "It's not right," Burkley protested to Mrs. Evelyn Lincoln, the President's personal secretary, who was also back there. "The President's personal physician should be much closer to him."

Still, Burkley's fussing seemed unwarranted. There was no sign of animosity anywhere, only an outpouring of warm and friendly folk. The motorcade, flanked by Dallas motorcycle police, crept slowly along Lemmon Avenue, into Turtle Creek Boulevard, down Harwood Street, and then made a right turn into the man-made canyon of Main Street, twelve blocks from Dealey Plaza. Now the crowd was gigantic. It greeted the sight of the motorcade with a roar, an undulating, rising, falling roar of voices that rolled like surf against the glistening skyscrapers and crashed down over the motorcade below.

From the rear seat of the lead car, a white Ford driven by Police Chief Jesse Curry, Special Agent Forrest Sorrels glanced back at the President's glistening limousine. It looked fine to him. Sheriff Bill Decker, seated beside Sorrels, thought he could see The Man waving in that odd, choppy fashion of his. Ahead, as far as Curry could see, stretched a surging sea of people on both sides of Main. Hundreds of faces peered out from the windows of office buildings. Main, at midday, was broiling hot. Sorrels fretted about all the open windows.

Not everyone had left *Air Force One* to go into town. Christine Camp and Sue Vogelsinger, two secretaries from the White House press office, stayed on the plane to run off press releases for the day's next event—a big fund-raising dinner in Austin. Pilot Swindal, occupied with the tasks of readying the aircraft for the next leg of the trip, declined an invitation to lunch in the terminal with Col. George McNally, chief of the White House Communications Agency. He settled for a roast beef sandwich from the galley.

Since the President and the First Lady weren't due back at Love Field for at least ninety minutes, many members of the crew decided to follow McNally's lead. From the airport restaurant, they could see the President's plane (SAM 26000) on the nearby ramp. Just beyond was *Air Force Two* (SAM 970) and the White House press plane, a chartered Pan American jet. Taking a lunch break was a normal occurrence whenever the rear guard had sufficient time. Besides, *Air Force One*'s communications center was in constant radio contact with the motorcade and with the White House Communication Agency's temporary signal board in the Sheraton-Dallas Hotel. From there, trunk lines linked the traveling White House with the real one in Washington, the Military Command Center in the Pentagon, the State Department, and Secret Service headquarters. Swindal, on the plane, could hear the agents' radio chatter as the motorcade inched its way through downtown Dallas toward the Trade Mart where the President was to speak. Swindal grinned pleasurably. The Kennedys were being inundated with flowers.

In the rear of *Air Force One*, George Thomas was tidying up the First Family's bedroom. For Kennedy's next appearance at Austin, the President's valet put out a lightweight suit and a fresh shirt, tie, and socks.

210

Flight steward Joe Ayres had wondered aloud how the Kennedys were going to like staying overnight on the LBJ ranch—and that gave Thomas a happy idea. To remind the President that he could have the rest of the evening off and Saturday too, Thomas also laid out a sport shirt, a pair of tan chino slacks, and a favorite Kennedy sweater. Thomas chuckled softly to himself. He could hear the President asking, "George, what am I supposed to do with this gear?" And he, George, would tell him. The President would like that. He always did.

At 12:30 P.M. Dallas time on *Air Force One*, a shout exploded over Charlie Frequency—and then another. Swindal stiffened. He recognized the voice of Roy Kellerman, the chief Secret Service agent riding in the President's limousine. Above the radio crackle, Swindal heard a third sharp cry: "*Dagger* cover *Volunteer!*" The radio became a babel of screeching voices. Then it fell silent.

Frustrated, with mounting alarm, Swindal tried swiftly to reconstruct what he had heard and what it might mean. Something clearly had gone wrong in Dallas. There had been surprise, even panic, in Kellerman's voice. *Dagger* was the code name for Rufus Youngblood, LBJ's chief agent on the trip. *Volunteer* was the Vice President. What was the emergency? Had Johnson been attacked?

Swindal's first thought was that a riot probably had occurred along the motorcade route. What was happening? The radio's silence was galling. Then, long moments later, an urgent telephone call came through to Swindal from Parkland Memorial Hospital. It was Brig. Gen. Godfrey McHugh, Kennedy's Air Force aide, with a cryptic order: refuel *Air Force One* immediately, cancel the Austin stop, and file a flight plan directly back to Washington.

Now Swindal knew the trouble, whatever it was, involved the President. Perhaps he had seriously injured his back; it was Kennedy's chronic problem, one for which he usually wore a brace. Maybe they were canceling the rest of the trip in order to rush Kennedy to Bethesda Naval Hospital. Voicing aloud his concern, Swindal strode back to the President's stateroom and flipped on the television. Alerted by his commotion, the others aboard—Camp, Vogelsinger, Ayres, and Thomas—gathered anxiously around the set.

Flight engineer Chappell was standing outside, in the shade of *Air Force One*'s port wing, talking with pilot Douglas Moody of the Pan Am press charter about having lunch in the terminal. Suddenly Swindal came scrambling down the stairs.

"Joe, get fuel on board," Swindal barked. "Get ready to go!" He rushed back aboard.

"I knew from Swindal's voice that something serious had happened," Chappell said. "My mind turned right away to some international crisis somewhere—Berlin, Cuba, something like that."

Moody quickly scrubbed the lunch idea. "If you're leaving right away, I guess we'll be going, too," he told Chappell. "I better see about my fuel." He started back toward the press plane.

At that instant, Swindal reappeared on the stairs, a stricken look on his face. "Hey, you guys! I just heard it—the President's been shot!"

At 12:36 Dallas time, ABC broke into local programs with the first network bulletin, based on United Press International's flash from Merriman Smith in the press pool car three vehicles behind Kennedy: "Three shots were fired at President Kennedy's motorcade in downtown Dallas." Four minutes later, Walter Cronkite came on CBS to say that the President had been hit and perhaps was "seriously wounded." NBC shortly added more to the horror.

On *Air Force One*, a numbness came over those huddled around the TV set in the President's cabin. The world stopped. They stared at each other in disbelief and shock, unable, unwilling to accept the awful news piercing the plane in staccato bursts from the glaring screen. The two women clutched each other and began sobbing wildly. Ayres pounded the bulkhead with his fist. Thomas, his own eyes brimming, wandered back to the bedroom and methodically began putting away Kennedy's clothes.

Lt. Col. Lewis "Swede" Hanson, *Air Force One*'s co-pilot, had taken advantage of the stop in Dallas to drive out and visit his ailing mother-in-law who lived there. When he heard the news, he raced back to Love Field to help Swindal.

In the airport restaurant, other members of the crew sensed a restlessness in the room, a strange and growing apprehension. The clatter of dishes seemed unusually loud; people were moving here and there, whispering nervously to persons at other tables. Even the waitresses seemed flustered; they were congregating in clusters near the kitchen doorway. Master Sgt. Joe Giordano, *Air Force One*'s baggage master, got up to check a report that the Pan Am crew had been summoned back to the press plane. Then the terminal's public address system came on with urgent calls for the crews of SAM 26000 and SAM 970. Giordano and the others hurried out into the brilliant sunshine and broke into a lope toward the White House planes, ignoring the puddles on the tarmac.

At 1:23 Dallas time (2:23 Eastern standard time), a radio bulletin announced that the last rites of the Catholic Church had been administered to Kennedy at the hospital. At 1:35 in Dallas, UPI and Associated Press flashed the incredible news to a stunned nation and the world: "President Kennedy is dead."

For one brief moment, an eerie calm settled over Love Field, as though it were caught up in the eye of a hurricane. Nothing moved. No one spoke. Then the agony, confusion, and fear that had stalked Parkland Memorial Hospital were swiftly transported to the field. *Air Force One* became the focus of frantic, disordered activity. "The United States government had been smashed at the top," *Newsweek*'s Roberts was later to write in his study of that black day, *The Truth About the Assassination,* "and for two hours no one seemed ready or able to pick up the pieces." William Manchester, in *The Death of a President,* a book authorized by the Kennedy family, speaks of police "running around with goofy looks." Others "who didn't look goofy *felt* goofy." If anyone was in charge at that moment, no one seemed to know who it was.

Alerted to prepare SAM 26000 for immediate departure, Swindal instructed Chappell to disconnect the ground air conditioner. Under the broiling Texas sun, the aircraft's interior soon became a sweatbox.

But the first arrival from the hospital was not the Kennedy entourage but the blood-drenched presidential limousine, now with its bulletproof top securely in place. It was destined for one of

213

the C-130 cargo planes. Furious Secret Service agents milled about the grim reminder of their failure to save the President, shouting that the back seat was too horrible to look at, hurling imprecations at the unknown assassin who had perpetrated the awful deed in Dealey Plaza. Dallas police cars and motorcycles guarded every entrance to Love Field. Armed officers ran nervously about the terminal and the tarmac, as though the murderer might be lurking somewhere in the vicinity of the plane.

Actually, there was a man at the helm of the government: the new President—Lyndon Baines Johnson. He had automatically succeeded Kennedy at the moment of death in Trauma Room One. Dr. Kemp Clark, Parkland's senior neurosurgeon, had fixed the time at 1:00 in Dallas. But Johnson and Lady Bird were being kept in guarded isolation in a barren cubicle at the hospital. Agent Youngblood feared a worldwide conspiracy against the leaders of the country, and he was taking no chances. He wanted to spirit Johnson out of there, away from Dallas, even before Kennedy was officially pronounced dead. But there seemed to be no safe, clandestine way to do it, nor could anyone *think* of a handy sanctuary. The press, the police, and the public were swarming around the hospital. Youngblood ordered Johnson to stay put.

Then, too, the Secret Service command structure in Dallas fell into disarray after the shooting of Kennedy. The White House security chief, who traditionally accompanied a traveling president, Gerald A. Behn, had elected to stay back in Washington during the Texas trip. In his place, Behn had designated Roy Kellerman, a senior agent, to run the Texas security operation. In ordinary times, the arrangement would have worked out fine—as it obviously had in San Antonio, Houston, and Fort Worth. But it proved inadequate for the crisis of Dallas, an error of judgment for which Behn would never forgive himself or be forgiven by others.

What made it transparently wrong was not a rivalrous competition between Secret Service agents, as suggested in Manchester's book, but the simple fact of the presence of the Vice President. Beyond the environs of Washington, the Vice President rarely accompanies the President. The reason is not only a matter of physical security but one of politics; they seldom have a

214

need to be seen together on treks around the country. Indeed, it is frequently the wiser political choice for the President and Vice President to remain apart, permitting each man to cater to his special constituency in the electorate. This political concept is rooted in the vice presidential selection process. Presidential candidates traditionally pick their running mates so they can geographically and philosophically "balance the ticket."

But Texas was a special case, the exception that proved the rule. Although Johnson had carried the state for Kennedy in 1960, LBJ was in political trouble at home in 1963. He had been unable to stop the wrangling between the liberal Democratic faction led by Senator Yarborough, which supported Kennedy, and the conservative Texas establishment led by Governor John Connally. Neither side trusted Johnson. Kennedy had decided to make the Texas trip for the specific purpose of helping Johnson reunite the fractious Texans. It was important to keep the state from going for Republican Barry Goldwater in the 1964 presidential election.

Under these unusual circumstances, with the President and Vice President traveling everywhere together except in the air, the chief of security should have been in Texas and in direct personal command of both groups of Secret Service men, the agents guarding Kennedy and the smaller detail guarding Johnson. Instead, when Kennedy was shot, the anguished Behn found himself in Washington, holding a telephone to his ear for fragmentary, sometimes conflicting reports from his men on the scene. And when Kennedy died, the *de facto* responsibility for presidential security at Parkland Memorial Hospital passed involuntarily from Kennedy's agents to Lyndon Johnson's, from Kellerman's detail to Youngblood's.

Behn's presence would have eased this transition for the Kennedy staff as well as for his agents. Wracked with grief over their fallen leader, some Kennedy aides watched bitterly as Secret Service men who had been guarding *their* President now began devoting attention to Lyndon Johnson and Lady Bird. The most obvious was Emory Roberts, Kellerman's deputy. In his book, Manchester suggests that ambitious agents were switching allegiance from Kennedy to Johnson even before the President was pronounced dead. But the truth is that at the hospital Kellerman

215

instructed Roberts and the 8-to-4 shift of agents to augment Youngblood's small contingent of Johnson bodyguards. Had Behn been present to issue the order himself, Kennedy's loyal aides might have better understood the necessity for it. As Youngblood observed in his memoirs, "the agents in Dallas did not have allegiance . . . to an individual. Their allegiance was to the mission itself. John Kennedy was dead. He was beyond the protective efforts of the Secret Service."

At 1:33 Dallas time, Love Field beheld a strange spectacle. Two unmarked police cars, led by a motorcycle escort, swept onto the airport concrete and raced toward *Air Force One*. Youngblood, physically shielding Lyndon Johnson in the lead car, recalls one of the most welcome sights he had ever seen— "the big, gleaming blue-and-white jet, with UNITED STATES OF AMERICA painted along the fuselage above the long row of windows and the number 26000 gracing the tail rudder." Pilot Swindal, alerted by radio, rushed out to salute his new Commander-in-Chief. Johnson, followed by Lady Bird, more agents, and several Texas congressmen, scrambled quickly up the rear stairs.

The interior of the plane was as hot as an oven, but Youngblood breathed easier. Conspiracy or no conspiracy, he told himself, he now had Lyndon Johnson in a secure place. The lanky agent had one remaining worry—a sniper on the terminal roof might get a shot at Johnson through the plane's windows. He ordered agents to pull down the shades.

Johnson strode past the Kennedy bedroom at the rear of the aircraft with a curt order to Youngblood: "I want this kept strictly for the use of Mrs. Kennedy, Rufus. See to that." Then he headed up forward into the presidential stateroom and office. The television was on and the room was already crowded with listeners. Suddenly the local station interrupted Cronkite's broadcast from New York with the bulletin from the hospital, officially announcing Kennedy's death 35 minutes earlier. (Johnson had ordered acting press secretary Malcolm Kilduff to hold up the public announcement to give himself time to get out to the plane.)

216

As Johnson entered the stateroom, everyone stood up and fell silent, even his own staffers and longtime Texas friends. "It was at that moment," Johnson said later, "that I realized nothing would ever be the same again. A wall—high, forbidding, historic—separated us now, a wall that derived from the Office of the Presidency of the United States." Those who had called him Lyndon before would defer to him henceforth as "Mr. President."

Much has been said over the years about Lyndon Johnson's rough-shod "seizure" of the presidency in those black hours of Dallas, how he "abused" the Kennedy people, dealt unfeelingly with Mrs. Kennedy in her unutterable despair, and generally behaved like a lout and a clod during *Air Force One*'s bleak flight back to Washington from Dallas—with Kennedy's body in a Texas coffin beside the rear door. But it is a myth, magnified by the passage of time and perpetuated by those who idolized Kennedy and who somehow blamed Johnson and Johnson's Texas for his death. Kennedy staffers seem to have gone out of their way to paint Johnson as crude, grasping, discourteous, and conniving in the takeover of the presidency.

There were, it is true, many misunderstandings between Johnson people and Kennedy's people at Love Field and on the flight home. Manchester is right when he says the transition of power seemed "needlessly cruel" to those who loved John Kennedy. He is accurate when he observes that "consolidating the two groups on one airplane was to prove extremely unfortunate"— at least it seemed that way to the grief-stricken Kennedy men. But although Manchester describes Johnson as being in a "torpor" and "a very understandable state of shock" that afternoon, that seemed—to reporters on the trip, persons on the plane and members of the crew—to be more descriptive of the reaction of close Kennedy staffers than Lyndon Johnson. Indeed, a dispassionate look at the record suggests that Johnson was the least agitated, most perceptive individual on the scene.

One of the two reporters on *Air Force One*'s tragic journey, Charles Roberts of *Newsweek,* notes that Johnson's takeover came under harrowing conditions—he was the first President to witness the murder of his predecessor. Wrote Roberts:

217

As an unbiased witness to [the takeover], now that questions have been raised, I might add something more: It was careful, correct, considerate, and compassionate. Considering that it occurred at a time when no one knew the full implications of Oswald's deed, and considering that there was no script to follow, it was a masterpiece of cool-headed improvisation. Johnson, in my eyes, was the coolest man in Dallas or aboard *Air Force One*.

Flight engineer Chappell, a presidential crew member from Kennedy's time to date, offered his own assessment of Johnson's performance. "That day on the airplane was probably his finest day—and I was there through all of them."

But if Johnson's takeover of the presidency had to be improvised (half the cabinet, including Secretary of State Dean Rusk, was in the air west of Hawaii en route to Japan), his takeover of *Air Force One* was a deliberate plan of action from the outset. Manchester quoted the distraught Kenneth O'Donnell as saying he was "dumfounded" by LBJ's decision, but the fact is that Johnson and his Secret Service men never contemplated using any other aircraft once Kennedy was dead. SAM 26000 was the big new Boeing Intercontinental jet acquired for the President in 1962. It had supplanted SAM 970 (*Air Force Two*) as the preferred presidential jet and it contained superior communications equipment for keeping a Chief Executive in touch with Washington and the rest of the world. In a time of national emergency— and Dallas surely had created one—it is inconceivable that the new President would use a backup plane so that SAM 26000 could serve as a hearse for the body of his predecessor.

Johnson, in fact, assumed he had made that clear in two conversations at Parkland hospital with O'Donnell. The first concerned the desirability of moving "the plane" (*Air Force One*) from Love Field back to Carswell for security reasons. The idea was scrapped because of the long drive from the hospital in Dallas to the base near Fort Worth. Love Field, after all, was less than ten minutes away by fast car.

And Johnson mentioned "the plane" again when O'Donnell informed him that Mrs. Kennedy "would not leave the hospital without the President's body." As Johnson recounted later, "I agreed that we would board the plane and wait until Mrs. Kennedy and the President's body were brought aboard.''

Unfortunately, that decision apparently was not conveyed at the outset to General McHugh, Kennedy's Air Force aide and pilot Swindal's superior. Emotionally wracked by the assassination and devoted to the Kennedys, McHugh simply assumed that Johnson ("the Vice President") would be flying on SAM 970 and the slain Kennedy ("my President") and the Kennedy group would be alone on *Air Force One.*

McHugh already had telephoned Swindal to have the plane ready to go and, in fact, had ordered the plane moved to a "safer" part of the field. "We ignored that," Chappell said. "A Boeing is a pretty big thing to hide. Besides, we would have lost our ground telephone lines. Swindal rightly figured he needed them for communication.''

Unknown to McHugh, Lyndon Johnson and his people already were aboard *Air Force One* when there ensued an incredible hassle at the hospital over possession of Kennedy's body. There had been a homicide, Dallas authorities firmly reminded O'Donnell and Dr. Burkley; the body would be needed for an autopsy. But Mrs. Kennedy would have none of that. She would not leave without her dead husband; they would fly back to Washington together—immediately. With Kennedy's angry aides and the Secret Service clearing the way, the 900-pound casket finally was rammed past the protesting officials and into the mortician's white hearse. Mrs. Kennedy darted into a jump seat beside the casket. McHugh and Burkley squeezed in behind with agent Clint Hill. With agent Andy Berger at the wheel, the hearse whipped out of the hospital driveway and sped to what McHugh expected to be a majestic, empty *Air Force One.*

On board, meanwhile, Rufus Youngblood was buttoning up Lyndon Johnson's security. He stationed agents at the stairs of the plane along with the regular Air Force guards. No one was to be admitted without his permission. He sent word to the cockpit that the aircraft was not to move until he gave the signal for the new President. And Youngblood was sticking to him like a shadow.

Johnson's immediate concern was not security but ceremony.

He wanted to be sworn in. It seemed, in retrospect, an odd choice. The mantle of the presidency had fully cloaked Johnson the moment of Kennedy's death, yet somehow that did not seem quite enough, not quite as official as the formal taking of the oath of office. It became a matter of heated discussion among those seated with him in the stateroom.

Several urged that he wait until he was back in Washington. Even the Texas congressmen were divided. Albert Thomas and Jack Brooks thought he should do it right away, there, on *Air Force One*. That squared with Johnson's natural urge to be doing something, anything, even in that dark moment when Youngblood still feared a conspiracy against all the leaders of the country and when nobody had yet heard of Lee Harvey Oswald, of the shooting of Officer Tippett, or of Oswald's capture in a Dallas theatre.

Perhaps, Johnson reasoned, the oath taking could be accomplished while he was waiting for Mrs. Kennedy to arrive with "the President's body." Johnson was President now and he knew it, but he plainly did not believe he looked that way in the eyes of the world, least of all in the eyes of those who revered John Kennedy. Perhaps a presidential investiture, while merely a reaffirmation of the vow he had taken as Vice President, would serve to publicly seal his right to govern the United States of America. Johnson's decision was odd because it was technically unnecessary. But it was psychologically astute. In that dark moment of history, Lyndon Johnson was more in tune with America's need than were those speeding Kennedy's body to *Air Force One*.

The crew was working feverishly to make room for the casket.

"When Swindal told me we were flying the body back, I knew right off it wouldn't be proper to put it in the hold," said Chappell. "We would have to put it in the passenger compartment. Swindal didn't think we could get a coffin through the rear door. I said we could do that all right, but we would have to pull out a partition in order to turn the coffin into the aisle and remove four seats on the left side to make room for it on the floor. So that's what we did, me and Ayres, with Swindal and Hanson helping.

220

We yanked out the seats and sent 'em over to the backup plane, and we finished up just moments before the hearse arrived.''

With sheer grit, the ponderous bronze casket was muscled up the narrow stairs into the tail compartment and pushed and tugged into its resting place, forward of the doorway and opposite the rear galley. It was an exhausting task. When Larry O'Brien straightened up, he was surprised to see the Johnsons consoling Mrs. Kennedy in the aisle outside the presidential bedroom. The Kennedy aide said later he was surprised "not because I thought it was bad taste or poor protocol or anything, except that none of us knew where the new President was at that moment.''

In the darkened, stifling hot interior of the plane, McHugh never saw the Johnsons at all. O'Donnell, fearful that Dallas authorities might yet try to reclaim Kennedy's body, instructed McHugh to get the plane into the air immediately. McHugh literally ran up the aisle to the cockpit. Swindal was ready; in fact he had already started the No. 3 engine.

But then commenced a series of incidents that would have been slapstick comedy had it been any other occasion. Mac Kilduff, apprised by Johnson of the swearing-in plans, burst into the cockpit and yelled, "Cut it off!" Kilduff was a Kennedy staffer, the trip's press secretary in the absence of Pierre Salinger. Swindal obeyed without asking for an explanation. Meantime, O'Donnell and Jackie Kennedy grew impatient with the delay. Cloistered in the rear with the coffin, they too were unaware that Johnson was waiting for the arrival of federal judge Sarah Hughes so he could be sworn in on the spot. Preoccupied with the urgent demands of his new office, Johnson had neglected to inform the young widow and her dead husband's chief aides of the ceremony about to take place in the presidential stateroom in the middle of the plane.

"It's so hot," Mrs. Kennedy kept telling O'Donnell. "Let's leave." Each time, O'Donnell had dispatched McHugh, Kellerman, even Major Gen. Chester V. "Ted" Clifton, the senior military aide, to get *Air Force One* moving. And each time, nothing moved.

For reasons he himself could not later explain, McHugh may

221

have been the last of the Kennedy men to know that Lyndon Johnson was aboard. Busily heeding O'Donnell's orders, the distraught general had dashed repeatedly up and down the plane's narrow corridor without ever bumping into the new President or ever being alerted to his presence. There is no other way, eyewitnesses agree, to account for McHugh's dramatic encounter with Kilduff near the flight deck.

"We've got to take off *immediately!*" McHugh shouted.

Kilduff tried to calm him. "Not until Johnson has taken the oath."

"Johnson isn't here," McHugh snapped. "He's on the back-up plane."

"Then you go back and tell that six-foot Texan he isn't Lyndon Johnson," Kilduff retorted.

The general flinched as if struck in the stomach. In a voice loud enough to rivet the attention of everyone in earshot, McHugh hotly announced: "I have only one President, and he's lying back in that cabin!"

Finally, through bits and snatches of overheard conversations during the first hectic fifteen minutes, O'Donnell, O'Brien, Dave Powers, and most of the other Kennedy staffers realized why the departure was being held up. The accepted it as inevitable, even if they didn't like it. After all, Johnson was now the President.

O'Donnell was too grief-stricken to make the adjustment. Between O'Donnell and Johnson there was a conflict of purpose—with Johnson clearly victorious—although not necessarily the grim struggle portrayed in some accounts.

Mary Gallagher, Jackie Kennedy's personal secretary, for instance, openly disputes Manchester's version. In her memoir, *My Life with Jacqueline Kennedy*, she observed:

> . . . I saw no division of JFK and LBJ people. I was certainly not angry at any time, as described by Manchester, using such words as "wrath," "blazing thoughts," "stiffened," "scowls," and "searing." Also, Evelyn Lincoln, Pam Turnure, and I did not decline something to eat from Marie Fehmer, Mrs. Johnson's secretary, because we were "angry" at her—we were just too numb to eat. Regarding the feelings of Kennedy men—and I con-

sider this of utmost importance—Kenny O'Donnell did not cover his ears to shut out the sound of the swearing-in ceremony of President Johnson. I saw him when he did this, and it was *before* the ceremony.

Jack Valenti, a new LBJ aide making his first trip on the presidential plane that day in Dallas, echoes Gallagher and Roberts in disagreement with the reports of "rampant hostility" aboard the plane. Valenti concedes that his loyalty to LBJ and his unfamiliarity with the Kennedy people at the time may make his opinion suspect. But in his account of his time with Johnson, *A Very Human President*, Valenti wrote:

> Could I have mistook what I thought was an immense sadness and dispirit for open hostility? No, I think not. I can understand now what I could not really perceive then. To sit in the White House, inside the magic inner circle where only the anointed of the President could freely move, to be there amid power and the celebration of power, to be the confidant and trusted emissary of the President, and now, by a freakish, ghoulish act of assassination to be isolated, alone, adrift, with the captain missing and a new helmsman in charge, this abrupt transition could not be managed by mere mortals. . . . I didn't see hostility. All I saw was grief—bitter, dry-teared grief.

The world's most memorable impression of the bitter grief aboard *Air Force One* was captured on film by White House photographer Cecil Stoughton in the stuffy, crowded presidential compartment. There stood a solemn Lyndon Johnson, right hand upraised and left hand on a small book held by a diminutive lady judge in a polka-dot dress, flanked by a dazed Jackie Kennedy and a somber Lady Bird Johnson. That stark moment of the swearing-in of the 36th President of the United States has been the subject of endless controversy and confusion among writers and eyewitnesses ever since. In many ways, it crystallizes the misperceptions and misunderstandings that abounded that day in Dallas.

The impression of many is that *Air Force One*'s departure was delayed interminably while Johnson waited for Judge Hughes to reach the airplane. Manchester describes Jacqueline Kennedy's

223

inner thoughts: "*An hour,* she thought. *My God, do I have to wait an hour*?" Some accounts reported that Johnson was kept waiting by Mrs. Kennedy, and that he was almost ready to fetch her personally when she showed up in the doorway. Tragedy has a way of heightening people's inner turmoil at such times; time itself must have seemed unbearable to those most intimately involved. Yet the record shows there were no interminable delays. Judge Hughes boarded the plane at 2:30 Dallas time, according to the log, only twelve minutes after Mrs. Kennedy. The ceremony took place at 2:38. Mrs. Kennedy, then, had to wait only 20 minutes at most. Furthermore, part of the delay in the ceremony was created by a couple of technical matters.

Stoughton, an experienced Signal Corps photographer, had momentary trouble with his camera. And then, in order to record the historic moment, he had to clamber upon a sofa and press himself against the rear wall of the small compartment. Even there he lacked room to capture the scene with his wide-angle Hasselblad lens, so he had to ask everyone to move back.

Even before Jackie showed up, a search was going on for a Bible to use in the ceremony. Johnson thought Judge Hughes was bringing one. She didn't. A Bible wasn't legally required as part of the oath taking, but its need, particularly in that anguished hour, seemed important to everyone. Steward Joe Ayres, according to Manchester, remembered that John Kennedy always carried a personal Bible under the lid of a table in the presidential bedroom and he went to fetch it. But it was Larry O'Brien, according to Roberts' eyewitness account, who came from the bedroom carrying what everyone assumed to be a small leather-bound Bible.

According to Roberts, it wasn't a Bible at all, certainly not the "personal" one that Manchester said Kennedy was in the habit of reading evenings on the plane. Roberts says he learned later from a Kennedy aide that the book on which Johnson took his oath was a Catholic missal, a thin volume of masses and prayers in English and Latin, which probably had been presented to the President shortly before arriving in Dallas. He reports that the book was still cellophane-wrapped in a cardboard box when found for the ceremony and obviously had not been opened. *The*

Washington Post claimed in 1967 that it had independently confirmed the use of the missal.

Unfortunately, the book is missing. Judge Hughes recalls giving it to an "official-looking person," as she left the plane following the ceremony. "I thought he was a security man," she says. Since the book has not turned up in the years since Dallas, the conclusive evidence is lacking. But whether Bible or missal, the volume in no way affected the validity of the oath taking. The Constitution and federal law is silent on the subject. If Johnson was the first President ever to be sworn in with his hand on a Catholic missal, he was not the first to assume office without employing Holy Scripture. Thomas Jefferson did not use a Bible for his oath-taking ceremony. Nor did Theodore Roosevelt or Calvin Coolidge—both of them, like Johnson, having moved up from the vice presidency upon the deaths of their predecessors.

Stoughton's official photograph of the ceremony, the one released by the White House and carried in newspapers and on television worldwide, lent further fuel to the reports of a crackling tension between Johnson people and Kennedy people aboard *Air Force One*. Manchester claims the photograph proves that the Kennedy aides did not want to be in the ceremony, certainly not in the picture. Stoughton's camera, he says, "did not report the presence of a single male Kennedy aide." But the fact is that the Stoughton negatives of his fifteen other pictures prove Manchester wrong. The pictures show six Kennedy men present: Kilduff, Dr. Burkley, General Clifton, Powers, O'Brien, and O'Donnell. Also there were Kennedy women staffers— Evelyn Lincoln, Pam Turnure, and Mary Gallagher. In all, there were twenty-seven persons in the small sweaty room, including several members of the crew, Texas congressmen, and Johnson aides Valenti and Bill Moyers.

The reason for the selection of this picture as the official swearing-in photograph was simple and human. Stoughton did not want to show Mrs. Kennedy's bloodstained pink skirt and hosiery, and this photo could be cropped just below her jacket. Moreover, on some of the other negatives there were hints of nervous smiles on the faces of several principals, including Lady Bird Johnson. Stoughton felt he had chosen a photograph that captured the historic moment as it should be remembered by the participants and the public.

There is no argument about Mrs. Kennedy's insistence on wearing the same bloody clothing she had worn when Kennedy was shot. In her ten-hour taping session with Manchester, Jackie conveyed the impression that "they" (meaning LBJ people) wanted her to look "immaculate" for the inaugural picture. But some of her own friends, including General McHugh and Mary Gallagher, had urged her to freshen up by changing her outfit as soon as she boarded the plane—even before the Kennedy people knew that there would be a swearing-in ceremony. She did, however, remove the blood spatters on her face and hair, a decision she quickly regretted. As she later recounted to Theodore White, the author and family friend, " . . . Everybody kept saying to me to put a cold towel around my head and wipe the blood off. . . . I saw myself in the mirror, my whole face spattered with blood and hair. I wiped it off with Kleenex. History! I thought, why did I wash the blood off? I should have left it there, let them see what they've done. If I'd just had the blood and caked hair when they took the picture. . . ."

The ceremony took only twenty-eight seconds, with Lyndon Johnson repeating Judge Sarah Hughes's somber intonation of the constitutional oath, "I do solemnly swear I will faithfully execute the office of President of the United States. . . ." She added, "So help me God," and the new President did the same. Eyewitness accounts vary about what he did next—whether he embraced Lady Bird and Jackie, whether he kissed both, or whether he only hugged Lady Bird—but are unanimous in what happened next. After a moment of awkward silence, Mrs. Kennedy returned silently to the casket in the rear of the plane where McHugh stood rigidly at attention. Lyndon Johnson drew himself up and commanded: "Okay, now let's get airborne."

Jim Swindal was in the cockpit and starting the engines even as Judge Hughes, some of the Texans, and several others hurried off. One of the latter was Sid Davis, White House correspondent for the Westinghouse Broadcasting network, who deplaned in order to brief the rest of the press corps on the swearing-in. It was Davis's watch that set the exact time at 2:38

P.M. Smith and Roberts had thought it occured at 2:37. But it was Davis's word that first went out to the world. The other two reporters, having failed to synchronize their watches with Davis on the plane, decided later to accept his time as factual.

Air Force One rose up from Dallas at 2:47, some of its windows still hooded as Swindal pushed the big Boeing into a steep, fast climb into the clean blue skies overhead. Those on board already had divided themselves into separate but logical groups. Some of the LBJ staff, morose Secret Service agents, and the two pool reporters went forward in the staff cabin. Johnson, Lady Bird, and close aides stayed in the presidential stateroom. The Kennedy people clustered protectively around the widow and the bronze box in the tail compartment.

Swindal leveled off at an altitude above 30,000 feet and set a 550-mile-an-hour course for Andrews Air Force Base. In the tail compartment, the brooding O'Donnell ordered a stiff drink of scotch and urged Jackie to have one, too. She hesitated, not ever liking the taste of it. "I'll make it for you," O'Donnell urged. She nodded wordlessly. The other men joined them, first one drink, then another, and more after that. There was so much to say to each other, but so hard to say anything beyond small talk, things of the moment. Looking ahead was simply impossible when the present was so incomprehensible. Not even the liquor helped. The LBJ staff, sensing their anguish, avoided intruding upon the black solitude of the aft compartment.

Air Force One was streaking eastward across Arkansas and Tennessee when Lyndon Johnson began asserting his presidency. From the executive suite, he placed a telephone call to Rose Kennedy at Hyannis Port to offer condolences on the loss of her son. He and Lady Bird talked by phone with Nell Connally, back in Dallas, to inquire of the governor's condition and wish him a quick recovery from his gunshot wounds. Johnson persuaded O'Brien to come forward to discuss the status of urgent congressional matters that might need his swift attention in the coming days. And he conferred repeatedly with McGeorge Bundy, Kennedy's national security adviser, who was running the White House Situation Room. Was there any evidence of an assassination conspiracy? Any hint that Moscow or Cuba might

227

attempt to exploit the national emergency? Each time, McBundy reported there were no such signs coming in over the nation's intelligence network.

Johnson summoned Moyers, Valenti, and Mrs. Elizabeth Carpenter, his executive assistant, to draft a brief statement he would need on arrival back in Washington. "I want to make it clear that the presidency will go on and I want to speak of my terrible sorrow which everyone else in this country feels," he told them. They labored over separate drafts and finally brought one in to him. Johnson read the paragraph, paused over the final sentence, then scratched it out in favor of his own phrasing. The statement was quickly retyped on a 3 x 5 card; he stuffed it in his inside coat pocket—it was to be his first public utterance as head of the nation:

"This is a sad time for all people. We have suffered a loss that cannot be weighed. For me it is a deep personal tragedy. I know the world shares the sorrow that Mrs. Kennedy and her family bear. I will do my best. That is all I can do. I ask for your help—and God's."

General Clifton, functioning now as the chief military assistant for the new President, also was busy on *Air Force One*'s air-to-ground communications. He relayed messages for the arrival ceremonies at Andrews and transfer of the slain President's body to Bethesda Naval Hospital. There would have to be a fork-lift truck at the airfield to lower the casket, he told the base. He was advised, too, of security precautions on American installations at home and abroad. Military forces everywhere were on the alert. The Pentagon's electronic ears were monitoring the airwaves for any reports of unidentifiable, armed, or stray aircraft in the vicinity of *Air Force One*, the backup Boeing (SAM 970), and the Pan Am press plane that were hurtling across middle America toward Washington.

Air Force One was streaking through the skies at a ground speed of nearly 600 miles an hour. The flight from Love Field to Andrews would take only two hours, twelve minutes. Up forward in the staff quarters, Smith and Roberts were frantically writing their separate but similar news accounts of the Dallas catastrophe. Roberts had a priority duty—preparing the pool report for the rest of their colleagues, those on the press plane and

228

those surely waiting at Andrews. It is a tradition that the pool reporter must turn in the report even before filing his own dispatches to his news organization.

But there were complications for Smith and Roberts, too. Smith had mislaid his portable typewriter in the confusion of the motorcade and the hospital. The crew helped him rig up one of the electric typewriters normally used on board by staff secretaries.

And then there were the visitors. Mac Kilduff, now serving as LBJ's press secretary, kept coming forward with bits of information from the new President and plans for the nighttime arrival at Andrews and what Johnson would be doing that evening and the next day. Through Kilduff, Mrs. Kennedy sent word that she had spent the entire flight keeping vigil over her husband's body. She felt it was important that the world know she was at *his* side, not sitting with the Johnsons.

General McHugh, Roberts remembers, was still angry over *Air Force One*'s failure to depart when he ordered it aloft: "He stopped at our press table, thumped his finger on my typewriter, and said: 'I want you to write that members of President Kennedy's staff'—he named O'Donnell, O'Brien, Powers, and himself—'sat in the rear of the plane with him and Mrs. Kennedy—not up here with them [the Johnsons].'"

The new President wanted to talk with the reporters, too. During the homeward flight he came forward several times to the table where Roberts and Smith were composing "instant history" while racing against the clock. On the first occasion, LBJ confided that he was going to ask all of Kennedy's cabinet and White House staff to stay on the job with him—a hint, Roberts recalls, of the "Let us continue" theme he would sound in subsequent days before Congress and the country. Johnson came up again to read the short statement he would be making before the television cameras when the plane landed at Andrews. He knew they needed it for their stories but he also was trying it out on them. He wanted it to be right. A bit later, Johnson passed on a report of his phone calls from the plane, his concern for the Kennedys, his worries about how the nation would weather its hour of crisis.

"We had so darn much work to do," an exasperated Roberts

229

recounted later in an oral interview for the John F. Kennedy Library. "I think that this was the only time in my life that I ever felt like saying to a President of the United States, 'Look, I know you want to talk, but I've got a lot of work to do.'"

For Smith, Dallas was a special ordeal. Smitty had been in Warm Springs, Georgia, when Franklin Roosevelt was fatally stricken in 1945. Now, on the Kennedy plane, he was unable to get over the fact that this was the second time he was riding back to Washington with a dead President. Smitty found himself talking to sorrowing Secret Service men, reliving the shock and grief of the earlier tragedy as well as the new one. And he was unable to mask his personal resentment against Kennedy's successor.

Smitty's reaction undoubtedly was typical of that of many persons that day, particularly those on Kennedy's staff. A very human and sensitive person beneath his gruff exterior, Smitty was simply disguising his personal grief under a cloak of antagonism—as he perceptively conceded in diary notes written in 1964 on the first anniversary of Dallas. "In JFK's death, my sense of loss had taken the form of simply being unable to accept in my guts the coarse image and patois of LBJ," Smitty wrote.

Later, Smith grew to respect and admire Johnson and, on occasion, even made speeches defending LBJ against his Vietnam critics (one of Smitty's sons was killed in the war). For Smith, the transition from JFK to LBJ was not unlike the personal accommodation he had to make for President Harry Truman after Roosevelt's death. The veteran White House correspondent eventually became fond of the feisty Missourian, but recalling his first meeting with Truman on the presidential railroad car on the day of FDR's funeral, Smith confessed to his diary: "My powers of recognition were blotted out by an inner rage—what were these *strangers* doing on *Roosevelt's* train?"

At 5:09 P.M., the strangers and friends on John Kennedy's airplane were over the Shenandoah Valley, already nestled in the twilight shadows of the Blue Ridge Mountains. Washington was only thirty minutes away; all thoughts now focused on what would happen at Andrews Air Force Base. Mrs. Kennedy passed word to agent Kellerman that her husband's personal bodyguards and staff men would remove the casket from the

230

plane, and never mind what the military or anyone else said—"I want his friends to carry him down." Johnson shaved, combed his hair, and put on a fresh shirt. He felt inside his suit pocket for the statement he would read on the ground; it was still there. Roberts and Smith continued to pound furiously at their typewriters.

From the cockpit, Swindal beheld a strangely beautiful sky. The hot sun of Dallas had fled beyond the western horizon, and the rim of earth was aglow with a magnificent halo. Then darkness fell over the eastern seaboard and, up ahead, he could make out the first twinkling lights of the Washington suburbs. Just beyond Middleburg, near the expensive mountain retreat Kennedy had built for Jackie, Swindal banked *Air Force One* to the right and began a long, descending glide past the District of Columbia, across the Potomac River, over the Maryland countryside, and into Andrews.

As the President's flagship thundered past the approach lanes for National Airport, flight engineer Joe Chappell noted something unusual. Although it was the height of the airline rush hour at Washington's busy commercial field, pilots of incoming craft in the area were voluntarily holding their patterns, waiting until *Air Force One* was on the ground. It was a spontaneous gesture, and Chappell knew instantly what it meant: *They're saluting Kennedy.*

There was a wisp of white smoke as *Air Force One*'s wheels met the concrete and a momentary shudder within the plane. Roberts felt it, looked up from his typewriter, and checked his watch. It was 5:59 in Washington, 4:59 in Dallas. Lyndon Baines Johnson had completed his first flight as President. John Fitzgerald Kennedy had finished his last.

Back in the tail compartment, brooding over the coffin, Kenny O'Donnell remembered a scene four months earlier at Shannon Airport in Ireland. The girls from Bunratty Castle, in their medieval dress, had sung one last chorus of "Danny Boy" as Kennedy waved and disappeared into *Air Force One*. Somebody in the crowd held up a hand-scrawled sign with the title of an old, sad ballad about a young Irishman who had gone away to fight— and to die. The sign had burned itself into O'Donnell's memory,

231

and he thought of it now as the same plane taxied slowly toward the floodlights across the field and the crowds that had gathered to mourn over Kennedy. The sign said simply:

JOHNNY, I HARDLY KNEW YE.

Chapter Eight
Hail to the Chief

During the Kennedy years, Vice President Lyndon B. Johnson quickly became the administration's premier traveler. A man of restless energy and with scant substantive work to do within the government, LBJ was constantly employed by Kennedy as an ambassador of goodwill abroad and a political emissary at home. The Vice President loved both his travel assignments and the handsome Boeings that Kennedy put at his disposal.

Nobody ever spent any time around Lyndon Johnson without coming away with yarns galore. Ralph Albertazzie flew Vice President Johnson on most of his trips during the Kennedy years and got to know the temperamental Texan better than he ever got to know President Nixon.

During Johnson's round-the-world flight in June 1961, LBJ was given a tremendous send-off at Manila after conferring with Philippine president Ferdinand Marcos. Johnson was already at the top of the stairs to the plane, waving and smiling and posing for last-minute pictures, when George Reedy, the burly White House press secretary, came straggling out of the crowd.

Reedy put one foot on the stairs. From the top came the voice of LBJ: "Now, George, just where in hell do you think you're going?"

"I'm coming aboard the plane, Mr. Vice President."

"Now, George," said Johnson, continuing to smile and wave at the crowd. "Now, George, you just get your fat ass down from there and get on over to the press plane. You're not coming on here."

"But, sir, my seat's on this plane! And all my bags are on it."

"George, you heard me. So get your fat ass out of there. If you keep coming up, George, I'm going to push you off the goddam stairs. If you want to go to Taiwan, well, you better get yourself on that press plane over there. Now git!"

Reedy looked up at the still-waving, still-smiling LBJ, sighed dejectedly, and lumbered off toward the Pan American 707 chartered by the traveling press corps.

Johnson was like that. He delighted in berating his staff, sometimes unmercifully and often in the presence of total strangers. But he would make up just as fast. Reedy was one of LBJ's respected assistants. He was accustomed to the routine.

Once, in the company of a couple of reporters, Johnson laced into Reedy in a way that would have signaled a permanent break between ordinary men. A bit later, after Reedy had padded away to lick his wounds like some huge St. Bernard, Johnson beckoned the reporters to accompany him "while we find ol' George and tell him about his vacation."

The reporters were incredulous. One of them remarked that the previous dressing-down seemed like an odd prelude to rewarding Reedy with a coveted vacation. LBJ disagreed. "You don't reward a man when he's feeling good—you do it when he's humbled and feeling rotten."

On his Asian tour for President Kennedy, Johnson's well-known penchant for secrecy was breached by an Associated Press report that he was bringing an offer of $27 million in U.S. aid to Ngo Dinh Diem, the embattled head of the South Vietnam regime in Saigon, who was still being propped up by the Kennedy administration.

The Vice President was furious with the AP reporter, Spencer Davis, and kept needling him all the way to Asia. At one point, he called out to then Ambassador (now columnist) Carl Rowan,

234

who had been borrowed to handle press relations on the trip, "Carl, do I look like I'm wearing glass pants?" Rowan replied that the vice-presidential trousers looked quite ordinary to him. "Well," sneered Johnson, "If I'm not wearing glass pants, how in the hell can Spencer Davis see $27 million in my pocket?" As it turned out, the assistance figure amounted to approximately $25 million.

In September 1961, Secretary-General Dag Hammarskjöld of the United Nations was killed in a tragic plane crash in Rhodesia. President Kennedy delegated Vice President Johnson to be the official American representative at the funeral to be held in Uppsala, not far from Stockholm.

Albertazzie planned to fly nonstop from Washington to Stockholm, but a day before departure he got word from the White House that President Kennedy wanted Adlai Stevenson, the U.N. ambassador, and the Swedish ambassador to the U.N. to accompany Johnson on the flight. So Albertazzie notified the Vice President's office that *Air Force Two* would have to stop at New York to pick up Stevenson and the Swedish diplomat, a woman, and then continue on to Stockholm. To his surprise, Johnson vetoed the plan.

"If they want to ride on *my* plane," the Vice President informed Albertazzie, "why, tell 'em to come on down here and leave with me."

Johnson often displayed disdain for the urbane Stevenson, twice the Democratic Party's standard bearer and a political rival of Johnson's in the 1960 convention. There is no evidence that Stevenson held Johnson in any higher esteem.

But Stevenson and the Swedish official complied with the Vice President's wishes. They were already aboard the Boeing 707 at Andrews Air Force Base outside Washington when the Vice President's motorcade, with flashing red lights, swooped onto the airfield and stopped at the ramp.

Albertazzie dispatched one of the plane's stewards to help Johnson with his luggage. A moment later, the steward bounded back up the stairs with a troubled look.

"I told the Vice President that Ambassador Stevenson and the Swedish lady were already aboard, waiting in the stateroom for him," he informed Albertazzie, "and now the Vice President is

235

doggone mad. He says he wants them out of there and he ain't going to get on the plane until they move.''

Albertazzie advised the steward there was nothing to do but inform Stevenson and the lady diplomat that Johnson wanted to use the executive compartment "in privacy for a while." Would they mind, please, taking other seats in the rear?

"Why, why, this is preposterous!" Stevenson sputtered. But he moved out, along with the puzzled Swedish woman, so Johnson could have his privacy.

No sooner had LBJ ensconced himself in the suite when he summoned a steward. "Go tell Ambassador Stevenson and that Swedish gal that I'd like to have them join me in here," he decreed. So, once again, they moved.

"Johnson was like that," Albertazzie recalled. "He was the senior official and he just wanted everybody to understand that this was his plane, his trip, and he was in charge."

The trip was an overnight flight. Johnson was a gracious host, ordering drinks all around and regaling his guests with one story after another. Johnson drank scotch and soda, insisting as usual that the steward open a fresh bottle of soda in front of him and pour it directly into his glass. (All that LBJ talk about "bourbon and branch water" was just part of the imagery of a Texas politician.)

The drinks and the stories continued well into the evening and long over the Atlantic. Stevenson, who couldn't get a word in and couldn't keep his eyes open, finally excused himself and sought out a row of seats toward the rear of the plane where he could sleep. After a few more scotches and some banter with the crew, LBJ generously surrendered the stateroom to the Swedish woman, grabbed a blanket, and went down the aisle seeking a place to stretch out his lanky frame. He spotted a pair of double seats facing each other, but there already was a body lying there beneath a blanket. Johnson beckoned a steward and, in a hoarse whisper, uttered a command. "Tell that sonofabitch to move over."

The sonofabitch stirred, pushed back his blanket, and looked up sleepily at Johnson. It was Adlai Stevenson.

"But he moved over," Albertazzie recounted. "The Vice President flopped down on a pair of seats beside him and the two slept side by side the rest of the night."

236

Johnson had told the crew that he wanted to be awakened about thirty minutes before arrival in Stockholm. Albertazzie doubted that would be sufficient for dressing and eating breakfast but figured the Vice President ought to know how much time he needed to eat breakfast, shave, and get into his striped trousers and cutaway coat, the required attire for the Hammarskjöld funeral.

Albertazzie had already put *Air Force Two* into the Stockholm landing pattern for its scheduled arrival at noon sharp, when a Johnson military aide came into the cockpit. Johnson wanted the landing delayed for thirty minutes.

"I was just ten minutes from touching down," Albertazzie recalled. "The Swedish government had assembled quite a crowd of officials and diplomats to greet the Vice President. They were already down there, waiting. But there was nothing to do but comply. Orders are orders."

Albertazzie grabbed his radiophone and hastily notified the tower at Stockholm that the Vice President's plane—by then clearly within view of people on the ground—would circle the airfield for half an hour.

"The Swede in the tower, in puzzled English, fired back a quick protest. Didn't the Vice President of the United States know that a sizable delegation was awaiting him? I said yep, he certainly did and he appreciated it, too, but the Vice President was 'occupied.' It would be impossible to land on time. Would the tower please pass on our apologies?"

When the tardy plane finally rolled to a stop before the impatient assemblage at the terminal, Albertazzie stepped out of the cockpit in time to see LBJ emerge from his stateroom, fully decked out in his formal regalia, and carrying a silk top hat in his hand.

"Captain," said Johnson, gingerly holding up the shiny topper, "what do I do with this thing—wear it or carry it?"

Albertazzie was no expert on diplomatic attire, but fortunately he had glanced out the window at the waiting group of dignitaries. All the men were bareheaded. "Sir," he replied, "you just carry it."

Johnson, greatly relieved, stepped out of the plane to greet his hosts.

Johnson's inexhaustible energy and incomparable ego would

237

have strained an ordinary marriage, but then Lady Bird Johnson was no ordinary woman. He loved her, respected her, and was immensely proud of her, but he had an admiring eye for pretty younger women and liked having them in his company and on his staff. Mrs. Johnson humored him, up to a point, and frequently arranged to seat attractive women on each side of him at dinner parties.

One of his favorites in the press corps was NBC's Nancy Hanschman (later Mrs. C. Wyatt Dickerson), a talented reporter who had been covering LBJ ever since his rise to power in the Senate. "I loved being with LBJ, but sex had nothing to do with it," she explained in her memoirs of twenty-five years in Washington, *Among Those Present.* "I enjoyed him because power is fascinating. Besides, he could be tremendously charming, witty, and downright funny."

After the Hammarskjöld funeral, Albertazzie assumed the Vice President would want to return directly to Washington. But Johnson had other ideas. No sooner had he reboarded *Air Force Two* than he ordered the radio operator to "get Nancy Hanschman on the phone. She's in Paris and that's where we're going."

Radio-telephone communications aboard the presidential planes are the best in the world, but they weren't good enough to find Nancy Hanschman in Paris. Informed she apparently was not in the French capital as he had thought, LBJ exploded. "Well, by God, then call NBC in Washington, or New York, and find out where she is. I want to talk to her."

While Albertazzie put the plane on a heading for Paris and notified the Air Force Command Post in Washington of the Vice President's changed itinerary, the radio operator began scouring the United States and Europe for a clue to Nancy's whereabouts. Finally, with LBJ growing more impatient by the minute, he located her in Vienna and got her on the phone.

The radio telephone, even from *Air Force Two*, is as open as any old-fashioned, small-town party line. It is a high-frequency voice system. Any radio operator sweeping the airwaves can listen in. If Johnson knew, he certainly didn't care.

"He started right in, pleading with her to leave Vienna and get to Paris," recalls Albertazzie. 'I want to take you to dinner, I want to entertain you,' he kept telling her. And Nancy, on the

238

other end, was saying, 'Oh, Mr. Vice President, that's sweet of you and I'd like to do it, but I'm here on vacation, and I just can't leave Vienna now.' But LBJ didn't want to take no for an answer. 'Honey,' he said, 'I've been just waiting for this opportunity to take you out in Paris, so you-all just come meet me now—please. We're going to have a good time.'

"Well, that conversation must have gone on for twenty minutes over the open channel, with the Vice President begging her over and over to meet him in Paris, and she, just as repeatedly, saying she'd love to, but she just couldn't leave Vienna. Finally, he realized he wasn't making any headway with her, so he hung up. I had heard a lot of stories about Johnson's interest in women, but this was the first time I was aware of it firsthand. What surprised me was how public he was about it."

Nor did Johnson make an effort to hide his fondness for the company of Mary Margaret Wiley, a pretty secretary who later married another LBJ aide, Jack Valenti. Johnson simply assumed that everybody understood his love for Lady Bird, and hers for him. Since there was no question about that in his own mind, he did not expect that people would see anything amiss with the flirtatious attention he delighted in paying other women. Lady Bird, secure in her own relationship with him, tolerated it all with rare good nature and some amusement.

On one occasion, what normally would have been a quick overnight flight out of Washington unexpectedly turned into a three-day safari. It was a classic example of Johnsonian whim.

Johnson had flown to Kansas City, Missouri, to address a Democratic fund-raising dinner. Since it was supposed to be a quick trip, only a handful of persons accompanied him: an ever-present pair of Secret Service agents, a military aide, and secretary Mary Margaret Wiley. Shortly after LBJ's arrival, a fire broke out in the kitchen of the hotel where the dinner was to be held, forcing cancellation of the event.

Albertazzie, who had given his crew the night off, heard about the blaze on a radio newscast while visiting friends in Kansas City. He hustled back to the airport, rounded up the crew, and hurriedly made preparations for what he supposed would be an immediate return to Washington.

As soon as Johnson and the others were aboard, Albertazzie

started the engines, activated his Washington-bound flight plan, and contacted the tower. The plane was already taxiing to the runway when a hand tapped his shoulder. It was LBJ's Air Force aide. The Vice President, he said, didn't want to go back to Washington. He wanted to go to the ranch instead.

So they flew to Texas, landing at Bergstrom Air Force Base outside Austin. Johnson and his companions drove to the LBJ ranch. Albertazzie and the crew stayed on the base, since Johnson had said he wanted to fly back to Washington early the next day.

Everything was in readiness the following morning, but departure time came and went—and no Johnson. Finally, Albertazzie got a call from the ranch from Stuart Knight, LBJ's senior agent who later became Secret Service director. "The man doesn't want to go to Washington," Knight said. "He wants to go to New York. He says he and Mary Margaret are going to see 'Death of a Salesman' on Broadway, then they're going to have dinner, and then we'll fly home after that."

The visit of a President or Vice President to New York City is a formidable undertaking even when it is unofficial. The city's politicians like to put on a good show and, of course, Manhattan's traffic has to be surmounted. That requires a substantial police motorcycle escort, the blocking of ramps and side streets, much flashing of red lights and the blowing of sirens. Then there was the matter of security, so extraordinary precautions had to be taken, including the placement of policemen on all the bridges and at key points along the route from the airport to the heart of the city.

New York's finest were all over Idlewild and the parkway when *Air Force Two* swooped in for LBJ's theatre date. The crew stayed aboard, since it would be only a matter of a few hours before the plane would be on its way again to Washington.

"Ten o'clock came, eleven o'clock came, and still no word," Albertazzie recalled. "Finally, about midnight, I heard from Stu Knight. The Vice President, he said, had decided to stay in New York overnight and would go to Washington the first thing in the morning . . . about nine A.M."

"So the cops were dismissed, and the crew and I moved the plane over to the Lockheed area for security and buttoned it up

240

for the night. We finally located some motel rooms and got to bed about 1:30 A.M. We were up again at 5:30 so we could get back to the plane and get it ready for departure at nine o'clock.

"Well, nine o'clock came and went and no sign of LBJ. About eleven o'clock, I located Stu Knight and asked, 'What's happening?'

" 'I don't know,' Stu said. 'Right now, the man is getting his hair cut. Then I think he's going to eat lunch. So it'll be some time after that before we get out of here. I'll call you if I find out.' "

Late in the afternoon, Albertazzie thought he detected increased police activity around the airport. Sure enough, about five o'clock, a motorcade with flashing red lights swept into view and stopped on the tarmac beside the plane. It was LBJ, along with Mary Margaret and the three aides. Albertazzie and the crew almost cheered.

Twenty minutes later, the plane was in the skies heading back to Washington. Johnson sent word up to the cockpit to "pour on the coal." He had a seven P.M. engagement and didn't want to be late.

"That's the way he was," Albertazzie said with a chuckle. "He was totally unpredictable, very demanding, and all that was quite unsettling. But he was so friendly with the crew, that you couldn't be angry or upset for very long. And what the heck, he was the Vice President. So we just did whatever he wanted to do."

When he became President, Lyndon Johnson luxuriated in the perquisites the White House afforded. Those who knew him, including reporters who covered him during his long political career, could not escape the imperious nature of the man. It was a natural quality with him; he considered himself superior to ordinary politicians, even while he retained a common touch and great personal vulnerability. He was a monarch with feet of clay.

Yet even the feet got royal treatment. Frank Cormier, chief Associated Press correspondent at the White House, wrote in his book *LBJ* that he once was startled aboard *Air Force One* to see Sergeant Paul Glynn, one of LBJ's attendants, kneel silently before the President and wash the man's feet. Johnson, talking

241

all the while, paid no heed as Glynn removed the presidential shoes and socks, cleansed first one foot and then the other, dried them, put on fresh socks, and replaced the shoes.

Lyndon Johnson lost no time in rearranging *Air Force One* to suit his expansive mood. The interior could accommodate about forty persons at the time of Kennedy's death. Johnson wanted several dozen more so that he could squeeze in additional senators, congressmen, and staffers to keep him company. He had the seats reversed so they faced toward the rear of the plane—toward his own compartment. He ripped out the cherrywood panels between the two and installed clear plastic dividers so he could keep an eye on everybody—and they on him. Johnson ordered a fancy chair that went up and down at the press of a button. The Secret Service called it the "throne," and there he presided high above the clouds. When he wanted privacy, the transparent panel could be covered with draperies.

Johnson loved to invite fellow travelers into his private compartment, where the seating space was cramped. So he asked the Air Force to remove the wall of his bedroom and replace it with an accordion divider that could be shoved out of the way. And he was proud as punch of the big kidney-shaped table, complete with telephone console, that served as his desk and gathering place aloft. It, too, went up and down at the press of a button. LBJ never tired of showing newcomers how it worked.

With Johnson as the new President, *Air Force One* practically wore a path through the skies between Washington and Texas, beginning with the Christmas holidays of 1963. Johnson loved to return to his native hill country and the LBJ ranch on the Pedernales River in central Texas. He flew home as often as he could get away from the White House.

"It's one place where they know if you're sick and care if you die," LBJ told reporters flying with him.

But he also wanted the rest of the country to know that he was a working President, even down on the ranch, and he had an idea just how the press could help him. He didn't like the prospect that the presidency would be covered in stories using the dateline of Austin, the Texas capital. "How about using Johnson City?" he asked.

"It's my home," Johnson added, explaining that his grand-

242

daddy had founded the town where he grew up and first ran for Congress. "Besides, it's my legal residence."

But the traveling press never yielded to that request unless LBJ actually went to Johnson City. After all, reporters were quartered many miles away in Austin, and the daily White House briefings were held there.

Johnson's all-embracing style was even more evident aboard *Air Force One* than around the White House. The magic carpet has a way of intoxicating Presidents, imparting a sense of power every bit as real as the jet engines outside the cabin windows. One moment he could be earthy, profane, selfish, devious, or rude, and then polite, considerate, affectionate, and downright charming. Whatever his mood, it was usually excessive.

In September 1964, LBJ interrupted his election campaigning long enough to escort Italian diplomat Manlio Brozio on a fast visit to the headquarters of the Strategic Air Command near Omaha. The distinguished guest had recently been named secretary-general of the North Atlantic Treaty Organization (NATO) and Johnson wanted to impress him with the stringency of U.S. controls over nuclear weapons. On the return flight to Washington, after several drinks, the President decided that the press had not had sufficient chance to interrogate the courtly Brozio. So LBJ strode to the rear of the plane and ordered the pool reporters to come up to his suite to interview "one of the wisest, most experienced . . . greatest statesmen of Europe."

Brozio was deep in conversation with Undersecretary of State George Ball when LBJ flung open the cabin door. Grabbing the surprised Brozio by the arm, he marched him into the adjoining bedroom, gravely introduced each of the reporters, and then bellowed over his shoulder as he retreated to the bathroom: "Now you-all interview the hell out of him while I take a leak!"

Returning from New York to Washington on another trip, Johnson encountered an unchewable hunk of gristle in the steak sandwich he was eating. The President put a hand to his mouth, removed the gristle, and hurled it across the compartment. It landed in a bowl of potato chips on the table between Lady Bird Johnson and Mary McGrory of the *Washington Star*.

During the 1964 presidential campaign, Johnson became so euphoric over the odds that he would beat Goldwater that he an-

243

nounced to reporters he would spend more time electing other Democrats to Congress and "unelecting" a few Republicans. He turned to the reporters aboard *Air Force One* and, to their surprise, insisted they give him the names of Republicans that "deserve to be defeated." The newsmen were reluctant to get trapped in that kind of game, but LBJ kept prodding. Finally, one blurted that he'd like to see Republican Congressman Bob Dole of Kansas defeated in November. Sure enough, a couple of days later, the President rearranged his campaign schedule to squeeze in an airport rally at Wichita on behalf of Dole's Democratic challenger. Dole won anyway.

On a visit to Australia in 1966, Johnson unabashedly reached across the table on *Air Force One* and forked up several strips of bacon from the plate of the wife of Prime Minister Harold Holt. LBJ was especially fond of the Holts. The Australian leader was a jovial chap who enjoyed Johnson's ebullience as a raconteur and often countered with some pretty spicy yarns of his own. Mrs. Holt was a pert, shapely woman, with a ready smile and a keen sense of humor. On another leg of that trip, LBJ put his arm around Mrs. Holt's shoulders and stared ostentatiously into the plunging neckline of her dress. Then, cupping both of his huge hands, he turned to the prime minister with a grin and said: "Harold, you sure know how to pick 'em." Lady Bird fixed LBJ with a reproving glare, but Mrs. Holt simply tossed back her head and burst into laughter.

Master Sgt. Joe Ayres had been Johnson's personal steward aboard *Air Force One* for some time when, one day, reporters learned that he had asked for and gotten a different assignment from Special Air Missions headquarters. It didn't take long to find out what had happened. The day previous, it seems, on a trip back to Washington, LBJ had developed an insatiable craving for diet root beer. In a short time, he had consumed all of the six bottles aboard. Ayres gave him the bad news and apologetically offered him a choice of half a dozen other diet drinks. LBJ exploded in anger, according to Frank Cormier of Associated Press. "How many times do I have to tell you that I want diet root beer on this plane at all times?" Johnson bellowed at the hapless Ayres. "It's not a difficult transaction. You can buy the fuckin' stuff anywhere. Sergeant, I want an order sent out to all

244

Air Force bases: stock root beer!'' The episode so unnerved the gentle Ayres that he requested a transfer.

Johnson's penchant for quibbling with reporters about the accuracy of their stories was part of the game he played. He wanted to make sure they put him in the best possible light, a natural attitude for any politician, but one that LBJ carried to extremes. Nor was he above suggesting that they fudge the truth a little if he feared that accuracy might reflect adversely on him.

Reporters aboard the President's plane got an early taste of the Johnson style on a flight back to Washington from Texas just six weeks after the Kennedy assassination.

The plane was barely off the ground at Bergstrom Air Force Base, near Austin, when LBJ appeared in the aisle beside the reporters' table and began to talk. Sensing that the President was warming up for a long conversation, Cormier gave LBJ his seat and described what followed in his personal account, *LBJ, The Way He Was:*

"I'm the only President you've got," Johnson told us, "and I intend to be President of all the people. I need your help. If I succeed, you succeed. We all succeed together or fail together. With your help, I'll do the best job that's in me for our country. I don't want Jack Kennedy looking down at me from heaven and saying he picked the wrong Vice President. But I can't do the job alone. I need your help."

Then, lowering his voice to an earnest drawl, Lyndon Johnson proposed how he would like to cut a deal with the press.

"I'll tell you everything. . . . You'll know everything I do. You'll be as well informed as any member of the Cabinet. There won't be any secrets except where the national security is involved. You'll be able to write everything. Of course"—and this shocked those among us who weren't accustomed to his verbal excesses—"I may go into a strange bedroom every now and then that I won't want you to write about, but otherwise you can write everything. . . . If you-all help me, I'll help you. I'll make you-all big men in your profession."

Cormier thought he ought to set Johnson straight on the role

245

of the press. There was no way reporters could transform themselves into the kind of cheerleaders that LBJ wanted.

"Mr. President," he began, "don't you realize that sooner or later every reporter around this table is going to write something that'll make you mad as hell?"

Johnson, surprised and injured, replied, "Why, I never got mad at a newsman in my life except for one NBC man—and he broke my confidence."

Presidential trips were a convenient vehicle for Johnson because the press pool was a captive audience. The pool that traveled with him normally consisted of a reporter for each national wire service—United Press International and Associated Press—plus representatives of the three radio-television networks and one or two poolers for the major newspapers and news magazines. Their responsibility was not only to provide coverage for their own news organizations but to report on presidential activities aloft to the correspondents following *Air Force One* in the chartered press planes.

Johnson's airborne attempts to handle the press were dramatized neatly after his Atlantic City speech to the United Steelworkers convention in September during the 1964 presidential campaign. Although LBJ normally avoided uttering harsh personal words about his Republican rival, Barry Goldwater, he was infuriated with the latter's accusation that the Johnson administration was "soft on communism." So LBJ, apparently carried away by the enthusiastic cheers of his audience, had gone beyond his usual campaign speech to declare: "You know, it takes a man who loves his country to build a house, instead of a raving, ranting demagogue who wants to tear one down."

By the time he was back at the airport, LBJ had misgivings about what he had said and its likely impact on the voters. He summoned pool reporters to fly back to Washington with him aboard the cramped presidential helicopter. Cormier quickly discovered why.

"You-all notice that in the speech back there I didn't say anything mean about Goldwater," the President insisted. "I talked about 'ravin,' rantin' demagogues,' *plural*. I wasn't referring to any single individual. I just thought you-all might have misunderstood."

Reporters listened politely, but remained convinced that they had heard him right the first time. Back at the White House, they persuaded Press Secretary George Reedy to replay the Signal Corps tape recording of the Atlantic City speech. Reedy came back with a forthright answer: "He said 'demagogue.'"

Four reporters in the press pool were sharing highballs with President Johnson in his airborne parlor on another occasion when LBJ began ruminating aloud about all the changes that had occurred in world leadership. He was in a buoyant mood, savoring his tremendous election victory over Goldwater in 1964.

"Look around the world," Johnson was saying. "Khrushchev's gone. Macmillan's gone. Adenauer's gone. Segni's gone. Nehru's gone. Who's left—de Gaulle?"

There was a sneering tone in Johnson's voice as he uttered the French president's name, Cormier said. Then, leaning back in his massive "throne chair," as the crew dubbed it, LBJ thumped his chest in Tarzan fashion and bellowed, "I am the king!"

As reporters left the plane, Reedy took pains to remind them that they had been the President's social guests and were not there as news gatherers. "Gentlemen," Reedy solemnly intoned, "you did not see the President of the United States tonight."

It was President Johnson's consummate curiosity that brought about the installation of a panel of three digital clocks in the presidential compartment of SAM 26000. Johnson was as fascinated as a schoolboy by the different stages of daily activity at any given moment in the various time zones around the globe. He incessantly wanted to know the time of day at his eventual destination, or the time back in Washington, or the time in the zone he was then flying through.

Presidential assistant Jack Valenti was LBJ's favorite time-keeper, as well as all-around Man Friday. He took to wearing several watches on his wrists, each timepiece set for the hour in a different place on earth.

"Jack!" LBJ would bellow, "what the hell time is it?"

The diminutive Valenti would dash up to the presidential chair and fall to his knees in a pose of worshipful attention.

"Where, Mr. President? In Washington? Where we're going? Or where we are right now?"

"Give me all of them."

247

Valenti would dutifully scan the watches on one wrist and then the other, repeating the times for the President. Johnson would grunt acknowledgment—and a short while later bellow again for Valenti.

In the course of a flight, the agile Valenti would be up and down on his knees before LBJ more often than an altar boy attending a cardinal at high mass. On long overseas trips, when human perception of time fades into a blur, Valenti sometimes would forget which watch told which time. That would necessitate scrambling back to his feet and dashing up to the cockpit to inquire of the crew. Meantime, the impatient Johnson would complain loudly about the inability of certain people on his staff to perform a simple task like telling time.

"I felt sorry for Valenti," said flight engineer Joe Chappell. "So I went to the drug store after one trip and bought three inexpensive alarm clocks with big dials and had the carpenter shop at Andrews build a small case around them that could be hung on the wall. The trouble was I would forget to rewind a clock, or one of the alarms would go off—and that would really annoy LBJ."

To solve the problem, the *Air Force One* crew eventually appealed to the Bulova Watch Company. It came up with a trio of electronic digital clocks in a handsome wall mounting, at no cost to the taxpayers. It also saved a lot of wear and tear on Valenti's kneecaps.

Lyndon Johnson rode his big jet like a range boss on a cattle drive, dashing here and there across the globe, rounding up stray prime ministers, dispensing his brand of Pedernales wisdom and money from the American chuck wagon, and radioing ahead for more root beer and Texas-size steaks.

In December, 1967, on short notice, he dashed off to Melbourne, Australia, for the memorial service for his friend, the late Prime Minister Holt. Thirty-six hours later he was airborne again, this time to Vietnam by way of Thailand, and then on to Karachi, Pakistan, followed by a long hop to Rome and a pre-Christmas call on Pope Paul VI before flying home to Washington, a four-and-a-half-day globe-girdling stunt that, as presidential aide Harry McPherson later said, "proved little more than the speed of *Air Force One*."

But LBJ loved every minute of the record he had set and the weight he had lost on board. He had brought along his exercise bicycle, which the crew bolted to the floor just forward of his presidential compartment. There, clad in his sweat suit, LBJ furiously pumped away while the huge Boeing sped across the South Pacific at 600 miles an hour.

LBJ had to surrender the airplane when he left office, but he managed to take a few souvenirs back to Texas with him. The Johnson staff obtained Nixon's consent to use it to fly LBJ home to the ranch following Nixon's inauguration on January 20, 1969. At Bergstrom, Johnson's people had the plane stripped of almost every passenger convenience.

"When I took over the plane after it came back from Texas, I found an empty larder," said Albertazzie. "We had no presidential china, no *Air Force One* silverware, no *Air Force One* cigarettes, no cocktail napkins, no towels—not even any paper products like toilet tissue. All these items were not stamped LBJ either, but were imprinted AIR FORCE ONE. But they were all gone.

"Even LBJ's special executive chair—the one we called 'the throne'—was unbolted from the floor and taken away. The presidential stateroom was bare of pillows, blankets, everything that bore the presidential seal. I couldn't believe my eyes."

All of the loot had been trucked away for deposit and eventual display at the LBJ Library, being constructed on the campus of the University of Texas at Austin. Especially missed by the crew was the matched set of presidential chinaware. It had been aboard since SAM 26000 was first given presidential status in 1962 under Kennedy, and had been specially ordered and selected by Jacqueline Kennedy—handsome beige plates with gold edging, each delicately embossed with the seal of the President of the United States.

Lyndon Johnson rode *Air Force One* only twice after he left office. President and Mrs. Nixon invited the Johnsons to fly with them from San Clemente to Arcata, California, for the dedication of the new Lady Bird Johnson Redwood Forest, a tribute to her efforts to beautify America. On the way back, instead of putting the Johnsons aboard the VIP jet that had brought them up from Texas, Nixon ordered Albertazzie to fly LBJ and Lady

Bird home in *Air Force One*. Johnson came into the cockpit shortly after the Nixons had left the plane at El Toro Marine Base outside San Clemente.

"I felt this big hand on my shoulder and it was LBJ," said Albertazzie. Johnson climbed into the observer's seat just behind the pilot, chatted with Albertazzie about flying the new First Family, inquired about members of the old LBJ crew, and spoke of the interior changes that Nixon had ordered. "I like your plane, Ralph," LBJ said. He sounded wistful.

Johnson's final flight on *Air Force One* occurred several days after his fatal heart attack, January 22, 1973, at the ranch. Returning the body from Washington, where LBJ had lain in state at the Capitol, pilot Albertazzie was tapped once more on the shoulder. It was Mrs. Johnson.

"Good to see you, Ralph," Lady Bird said quietly. "Lyndon would have been happy to know you were flying him home on his final trip."

Air Force One was nearly seven years old when Richard Nixon became its master on Inauguration Day in January 1969. It had already outlasted and outflown every previous presidential aircraft. But it was in mint condition, thanks to the extraordinary maintenance provided by the Special Air Missions ground crews at Andrews Air Force Base. And it was electronically superior to every other Boeing 707 flying anywhere in the world.

Still, even near-perfect machines can develop an unsuspected weakness at some unexpected moment—and that would not do for the airplane that carried the President of the United States. So in March 1969, SAM 26000 went back to the Boeing factory for its first major overhaul. It was to be almost totally dismantled, from the cockpit to the lavatories in the tail section. The handsome interior was removed and the fuselage stripped to its metal shell while aeronautical engineers with complicated testing equipment checked its structural soundness and sleuthed about for minor flaws or hints of metal fatigue. All the systems aboard—communications and navigation gear, electrical wiring, fuel lines, engines, hydraulic power units, and the like—were minutely examined and either reinstalled or replaced with newer, more advanced systems. It was an expensive, time-consuming process, that ran to several millions of dollars. It took *Air Force One* out of service for nearly three months.

To this day, stories abound that Nixon could hardly wait to get his hands on *Air Force One* so he could redesign the interior to suit his fancy. Such talk, repeated even by ex-staffers like John Dean, may fit the popular image of Nixon but it does not fit the facts. A reconfiguration of the big Boeing was already in the planning stages during the final months of the Johnson administration in 1968.

The Air Force had notified the White House that SAM 26000 was due for its first overhaul in March 1969—regardless of whether Nixon or Democrat Hubert H. Humphrey won the election. Nixon first learned about it from President Johnson during one of their post-election transition chats.

"If you're planning any major trips early in your first year," LBJ informed his successor, "you ought to know that the Pentagon wants to send *Air Force One* back to Lockheed for overhaul in the spring. It hasn't had one for six years—and I guess you know I used it pretty hard."

Actually, some Special Air Missions brass had hoped to get at the overhaul sooner—during the final months of the Johnson presidency, after LBJ announced he would not seek reelection. But such hopes didn't reckon with Johnson's own travel plans for his last year in office. And there was another reason, too. Whoever won the presidency, cooler heads observed, would probably want to make some internal changes anyway in his special airplane. Why not postpone the mechanical overhaul until the new President was in the White House so that the redesign of the interior could be accomplished at the same time, without requiring further out-of-service time?

Nixon delegated the task to Haldeman, his chief assistant, who accepted it with alacrity. Before long, the President's military assistant, Col. James D. Hughes, pilot Albertazzie, and Lockheed designers were busily fashioning a new interior for *Air Force One* that would do justice to the President of the United States.

They had ample precedent for thinking big. During the Kennedy and particularly the Johnson years, SAM 26000 had received more than $5,000,000 in technical and physical altera-

251

tions. Lyndon Johnson had been the biggest cosmetician of them all.

"Seems like he wanted interior changes made before—or after—nearly every trip," chuckled one crew member.

After such profligacy, the Nixon staff had little reason to pinch pennies in the redesigning and outfitting of *Air Force One.* Nearly $800,000 was spent on the new interior alone. But they did more than throw tax dollars at the airplane. They came up with a layout that worked equally well for the First Family, the presidential staff, and the crew. In the process, Boeing and the White House conceived a floor plan that has remained basically unchanged to this day, and eventually would serve as a model for the configuration of SAM 27000, the newest presidential plane.

The heart of the scheme was the creation of a special three-room suite of private quarters for the President and his family up forward over the wings, the most stable and quiet area of the Boeing 707. The suite consists of a combination office and sitting room for the Chief Executive, a smaller sitting room for the First Lady, and a large lounge that affords them a place to sit together as a family or with friends—or may be used as a conference room by the President, key staff persons, or accompanying dignitaries. The presidential suite has its own lavatory and ample closet and storage room.

A second feature was another distinct departure from the old layout of SAM 26000. A special aisle was designed along the left side of the interior so that fuselage traffic could move past the First Family's quarters without intruding on their privacy.

Just forward of the presidential suite is the seating area for the Secret Service detachment traveling with the President. Between this security compartment and the cockpit, SAM 26000's new interior featured an elaborate presidential communications console along the left side of the fuselage. On the right is the forward galley, where the First Family's meals are prepared, plus another lavatory for crew and staff.

To the rear of the presidential suite is a roomy staff compartment the width of the fuselage, with two built-in typing stations for secretarial work. Behind that is an eight-seat guest suite for VIPs traveling with the President, followed by a compartment shared by the handful of news reporters usually present on every flight and *Air Force One*'s security guards. A larger galley and additional lavatories occupy the tail section.

All in all, it is an extremely functional layout, vastly superior to the original Kennedy configuration and Johnson's altered version. It even includes a trap door, concealed in the aisle floor forward of the presidential suite, which allows flight communicators to have access to the secret encoding equipment in the hold below. It also permits a flight steward to dash down to the onboard freezers for a special steak for the President or a change of clothing for the First Lady.

The color scheme retained the soft beiges, sand tones, and golds that Lady Bird Johnson had used during one of LBJ's redecorating ventures. Its western or desert theme, accented here and there with a splash of bright yellow, orange, green, or blue, appealed equally to Pat Nixon.

Nixon's favorite seat in the lounge of SAM 26000 was just inside the internal doorway on the right side of the plane. It faced to the rear, enabling him to command the room since all the other seats faced forward. There was one exception—an identical chair on the opposite side of the doorway. It was one of Mrs. Nixon's favorite spots as well as a seat that Henry Kissinger preferred because it put him closest to the President. On the wall behind this chair was a splendid replica of the Great Seal of the President. And behind the seal lies a story.

The White House staff had authorized *Time* magazine to photograph the new President at work aboard his freshly redone airplane. The photos came out beautifully, or so almost everyone thought. But not Bob Haldeman, the White House staff boss. He took one look at the magazine and immediately put through a telephone call to *Air Force One*, which just happened to be aloft on a crew proficiency flight.

"You know that seal on the wall in the lounge?" Haldeman asked chief flight engineer Chappell. "Well, I want it moved to the other side of the doorway. Right away."

When Chappell glanced at the latest *Time,* he knew instantly what had upset Haldeman. One photograph showed Nixon and Kissinger conferring together in the lounge, each sitting in his favorite spot. The wall behind the President was blank, while

253

clearly visible behind Kissinger's head was the presidential seal. Haldeman plainly did not want to see any more photographs like that.

Chappell obligingly unscrewed the seal and shifted it to an appropriate spot on the wall in back of the President's chair. But that left a problem: three very unattractive holes in the wall where the seal had hung. Replacing that small section of the compartment wall would cost the Air Force several hundred dollars or more.

"I just happened to be in a gift store a day or so later when I spied my answer," said Chappell. "There, up on a shelf, slightly dusty, was an American eagle plaque made out of plaster. I bought it. It cost the government $13 plus tax. And it covered the holes perfectly. Even Haldeman liked it."

The newly furbished Boeing came back from her factory overhaul in good time for Nixon's thirteen-day round-the-world flight to the Philippines, Indonesia, Thailand, India, Pakistan, Rumania, and Britain in July 1969. At the big hangar at Andrews they waxed the wings, polished the fuselage, and restocked the passenger compartments with the matchbooks, cigarette packs, and notepads that say AIR FORCE ONE. Preparations in the galleys were even more extensive. Chief steward Shell planned the menus, supervised food preparation, stowed it all in *Air Force One*'s cargo freezers, and served nearly 800 individual meals to the President, the staff, and the crew.

In mid-1971, when the nation began looking ahead to its bicentennial birthday in 1976, Nixon officially named his plane *The Spirit of '76*. That seemed like a nifty idea to the President and his staff, but it never quite caught the fancy of the public or the press. While the White House and the Pentagon officially referred to SAM 26000 as *The Spirit of '76* in all public announcements and press releases, everyone else just kept on calling it *Air Force One*. Somehow that seemed to symbolize the American spirit and heritage just as aptly as the Revolutionary slogan.

But even a magic carpet as magnificent as SAM 26000 created some problems for both the President and the Air Force. Perhaps the biggest was that it was the only intercontinental Boeing in the government's transport fleet. It could outfly and outdistance the other Boeings, which were the original 120 series 707s.

254

The pilots called them "short-legged." They lacked 26000's fuel capacity for long nonstop flights. Moreover, they were limited in performance because they required longer runways than 26000 with its more powerful jet engines.

These shortcomings robbed *Air Force One* of some of its performance potential because one of the older Boeings, usually SAM 970, had to serve as the backup aircraft for the primary plane. *Air Force One*'s superior performance capabilities had to be downgraded to compensate for the limitations imposed by the less powerful, shorter-range Boeing 707-120's. Flight schedules had to be adjusted to accommodate more frequent refueling sites, and trip planners had to rely on stops at the major airports of the world because the backup plane couldn't use the shorter runways that might be closer to the President's actual destination.

It wasn't long before the Air Force began planning for the day when SAM 26000 no longer would be handicapped by the lesser capabilities of its companion airplane. That day loomed in 1972 as the Vietnam war drew to an end. The Air Force now had money it didn't have to spend on bombers, fighters, and ammunition for the conflict there. At long last it seemed reasonable to place an order with Boeing for a successor to the ten-year-old SAM 26000. The Boeing Company was only too happy to comply. So, too, was Nigerian Airways.

Boeing already had laid the keel for an intercontinental Boeing 707-353 for the Nigerian government's airline when the order for a new *Air Force One* came in from Washington. Boeing's sales force and American diplomats persuaded Nigeria to transfer its deposit to another Boeing to accommodate the White House.

When SAM 27000 finally arrived at Andrews Air Force Base two days before Christmas 1972, only someone spotting the tail number would have known it was a new *Air Force One*. Outwardly, it was a twin of SAM 26000. It was the same length, had the same wingspan, was powered by identical (and interchangeable) jet engines, and sported the same exterior markings.

There were similarities internally, too. The cockpit configuration and instrumentation of SAM 27000 and 26000 are identical, as well as the navigation systems, the oxygen systems, even the complex communications center, the galleys, and the trap door

255

that gives access to the secret coding equipment, the freezers and First Family wardrobe storage in the cargo hold. SAM 27000, delivered at a cost of $12,900,000, courtesy of the taxpayers, was not a better plane than SAM 26000—only newer.

Its price tag, in fact, would have been even higher had not Albertazzie persuaded the Air Force in 1969 to retain in the inventory a set of four Pratt & Whitney JT3D-3B turbofan engines that had been purchased six years before as spares for SAM 26000. When the Air Force bought them in 1963, the price per engine was about $100,000. Their cost in 1972 would have been approximately $1,000,000 apiece.

Now SAM 26000 was relegated to a backup role. President Nixon transferred the name *Spirit of '76* to his shiny new *Air Force One* and flew off to San Clemente on his first flight on February 8, 1973. He apparently enjoyed it, but word soon filtered out that other members of the First Family were quite unhappy with the interior layout masterminded by Haldeman.

The fuss came as no surprise to Albertazzie. Back in the early planning stages, a model of the new plane's floor plan had been displayed in the White House theatre for Mrs. Nixon to consider the color scheme and fabric selection.

"Is this the way Dick wants the airplane?" she inquired.

"Well, this is the way Mr. Haldeman said the President wanted it," Albertazzie replied.

The First Lady examined the plan again and made a face. "I don't think Dick is going to like it," she said.

Haldeman had placed the big staff compartment—his own domain—directly behind the President's office and the First Lady's tiny sitting room. That meant that the presidential lounge, a favorite gathering spot for Mrs. Nixon and daughters Tricia and Julie and their husbands, would no longer be adjacent to the presidential suite as it was on SAM 26000.

"In effect, the First Lady was being forced to travel through the staff compartment each time she wanted to enter or leave the lounge," said Albertazzie. "She took a pretty dim view of that."

Whatever her objections, they apparently did not impress the President at the time.

"Construction of the interior proceeded in line with the Haldeman blueprint," Albertazzie said. "After the first few trips in 27000, there were some family huddles about the awk-ward layout. During one flight, the stewards told me that the President, Mrs. Nixon, and Julie were deep in conversation about the disadvantages of having the staff compartment be-tween the First Family's quarters and the lounge.''

If he knew about the grumbling, Haldeman simply turned a deaf ear. The new floor plan was functioning exactly as he had intended.

From his big swivel chair at the first table in the staff section, he had easy access to the President's door, noting whom he sum-moned in, and how long they remained together. It was all part of Haldeman's *modus operandi*. He wanted Nixon under tight surveillance. Haldeman's deputies, Dwight Chapin and Larry Higby, were under orders to keep a log of everything Nixon did aboard the plane, with whom he talked, how long they talked, and, if possible, what they talked about.

"Julie Eisenhower had another gripe about the configuration of 27000," said Joe Chappell, the senior flight engineer. "Her own Secret Service man had asked her to come back to see how tightly the eight agents were jammed together in their compart-ment toward the rear. She told me she had mentioned that to the President, too. Those poor guys practically had to be shoe-horned into their seats.''

Nixon himself never inspected the faulty layout nor men-tioned the family's complaints to Haldeman within earshot of others aboard. But stories about Mrs. Nixon's discontent soon hit the papers. Within a few weeks, the White House Military Office dispatched a memo to Albertazzie's office at Andrews Air Force Base.

"At the first opportunity, meaning the next time SAM 27000 was out of service for maintenance, the President wanted us to install the same kind of configuration we had aboard SAM 26000," Albertazzie said. "In other words, the staff compart-ment was to be moved back and the lounge was to be moved for-ward and made a part of the presidential suite. That's what we did. The bill came to about $750,000.''

Although SAM 27000 had become the primary presidential air-craft, Mrs. Nixon much preferred the privacy afforded by SAM 26000 and saw that it was used as *Air Force One* whenever the

First Family wanted to relax together. On such occasions, SAM 27000, the new airplane, took up the backup role.

In contrast to the desert tones of 26000, the basic interior color aboard 27000 is blue. The President's personal chair is a deep solid blue and there is a deep blue top on his desk. In the First Lady's sitting room and the presidential lounge, crushed velvet upholstery was selected in a Wedgwood blue. Textured fabrics and crushed velvet were used to cover the massive chairs in the staff compartment. The staff tables are inlaid with leather. Muted blue plaids and textured materials dominate the Secret Service compartment and the rear areas for the press pool and Air Force security guards. Blue-gray carpeting in a marbled pattern runs throughout the airplane. SAM 27000 also has the sculptured look and enclosed overhead racks of the latest model Boeing jets, giving the interior a sleek and modern feeling.

Mrs. Nixon selected most of the colors during several sessions with the interior decorators in the White House theatre, sometimes getting down on her hands and knees to match and mix color swatches to obtain the effect she wanted.

Richard Nixon was a man in constant motion. He had been in office barely a month when he set out on his first foreign trip in *Air Force One*—a whirlwind tour of six European capitals in seven days. Before his first year was up, he made two more long overseas flights, one to Midway Island in the mid-Pacific to meet with South Vietnam's President Thieu and chart the beginning of his plan to "de-Americanize" the war, and then a round-the-world visit to Asia, Vietnam, the Balkans, and Britain, with time out to greet the Apollo 11 moonmen after their Pacific splashdown. He went abroad three times in 1970, twice in 1971, and topped it off in 1972, a reelection year, with three more foreign visits, including the historic flights to China and the Soviet Union.

And when he wasn't flying abroad, Nixon was flying around the country or heading for his homes in Florida and California. By the end of November 1973, Nixon had managed to stay in the White House only four of the forty-four weekends of his second term. Weary reporters were beginning to write of Nixon what had been said of Lyndon Johnson near the end of his tenure: "The President arrived in Washington today for a brief visit."

The *Congressional Quarterly*, the respected journal of governmental activity, took occasion to note in June 1974 that "it sometimes seems as if the Nixon presidency is almost perpetually airborne." Albertazzie and his *Air Force One* crew could vouch for it. The Nixon staff, however, was quick to add that, for all of his traveling, the President was still presiding. The White House, it was said, is wherever the President happens to be.

After flying Lyndon Johnson, it took the crew a while to adjust to the contrasting temperament and aircraft lifestyle of Richard Nixon.

"They were such different men," Albertazzie noted. "Johnson was always up and down the aisle. He had the plane arranged so he could see a lot of people, and they could see him, even when he was in his special suite with the 'king' chair. And he frequently came into the cockpit to talk to us, to ask about the instruments, to check on things."

Nixon was less visible and much more reserved. "He didn't wander around the plane. He stayed pretty much in his cabin, and the door was usually closed. I don't recall that he ever came up into the cockpit to chat in the five and a half years I was his pilot."

What was noticeably lacking aboard *Air Force One* during the Nixon years was precisely what was absent from his Oval Office in the White House—a sense of joy, a sense of humor. "Life is real, life is earnest," Longfellow said, and it aptly portrayed life aboard Nixon's airplane.

The President's principal assistants, H. R. Haldeman and John Ehrlichman, were also men of steely determination. Haldeman, in particular, let nothing stand in his way, not even security precautions.

For weeks, during the 1972 campaign, Haldeman had been unhappy with the Secret Service guarding the President. Although the opinion polls showed Nixon far in the lead over the Democratic senator from South Dakota George McGovern, Haldeman felt the President was being portrayed in the press as a "plastic

259

man appearing before plastic audiences." He wanted some enthusiastic crowd scenes on television and in the papers. Since they were not occurring, Haldeman decided to arrange a few. At the Providence Airport, Haldeman quietly passed the word to his political advance agents—at the proper moment, drop the ropes so the crowd could surge around Nixon and thus create the image of a popular President being mobbed by happy voters.

Robert Taylor, chief of the White House Secret Service detail, was furious when he heard of Haldeman's order. That would be a security risk, he hurriedly told Haldeman, and if Haldeman's men failed to keep the crowd behind the ropes, he personally would arrest Haldeman.

That cooled the plan for that night. But Haldeman was not to be deterred. The following day at Greensboro, North Carolina, the political advance men dutifully lowered the ropes and clamoring Nixon supporters rushed for the presidential limousine, engulfing the surprised Nixon and his Secret Service bodyguards.

"They even reached the airplane," Albertazzie remembers, "and I began to worry about damage to *Air Force One*—whether we would still be able to evacuate the President. It was a regular mob scene."

Taylor finally pushed Nixon aboard the plane and a grateful Albertazzie slowly eased the aircraft away from the ramp. Haldeman was delighted with the "spontaneous" crowd reaction he had arranged. Taylor was bitter. The incident festered. Later, during Nixon's inaugural parade, millions of TV viewers saw Taylor remove his coat and place it around Nixon to shield him from the January wind. And then Taylor disappeared from the White House. Haldeman had obtained Nixon's permission to fire him.

The news disturbed even the most loyal members of the Nixon staff. Highly respected among his colleagues and well-liked by the First Family, Taylor had often risked his own life to protect Nixon's. He had guarded him for years. It was Taylor, during Nixon's vice-presidential days, who had saved him from the angry rioters trying to overturn his automobile in Caracas, Venezuela.

Taylor left the Secret Service to take charge of security for

New York's former Governor Nelson Rockefeller and his family. But his departure from the White House—without a parting word of commendation from the President—puzzled even members of the Nixon family.

Flying out to California aboard *Air Force One* a few weeks later, Mrs. Nixon remarked to Albertazzie, "Isn't it terrible what they did to Bob Taylor? I don't know why Dick let them get away with it." Julie Nixon Eisenhower told a flight steward that she couldn't understand her father's decision. Rose Mary Woods, the President's secretary, complained openly about "the hatchet job on Bob Taylor." The career of a presidential security man, it seems, is not always a secure one.

In the Nixon years the atmosphere in flight was puritanically grim. The emphasis was on decorum, efficiency, keeping the schedule, finishing one's assigned task, and dutifully turning to another. If the irrepressible Henry Kissinger sometimes evoked a guffaw from an aide at his staff table, it was invariably squelched by a raised Ehrlichman eyebrow or a Haldeman scowl.

"My God, no—we weren't supposed to have fun!" said Stephen Bull, one of the few Nixon aides who managed to stay relaxed about things. "Haldeman and Ehrlichman never had a drink either, and at times the tensions in the staff section got pretty tight."

Whenever he could, Bull would contrive an excuse to leave his seat. Sometimes he would stop by the galley for a generous belt of bourbon (surreptitiously poured into a white paper coffee cup) before strolling back to one of the rear compartments for a welcome change of faces.

Yet even the most sober of presidents can have one too many.

Nixon's time occurred the night of November 17, 1973, following his appearance before the convention of Associated Press Managing Editors at Disney World, near Orlando, Florida. There, in an unforgettable defense of his conduct in the White House, he had said: "People have got to know whether or not their President is a crook. Well, I'm not a crook."

The trip back to Key Biscayne was a short one, but long enough for the President to gulp several stiff drinks in his cabin.

261

As he left the plane at Homestead Air Force Base, a jovial Nixon confided to Albertazzie that he'd "had a couple of good belts."

At the bottom of the stairs stood the base commander, resplendent in uniform and frozen in a stiff salute to his Commander-in-Chief. Nixon glanced at the general—and bowed from the waist, grandly, magnificently, with great flourish.

The flustered officer didn't know how to respond to such an unusual gesture by the President of the United States. So he held his salute. Nixon stayed at his bow. After what seemed an eternity but actually lasted no more than thirty seconds, the general dropped his right arm and thrust out a hand to shake the President's. Nixon grasped it, straightened up, gave forth with a cheery "Good evening, sir!" and headed toward his limousine.

Reporters in the press pool had already left the plane through the rear door and missed the scene. "That was the only occasion I remember when the President overindulged," Albertazzie said later.

Nixon was never easy with the press and the layout of *Air Force One* enabled him to keep them at a distance, physically as well as mentally. Sometimes he threatened to ban the press pool from the plane to show his displeasure with their coverage of him. Occasionally, however, he was in a more expansive mood.

One day in July 1969, when he was winging across the Pacific to welcome the Apollo 11 astronauts back from their moon landing, he decided to pay a rare surprise visit to the pool reporters seated in the rear of *Air Force One.*

Ron Ziegler, Nixon's press secretary, said Nixon had come by for "small talk," nothing serious. But reporters knew Nixon planned to visit Vietnam the following day and they were starving for something solid to write in advance of Saigon. Vietnam was the first subject that was raised.

The President shifted his gaze and then out of the blue remarked: "You know, the Senators and my friend Ted Williams have gone into a little slump. What they ought to do is make some trades."

For the next few minutes, it was Nixon the baseball fan, talking learnedly about the problems of the Washington ball club. A question about the economy back in the States drew from Nixon more baseball talk. A question about the Russian space program somehow started him on an analysis of the football-passing difficulties of Sonny Jurgenson, the aging quarterback of the Washington Redskins.

With that, Nixon departed up the aisle toward his own suite, leaving eight reporters empty-handed and completely puzzled.

During the Nixon years, members of the press pool were confined to their seats in the tail area. Only rarely were they permitted to go forward into the staff or VIP sections, and then only for a specific purpose and always with a staff escort. But the VIPs occasionally wandered back to the tail to use the lavatories, and when they emerged the reporters were waiting to ply them with questions.

UPI's Helen Thomas believes Martha Mitchell first strained Nixon's affection for her on just such a trek to the rear. It happened in September 1970 when Attorney General John Mitchell, Secretary of State William P. Rogers, and their wives were returning to Washington with Nixon.

Helen, who had established a strong and lasting friendship with Mrs. Mitchell, began by asking what she thought of the latest calf-length skirts for women and other trivialities.

"Oh, Helen," Martha interrupted, "why don't you ask me something important?"

"Okay," said Helen, "what do you think of the Vietnam war?"

"It stinks, and if it weren't for Senator Fulbright, we'd be out of it," Martha snapped.

With other reporters now joining in, Mrs. Mitchell made her point even stronger.

"If this country would stick together . . . if everyone felt a common cause in Vietnam, we would have been out sixteen months ago, and it makes me so mad I can't see straight. . . . We shouldn't have gotten into the war in the first place. The Nixon Administration inherited it and they're trying their best to get out of it."

By then, Thomas recounted in *Dateline: The White House*, other officials had appeared in the press area, anxious to quell the loquacious Mrs. Mitchell. "Martha," interposed Rogers, "why don't you stick to the Justice Department and I'll take

263

care of foreign affairs." John Mitchell, asked if he would like to hear what his wife had just said, rolled his eyes upward. "Heavens, no!" he replied. "I'd jump straight out of the window."

The story of a cabinet wife's unhappiness with the war made headlines the next day. Mrs. Mitchell never again was permitted to fly aboard *Air Force One.* The word within the White House was that Nixon personally had grounded her.

Grounding the First Family, however, was a more complicated matter, and this time the villain was not the press, but inflation. When congressional penny-pinchers like Senator William Proxmire of Wisconsin and some newspapers began zeroing in on White House "perks," Nixon decided that members of his family should cut down on their use of the Air Force Jetstars for personal trips to New York, Boston, Florida, and California. The Air Force was billing the White House for the family's unofficial flights and the staff was passing the bills to the President as personal expenses requiring reimbursement. And the tab was steep—about $487 per hour.

Mrs. Nixon and Julie Eisenhower readily assented. Julie, who was then living in Washington with her husband David, began traveling on commercial aircraft to her magazine job in Indianapolis. But Tricia proved stubborn.

While flying the President back to Camp David after a Jetstar inspection flight of Hurricane Agnes's damage around Wilkes-Barre, Pennsylvania, on September 9, 1972, Albertazzie felt a tap on his shoulder. It was John Ehrlichman.

"The President would like to talk with you if you can leave the cockpit," Ehrlichman told him.

Albertazzie turned the controls over to his co-pilot, Lt. Col. Carl Peden, and clambered back to the President's cramped quarters in the handsomely appointed little jet.

"I'm trying to persuade Tricia to use a less expensive airplane than this one," Nixon began. "What could she use?" Tricia, as Albertazzie knew, was commuting almost every weekend to Washington from New York, where she and husband Ed Cox were residing. The round trip was costing Daddy about $900.

"Well, sir, she could fly commercially without any difficulty," Albertazzie told the President, referring to the Eastern Air Lines shuttle schedule and the American Air Lines flights. "But if she has to travel on a government plane, our Convair 580s would be better suited than a Jetstar, and less expensive, since they're propeller craft.''

"Fine," said the President. "The next time Tricia asks for an airplane, you tell her that all you have available is a Convair.''

Albertazzie relayed the President's instructions to the White House Military Office, which handles First Family air transportation. But Tricia was not deterred. She knew Jetstars were available and she would fly in no other airplane. Since the President had not flatly prohibited her use of the Jetstar, the Military Office gave in—and kept passing the bill on to Nixon. It took the Arab oil embargo and a government-wide crackdown on the use of government aircraft before Tricia, in the latter part of 1973, also began using commercial airlines for personal traveling.

Air Force One trips during the Nixon-Ford era were livelier with Kissinger aboard. His presence lent an air of excitement and frequently a touch of humor.

Kissinger loved to joke with members of the crew and frequently poked his head into the cockpit to needle Albertazzie. "I suppose you are delaying lunch until you find some bumpy air," he would joke. On a flight to San Clemente, he might propose that Albertazzie swing low over Hollywood and waggle *Air Force One*'s wings. "I promised Jill St. John I would let her know when I was arriving.''

Flying back to Washington one Sunday afternoon from California, Albertazzie needled the keg-shaped Kissinger about a public opinion poll in that morning's *Los Angeles Times.* It showed that while 78 percent of the men recognized Kissinger's name, only 74 percent of the women attached any significance to it. Knowing Kissinger's vanity and his celebrated reputation as a ladies' man, Albertazzie asked how he interpreted the poll. "Hmph," sniffed Kissinger, "that survey obviously was not taken in Beverly Hills.''

Kissinger's reputation as a Lothario accompanied him on presidential trips, and occasionally provided international mirth. After the Moscow visit in 1972, *Air Force One* took Nixon and Kissinger to Iran for an overnight stop and a meeting with the Shah. While the President remained in the palace at Teheran, the Iranian prime minister, aware of Kissinger's legendary appeal to women, invited him to a night club performance by Nadina Parsa, the country's most famous belly dancer. There, to the howling amusement of his Iranian hosts and White House reporters, Nadina wound up her act by plopping affectionately in Kissinger's lap. Kissinger took it all in stride.

Aboard *Air Force One* the next day, reporters ribbed Kissinger about his latest conquest.

"She was a charming girl," he said with a straight face. "Very interested in foreign affairs."

"Really?"

"We discussed strategic weapons, the SALT talks. I spent some time explaining how you convert an SS-7 into a Y-class submarine."

"You don't say!"

"Of course, what else? I want to make the world safe for belly dancers."

But Kissinger's sense of humor did not extend to situations that he felt threatened his supremacy over foreign policy making. He saw nothing funny in the reports that Donald Rumsfeld, Ford's White House staff boss, was attempting to diminish his authority within the Oval Office and the National Security Council. White House Press Secretary Nessen unintentionally created a flap on a Ford trip to Brussels by joking to *Air Force One*'s press pool that since Kissinger was on another airplane, Rumsfeld would serve as the "senior American official," a sobriquet that Kissinger often used when providing background information to reporters. When some of the news media took Nessen's crack as a serious indication that Kissinger was losing status, Kissinger accused Nessen of being part of a plot to get him.

On a later *Air Force One* trip to Paris, Nessen said, Kissinger asked him to step into the empty presidential bedroom where he spent fifteen minutes berating Nessen for allegedly leaking anti-Kissinger stories to the press.

Kissinger's star status irked Nixon loyalists like Bob Haldeman, the White House staff chief. Albertazzie once had started up *Air Force One*'s right-side engines for departure from Andrews when chief steward Vernon Shell notified the cockpit that Kissinger was not yet aboard. Instead of accompanying Nixon on the helicopter ride from the White House, he was motoring out by limousine. Albertazzie asked for instructions. Did the President wish to wait? Back came word from Haldeman: "Give Henry two minutes and if he isn't here, we'll take off."

The two minutes passed with no sign of Kissinger. Albertazzie started up the other pair of engines and ordered the boarding stairs pulled away from the plane. "Just as I was about to release the brakes, the black limousine came into view. So I shut down Number 1 and 2 engines, we opened the door, and brought back the stairs so Kissinger could get on board. He was pretty upset that the plane was about to leave without him, and exchanged sharp words with Haldeman. A steward told me later that Haldeman hadn't wanted to wait at all. It was the President who suggested giving Kissinger a couple of extra minutes."

Haldeman could faze every other member of the Nixon staff but not Kissinger. Coming in for a landing at one foreign capital, Haldeman burst out of Nixon's suite with a three-page arrival statement that Kissinger had drafted for the President.

"It's too long. He wants this cut down to two pages," said Haldeman, thrusting the statement at Kissinger. "Get on it."

Kissinger took the papers and coolly handed them to his secretary. "Retype it on two pages," he said, walking away.

Of all the status symbols of presidential flights, none was comparable during Nixon's days to "the jacket."

It was not expensively tailored and it looked pretty much like a casual windbreaker, something to knock about in. Albertazzie had one made up by the Air Force's clothing laboratory at Wright Patterson Air Force Base in Dayton, Ohio, as a crew gift for the Commander-in-Chief. It was a replica of Albertazzie's pilot's jacket, but with the presidential seal embroidered atop the left breast pocket and the President's name embroidered over the right pocket. Nixon put it on. Nixon liked it.

"Suddenly, all the President's men decided they had to have jackets, too. And, just as suddenly, what had been a prerogative of ours was taken over by the White House staff and became a prerogative of theirs in determining who was entitled to wear the *Air Force One* jacket," Albertazzie remembers.

On boarding *Air Force One*, Nixon's men instantly shed their business coats and donned their special flight jackets. When they left the plane, the jackets would remain on board, stowed away by the stewards until the next trip. No matter that the jackets all looked alike, save for the individual's name imprinted in silver on a black breast patch. What mattered was what it signaled: The wearer was a member of the elite on a very elite airplane.

Haldeman got one. So did Kissinger and Ron Ziegler. John Ehrlichman, an ex-Air Force man, insisted that his jacket also display his navigator's wings and his "jump" wings. Although an Army general, Alexander Haig had to have one of the Air Force's special jackets. Another was made up for his assistant, Major George Joulwan, who walked in Haig's shadow. (Later on, as a matter of petty discipline by Gen. Richard Lawson, Nixon's military assistant, Joulwan's jacket was briefly removed from *Air Force One*.)

Soon the jacket became a way of denoting special people who were important to the President. Attorney General Mitchell, a favorite before Watergate, was presented with his very own jacket. So were Bebe Rebozo and Robert Abplanalp, Nixon's millionaire pals who helped finance the purchase of his houses in Key Biscayne and San Clemente. Vice President Spiro Agnew got one, as did David Eisenhower and Edward Cox, the Nixon sons-in-law.

Oddly enough, Nixon didn't wear his jacket on every flight, preferring a well-worn sport coat that steward Lee Simmons kept ready in the presidential suite. But jacket fever never abated among Nixon's senior aides. Albertazzie was able to dissuade them from having the Air Force make up extra jackets for the on-board pleasure of VIP guests. That would be very expensive, he told them. Besides, it would have diluted the exclusivity they prized.

As time went on, Albertazzie found himself caught in the middle of the rivalries and jealousies that periodically swept through the Nixon staff at the White House. The distrust mounted noticeably as the Watergate scandal worsened. The Military Office, quartered in the East Wing and successively headed by Generals Hughes, Scowcroft, and Lawson, fretted regularly about Albertazzie's associations with the civilian staffers quartered in the

West Wing, where the President's office was located. At one time, Albertazzie was ordered to "stay away from Ziegler," with whom he had struck up a casual friendship.

When General Alexander Haig took over as Nixon's staff chief on May 4, 1973, after Haldeman's resignation during the Watergate era, Haig suddenly became a suspect figure within the Military Office.

"Lawson put out a memo to Special Air Missions that I was to be dissuaded from doing any flying of General Haig except when he was accompanying the President," Albertazzie said. "As a matter of fact, Lawson sent a memo to the Air Force asking that he be advised anytime I flew anywhere, except with the President. I'll never understand why, or why he didn't just ask me to tell him if there was any reason to know. There was a kind of underhandedness about things."

As the Watergate paranoia settled over the White House, it became increasingly difficult for Albertazzie to find out more than twenty-four hours ahead whether the President would be going to Florida or to his home in California.

Then, suddenly, clues started coming from an unexpected source—Dr. John Handwerker, a Key Biscayne physician and golfing partner of Albertazzie's.

"Hey, I hear you're going to be down here this weekend," Handwerker telephoned Albertazzie one day.

"We are?" asked Albertazzie. "Nobody's told me."

"Well, I heard it at the Shell station," Handwerker replied. "They've been told to lay in extra gasoline for White House cars."

Sure enough. The next weekend found *Air Force One* down in Florida and Albertazzie out on the golf links with Handwerker.

The doctor's tip service eventually proved to be too much of a good thing. Bebe Rebozo, Nixon's best pal, always knew well in advance when the President was going to Key Biscayne, but he never told anyone. Rebozo also happened to be a friend of Handwerker's. The first time Handwerker mentioned that he'd heard the President was flying down, Rebozo merely nodded agreeably. The next time, Rebozo became suspicious. He surmised the doctor was getting his information from his buddy who flew the President's plane. Before long, Albertazzie received a call from the White House, scolding him for telling "outsiders" about Nixon's travel plans.

"You've got it wrong," Albertazzie chuckled over the telephone to General Hughes, the President's military assistant. "I'm not telling the doctor—he's telling me. And he gets his information from a gas station on Key Biscayne because somebody in the White House is more concerned about having fuel for the cars this weekend than about advising the President's pilot to get the airplane ready."

Additionally, the disclosure of presidentially sanctioned wiretaps on some of Henry Kissinger's assistants and Washington reporters—plus the disclosure of Nixon's own secret tape-recording apparatus—began to gnaw at the crew of *Air Force One*. Albertazzie had a White House phone in his residence at Andrews Air Force Base to keep him in constant contact with the White House signal board. His wife, Carol, frequently would tell him, "I think the line is tapped," and urged discretion in what he said over the telephone.

For a long time, Albertazzie pooh-poohed her suspicions. But after a while he began to wonder himself. Generals Hughes and Scowcroft, the top White House military assistants, took to calling him on a separate Pentagon line or an outside commerical telephone whenever they wanted to ensure privacy in their conversations. Albertazzie became even more convinced of a phone tap after passing along a confidential word to Lt. Col. Gene Boyer, commander of the Army helicopter detachment that served the White House. Boyer had been at odds with Marine Major Jack Brennan, Nixon's favorite aide.

"The next thing I knew I was called on the carpet by Gen. Dick Lawson (Hughes' successor) for what I had said—privately I thought—to Boyer, a longtime friend. That really bothered me. Then I remembered Lawson had told me earlier, in no uncertain terms, that he had 'the means' to monitor everything. I'm sure now, given all the suspicion pervading the White House during the Watergate period, that we were all monitored. There were too many 'private' conversations that were later, in some context, reported."

Albertazzie was totally baffled when the existence of Nixon's White House tape-recording system came to light during the Watergate hearings. "It didn't make sense to me, no matter how I looked at it," he said.

In the first place, the Nixon he knew was a man of ten thumbs. No matter how frequently Nixon flew aboard *Air Force One*, for example, he never mastered the simple controls that adjusted his presidential chair. He couldn't figure out how to operate the various spotlights over his chair and desk. And the stereo system in the presidential compartment remained a complete mystery to him.

"It got to be a kind of game whenever he came aboard. The stewards used to kid each other, asking how long do you suppose it'll be before he calls one of us for help? And it was never more than a minute or two. It just seemed that he could not understand the mechanical aspects of those simple things. So how in the world could he ever figure out a secret taping system in the Oval Office?"

Albertazzie, incidentally, thinks Nixon's lack of technical comprehension was the prime reason why, unlike other presidents, he never visited *Air Force One*'s cockpit during his years as Commander-in-Chief. "All those instruments represented an environment he didn't understand and in which he would have felt inferior. Therefore he just wasn't going to put himself in such an environment if he could avoid it."

Albertazzie was equally puzzled by the disclosure that the Oval Office taping system was a relatively inexpensive one, lacking the voice quality and fidelity of a professional tape-recording system.

"The White House Communications Agency had the men and the know-how to install the most sophisticated electronic equipment imaginable. They could have done it right.

"And there is unlimited money available for just such things. Look at what's aboard *Air Force One*! We had the most elaborate of telephone systems, capable of voice communication from the plane to any place on earth. The Air Force spent a small fortune ensuring that the President and his people could talk with reliability and clarity. That could have been done at the White House, too, but wasn't."

271

Nor does Albertazzie accept the argument that Haldeman decreed a low-budget taping system because he didn't want to use Department of Defense equipment or personnel to achieve a quality operation.

"The White House uses DOD [Department of Defense] equipment for everything, everywhere. For instance, we had DOD television sets all around, on the plane, in the White House and up at Camp David—all bought and paid for by the Army Signal Corps."

Albertazzie likewise discounts the notion that the White House staff felt it would be illegal to ask the Defense Department to install a White House taping system to record conversations useful for Nixon's memoirs.

"Bob Haldeman was a home movie fanatic. Everytime you turned around, he was taking pictures of historic places with his own camera, even if it meant getting in the way of the news photographers. If he discovered that we were taking pictures, however, he would put out a memo saying we couldn't do that. But he would get his film by the case from the Navy Photographic Laboratory [which serviced the official White House photographers] and they would process his film for him. He didn't have any hesitancy about getting film rolls from the Navy, which was a very questionable practice since they were for his personal use."

"So if he had called in the White House Communications Agency and said, 'We want a first-class tape recording system in the White House for the President's memoirs,' why, it would've been done like that," said Albertazzie, snapping his fingers.

In Albertazzie's view, the greatest inconsistency of all is rooted in a fact not heretofore made public.

When Richard Nixon inherited *Air Force One* (SAM 26000) from Lyndon Johnson on January 20, 1969, he also inherited a telephone monitoring system. All incoming and outgoing conversations between persons aboard *Air Force One* and the outside world were secretly tape-recorded during the Johnson presidency. At the conclusion of every trip, the radio operator would gather up all the tapes and deliver them to the White House—for whatever use Johnson or his aides might desire.

Albertazzie discovered the existence of the airborne taping system shortly after he took over SAM 26000 as the new presidential pilot. He sensed it was an unusual "extra," not a piece of standard *Air Force One* equipment.

"I immediately went to Colonel Hughes [Nixon's Air Force aide at the White House] and said, 'Hey, we have this nice little taping system aboard the plane that was used during the Johnson years. What do you want me to do about it?'

"Hughes said he would have to check with Haldeman. And the word came back a little later that Nixon didn't want it. So I had it removed. The result was that during the Nixon presidency, no telephone conversations between *Air Force One* and the ground were recorded aboard the plane. They could have told me to leave the one in the plane in service. They could have told me to leave it in place but to disconnect it. Instead, I was given authority to remove it, which I did.

"They wouldn't have had to invent an excuse to put a system aboard, because it was already in place. And it was a very fine taping operation, much more sophisticated than the kind they apparently used in the White House."

Even harder to understand is why Haldeman, having wired the President's office in the White House, did not choose to augment that taping operation by recording the important conversations that occurred between President Nixon and the politicians, diplomats, and aides who conferred with him in his private quarters aboard *Air Force One.* That would have been quite easy to do, given the telephone tape-recording system already put in by Lyndon Johnson. And it would have furthered the historic purposes for which Nixon tried to justify the White House system.

But it wasn't done. The existing LBJ system aboard *Air Force One* was yanked out on Haldeman's orders.

That decision apparently stemmed from an occurrence shortly after the 1968 election as Nixon began his transition to power as the president-elect.

On November 12, 1968, flying from Key Biscayne to New York after a brief post-election rest, Nixon stopped off in Washington to discuss the procedures of transition with the Johnson staff and to learn how the White House functioned. It was then,

273

Theodore H. White noted in *Breach of Faith*, that Nixon first learned about the Johnson taping system in the Cabinet Room and the Oval Office.

During the hop to New York, with Albertazzie in the cockpit of the government-assigned plane, Nixon confided to his assistant Robert Finch that the first thing he planned to do was to remove the Johnson taping apparatus. He felt that no one should be "bugged" in the President's office.

Thus, on February 15, 1969, three weeks after Nixon took office, the Army Signal Corps ripped out the LBJ microphones and wiring that led to the hidden tape recorders.

Nixon's distaste for taping his office conversations lasted two years.

In February 1971, on Nixon's orders, the Secret Service installed a much more elaborate recording system than Johnson or Kennedy had ever employed. At first it covered only the Oval Office and the Cabinet Room. On April 16, 1971, it expanded to include the President's hideaway in the Executive Office Building as well as three White House telephones Nixon customarily used. A year later it was extended to the presidential lodge at Camp David.

But despite all the tape recording that now went on secretly in Nixon's quarters on the ground, there was no move to reinstall a taping system in *Air Force One*. And that remained the case, even though Nixon became the most peripatetic President in history, visiting more countries and traveling more miles outside the United States than any previous President—not to mention his constant flights around the country and to his homes in Key Biscayne and San Clemente in the five and a half years of his tenure.

Thus the decision to forgo a taping system in *Air Force One* must be set down as another of the enduring inconsistencies of the Nixon presidency.

Chapter Nine
Cherchez La Femme

The flight controllers in the tower at Frankfurt's Rhein-Main Airport were puzzled. Darkness had already fallen across the German countryside when a White House plane came in for a landing. Then, quite unexpectedly, it was followed by the Mystère 20 jet of French President Georges Pompidou. The smaller French craft turned off the runway and taxied over to the U.S. Air Force side of the airfield where the American Boeing 707 was rolling to a stop. Suddenly, as if on signal, all the field lights in that area were doused. Nine minutes later, the Mystère notified the tower that it was ready for takeoff. The sleek French craft sped down the runway, climbed steeply, and flew off on a westerly course toward Paris. One of the controllers watched its blinking lights until they disappeared in the night sky. Then he reached for the telephone.

Early the next day, March 16, 1970, a German air attaché stationed in Paris found himself driving through morning traffic and south of the city to Villacoublay Airport, where President Pompidou's executive jet was kept. This was not what he had planned to do on a Monday morning, but then, of course, he had not anticipated the urgent query from German intelligence.

275

Within the hour, he presented himself at the office of Colonel Calderon, Pompidou's personal pilot.

Calderon was not surprised at the arrival of his visitor. He had warned the Americans that the Germans would surely ask questions. He ushered the attaché in, motioned him to a seat, and proffered a cigarette.

The German took his time. He settled himself in the chair, crossed his legs, and, out of habit, ran a thumb and forefinger along the crease of his trousers. He looked up casually at Calderon and addressed him in fluent French.

"That flight last night, *mon colonel*. What was that all about?"

Calderon measured his visitor. Perhaps the German knew less than he did. Calderon smiled. "Oh, that flight—you mean the one last night to Rhein-Main?"

The German attaché was not to be put off so lightly. His voice became urgent.

"Last night German air space was penetrated by an executive aircraft bearing the insignia of the government of France. No flight plan had been filed. There was no clearance. Without advance notice, this aircraft flew into Rhein-Main."

He paused to let his words sink in. Calderon's face was bland. The attaché pressed on.

"The aircraft then taxied over to the American side of the airport where a Presidential plane from Washington had just arrived. Your aircraft—*the plane of the President of France*—remained on the ground only a few minutes, nine to be exact. It then flew off again, presumably back to Paris. Really, *mon colonel,* this is a very serious matter. I have been requested to ask you for an explanation."

Calderon sighed contritely. "*Ah oui, mon ami,* the protocol of things—it is always, how shall I say it, always so important to persons such as you and me who are in the service of our countries."

He was leading up to the answer he had been advised to give. But he was also enjoying his role in the mystery of the previous night. "Protocol, the formalities of flight plans and advance clearances—it is very difficult these days for a man to be romantic in a world that worships regulations."

The German air attaché sat erect. "Romantic? What is romantic about violating the air space of the Federal Republic of Germany?"

Calderon leaned across his desk and, with a finger, beckoned the German closer. "Last night's flight," he whispered *tête-à-tête,* "involved a woman."

"A woman!" The German almost shouted the word.

Calderon put a finger to his lips and glanced warningly toward the door. "The flight to Rhein-Main last night involved a woman."

Now it was the German's turn to smile. "You Frenchmen," he said, his voice registering admiration and astonishment. "You mean—?"

Calderon nodded encouragement. The ploy was working. "A woman," he repeated with an expressive shrug. "Is that not what nights—and flights—should be all about?"

The German air attaché was beaming. He could hardly wait to get back to his embassy in Paris. He took Calderon's hand and pumped it vigorously. "A woman," he said aloud to himself. "A woman." At the door, he turned back to Calderon and shot one final question. "This woman—is she German?"

Calderon's eyes widened with innocence. "I am but a pilot, *mon ami.* I only fly the airplane."

Smuggling is illegal. It also is lucrative, sometimes dangerous, and, most times, exciting. Customarily, it involves the transporting of illicit goods in a secret manner to evade the laws of another country or to avoid payment of import duties. Smuggling a person into a country is vastly more complicated, especially if that person not only has to be smuggled in but must also be smuggled out. And not just once, but repeatedly—each time with the same destination. When Ralph Albertazzie signed on with the White House as presidential pilot in 1969, he had no clue that he was about to become one of the prime smugglers of his day.

Back in his youth, he had unwittingly worked for a man who made a good living by flying moonshine out of the hollows of West Virginia. But now, wearing the silver wings of the U.S. Air Force, Colonel Albertazzie was about to go into smuggling in a big way—and with his own full knowledge and eager participa-

277

tion. He would be using the airplane of the President. He would be responsible for secretly inserting Henry Kissinger into France, England and Germany, and then secretly extracting him a day or two later. He would not even be able to tell his Air Force superiors in the Pentagon.

The orders came directly from President Nixon. Summoned to a clandestine meeting in the White House in the summer of 1969, a few months after Nixon's inauguration, Albertazzie found himself seated at the mahogany table in the Roosevelt Room, across the hall from the Oval Office. Already there were Col. James Hughes, the President's military assistant, and Alexander Haig, then serving as deputy to Kissinger. Later Kissinger himself joined them.

Albertazzie has since described the session: "There had been many public meetings between American officials and the North Vietnamese in Paris during the Johnson administration. They always turned into propaganda forums for the other side. Now Mr. Nixon wanted to try a secret track, using Henry Kissinger, to see if Hanoi and the United States could privately work out some means of settlement."

Kissinger, without going into excessive detail, observed that "the groundwork for private talks already has been laid." What he didn't say was that in response to a letter Nixon had sent Ho Chi Minh in Hanoi, shortly before Ho's death, Kissinger had already held a preliminary secret meeting with Xuan Thuy in Paris. On the way home from Nixon's globe-girdling trip in July 1969, Kissinger detoured to Paris, ostensibly to brief French officials on the President's travels. But the side journey was primarily an excuse to explore North Vietnam's interest in private negotiations. Xuan Thuy's response had been positive.

"But how can we do it without the whole world knowing?" Kissinger asked. The world's press was not the only problem. In fact, the President did not even want the Defense Department, the State Department, or the Central Intelligence Agency to know that he would be sending Kissinger to Paris for ultra-secret meetings with the North Vietnamese. There was only one way to ensure that kind of secrecy—and that was to keep the matter privy to a small handful of persons working directly with the President at the White House. Albertazzie figured in the scheme for a very obvious reason: *Air Force One.* It and its backup version, SAM 970, were the only long-range aircraft under direct control of the man in the Oval Office. He could send Kissinger anywhere he wished on a presidential jet. But how to do it without arousing Pentagon interest and outside curiosity?

Kissinger explained that he would take care of masking his own absence from Washington whenever a trip became necessary. It would be up to Hughes and Albertazzie to find a way to account for the absence of the President's plane from Washington and for its arrival in Europe.

"That particular Boeing isn't going to be easy to hide," Haig observed as the meeting broke up.

Hughes walked Albertazzie to the door. "Well, Ralph, all you have to do is concoct the perfect alibi for the world's best known airplane. It better be good."

The answer came to Albertazzie one day while fretting about the unreliability of *Air Force One*'s "voice scrambler" system. "We had on board this $25 million contraption which had been installed during Lyndon Johnson's days. They called it the High Frequency Scopesafe system. It was the creation of a lot of high-powered people in the Air Force who, by God, were determined to make it work. It was going to be a feather in their caps. But frankly it never performed properly and I wanted something done about it. It weighed about 1,700 pounds and I felt we could put that weight to better use.

"The purpose of the voice scrambler was to make it possible for the President, in complete privacy, to communicate by voice radio on very sensitive subjects and be clearly understood on the other end. The scrambler was supposed to thwart eavesdroppers. Ordinarily voice communications from the airplane can be intercepted by anybody. We always warned people on the aircraft that they were not talking over a secure system."

The voice scrambler, however, rarely performed as intended. It did not operate all the time. Sometimes its voice traffic was so unintelligible as to be useless.

"I felt that the Air Force ought to make sure that the system had both intelligibility and reliability. I didn't want the President's conversations to break down in the middle and I didn't want the President to be misunderstood. If the President called

279

the Secretary of Defense about some emergency, I wanted the Secretary to be able to know whether the message was 'start the bombing' or 'stop the bombing.' That's a pretty important difference.''

Albertazzie went to Hughes to explain what he had in mind. With the voice scrambler as the excuse, Albertazzie could take up the presidential planes on long overseas flights to test out the communications systems and simultaneously maintain navigational proficiency and improve crew performance. The Pentagon, the White House Communications Agency, and all the logical overseas air bases could be notified that SAM 26000 (*Air Force One*) and its backup, SAM 970, would be undertaking a series of training missions. Besides, the passenger manifest on presidential trips did not have to be divulged to anyone. Henry Kissinger's presence could easily be kept secret.

"I think you've hit on it," Hughes replied. He suggested a few refinements.

One problem that concerned them was the matter of "space-available" passengers. As a cost-saving feature, it was customary for the Air Force to permit military personnel to travel from one base to another aboard transports with empty seats. But space-available passengers were the last thing Kissinger needed on his secret trips abroad! At the same time, Hughes knew, it would arouse curiosity in Air Force headquarters to ask for an exemption from standard practice. He suggested that Albertazzie couch his agreement to take space-available traffic in language that clearly reserved his right to bump them. That, he felt, would discourage applicants.

"Send me a memo outlining your proposal," Hughes instructed Albertazzie. "I'll respond with your authorization."

Kissinger's first secret flight aboard the President's plane took place over the weekend of February 20–21, 1970. He was to meet with Le Duc Tho, the silver-haired North Vietnamese diplomat, in a private villa near Paris. Getting away from Washington turned out to be easier than even Kissinger had anticipated a few months earlier—and quite by accident. He had become a social celebrity.

During the autumn of 1969, a young reporter for *The Washing-*

ton Post, Sally Quinn, had spied the portly presidential assistant at a Georgetown cocktail party in honor of Gloria Steinem. Quinn invited bachelor Kissinger to be photographed with Steinem. He accepted with such alacrity that Quinn joshed, "You really are a swinger underneath it all, aren't you?"

Kissinger parried, undoubtedly remembering he worked for a very square and Republican President. "Why don't you just think of me as a secret swinger?" he ventured.

The picture, Quinn's story, and Kissinger's quote in the morning *Post* and many other papers across the land made Kissinger famous as a ladies' man long before he gained recognition as an international diplomat. Before the winter of 1969 was over, he was being seen in the company of pretty, prominent women at fashionable parties in Washington, New York, and Los Angeles.

And that gave him a perfect alibi.

On the evening before a clandestine departure, Kissinger would make certain he had been seen, quoted, and photographed at some social affair in Georgetown, usually with a beauteous creature on his arm. The following morning he would fly secretly to Paris, spend fourteen to eighteen hours there, and immediately return to Washington. As soon as he got back, Kissinger again would turn up at a public or social function to make sure he had been seen. No one, least of all the press, ever suspected that he had been to Paris in the interval. The pattern worked beautifully every time.

The tricky part fell to those who had to transport Kissinger to Paris and back. The missions always began and ended with the crew of the presidential airplane. But the shepherding of Kissinger inside France was the responsibility of Major Gen. Vernon "Dick" Walters, the Defense Department attaché at the American Embassy in Paris, who later would become deputy director of the CIA. Fluent in a half-dozen languages and a frequent interpreter for U.S. Presidents, Walters masked his skills as an intelligence officer within the hearty exterior of a traveling salesman. His key role in Kissinger's secret negotiations in Paris remained hidden from public view until he retired from the Army in 1976 and wrote his memoirs, *Silent Missions*.

The plane of the President of the United States could not simply take off and fly to Paris on a training mission. The French government, under the late Charles de Gaulle, had reacted sharply to American domination of NATO. As an assertion of France's sovereign independence, he demanded that American military aircraft henceforth obtain special permission before flying over French soil.

"De Gaulle had gotten pushed out of shape because our B-52s were flying over France without clearance. All of our NATO-based military craft were constantly flying back and forth," said Albertazzie. "So they restructured the whole system of air control. We had no U.S. Air Force installations in France anymore, so we couldn't head directly there. In order to land the President's plane at a French base, the French required that we have some overriding reason of an official nature. Given the covert nature of the Kissinger trips, we didn't want to get into that."

What to do?

Enter Dick Walters. As Kissinger later acknowledged, Walters convinced him that it would be wise to take French President Pompidou and his chief assistant, Michel Jobert, in his confidence. France's superb intelligence community would surely sniff out Kissinger's comings and goings with the North Vietnamese in Paris and that information would upset Pompidou and the high French officials. So Kissinger, with the authority of President Nixon, met privately with Pompidou to explain the nature of his diplomatic trips. He asked that the information be restricted to the highest levels to preserve the necessary secrecy. Pompidou appreciated Kissinger's overture and, in fact, offered discreet assistance. Through Pompidou's office, Walters obtained blanket clearance for Albertazzie to land *Air Force One* at several obscure French airfields long enough to drop off Kissinger and pick him up later. From these points, Walters would arrange for his own Defense Department courier plane or a French military craft to airlift Kissinger to Villacoublay, or another airport on the outskirts of Paris.

On some occasions, SAM 26000 or the backup SAM 970 would fly Kissinger to an American military installation in Germany or a military airfield in Britain. From there he commuted to Paris aboard an Air Force plane attached to the European Command and thus unlikely to attract attention. The French also provided an out-of-the-way parking spot for a military aircraft at busy Orly Airport.

Indeed, without the quiet cooperation of the Elysée Palace, it is likely that the Kissinger missions to Paris would have foundered at an early stage, aborting secret peace negotiations and extending the Vietnam conflict for more agonizing months. At a time when much of the world deemed Franco-American relations to be rather strained, Pompidou proved to be a valuable backstage friend of the White House.

For Dick Walters, the difficult part of the assignment lay in keeping Kissinger's presence a secret in Paris. He even put up Kissinger and his assistants, usually two National Security Council aides, at his own small apartment in Neuilly. Walters employed all the wiles of the intelligence trade to keep Kissinger from being recognized. Kissinger, not much given to complimenting subordinates, later thanked him generously in a letter. He told the authors that Walters's role as escort and interpreter had been "indispensable" to the success of his Paris missions.

For Albertazzie, the difficulty of the assignment lay not so much in keeping Europe unaware of Kissinger's travels as in keeping the Pentagon and the State Department in the dark. Those were the orders of his Commander-in-Chief. He was not worried about *Air Force One*'s crew members; they were sworn to secrecy. The risk lay in filing the required flight plans and obtaining landing clearances without alerting the high command in the Air Force and the Defense Department to the fact that he was making some rather unusual side trips and detours for what were supposed to be normal "crew training missions."

The first secret trip on February 20, 1970, was a classic example. On the record, the President's plane was going to fly from Andrews Air Force Base outside Washington to the U.S. base at Wiesbaden, Germany. But what Albertazzie couldn't tell Flight Control at Andrews or the *Air Force One*'s special tracking center in the Pentagon was that he was going to veer southward over the Atlantic to drop off Kissinger at the French air base at Avord, one hundred miles south of Paris.

Avord was an interesting choice. It was far enough from Paris to avoid easy detection, yet close enough for Kissinger to be whisked there in twenty minutes. Additionally, Avord was the base at which the French stationed the tanker aircraft that serviced their nuclear bombers. To a casual night-time observer, the presidential plane would appear to be just one of the tankers.

To reach Avord, Albertazzie had to crank an extra hour into the normal seven-hour flight time from Andrews to Wiesbaden. But he knew from experience that this alone would not intrigue Trans-Oceanic Control. "An extra hour's flying time across the Atlantic is not unusual. You may run into heavy winds or heavy air traffic may divert you to a slightly longer route. It happens frequently."

Albertazzie, of course, was counting on no such problems. But another one cropped up even before the plane left Andrews. Kissinger, as usual, was late.

"We were supposed to leave Andrews at ten o'clock in the morning, but he didn't show up until nearly ten-thirty. The time was critical. We were due to rendezvous in the nighttime at Avord with Walters at a certain hour. Now our flying schedule was tighter than ever."

En route over the western Atlantic, the crew dutifully filed all the normal flight information with Trans-Oceanic, Air Force-FAA, and the Defense Department office that follows the presidential plane whenever it is aloft. But as the blue-and-silver Boeing flew high over Land's End at the southern tip of the British coast, control over the international flight had shifted from Trans-Oceanic in New York to Shannon Control in Ireland. And Albertazzie executed his first little act of subterfuge.

"Shannon, this is SAM 26000. Request change in routing to Wiesbaden. Over."

An Irish voice came over the cockpit radio. "Roger, SAM 26000, say your flight plan change, please."

"Shannon, SAM 26000 requesting change in routing from Land's End to Wiesbaden via Paris and Luxembourg. Over."

"SAM 26000, Shannon has your request and will advise. Over."

Albertazzie knew exactly what was happening on the ground. Shannon Control was checking with Paris Control to see if the President's plane had been issued an overflight clearance for France. If Dick Walters had done his job, the proper document was on file. Albertazzie didn't have to wait long for the Irish voice to come back on the radio.

"SAM 26000, this is Shannon. You are cleared to Wiesbaden via your new routing: Jersey, Paris, Luxembourg, Wiesbaden. Have a good flight."

So far, so good. Albertazzie knew Shannon would not notify Trans-Oceanic in New York or Andrews of the change in routing so long as the final destination of the flight remained Wiesbaden. Since he had used only his short-range radio, he knew Washington could not have monitored the conversations with Shannon.

Over the Isle of Jersey, flight control shifted briefly from Shannon to London. A few minutes later, he picked up the lights along the French coast near St.-Lô. Now the plane was under Paris Control. It was time to tamper with the flight plan again.

"Paris, this is SAM 26000 requesting a change in routing to Wiesbaden. Over."

"Go ahead 26000, this is Paris."

"Paris, SAM 26000 requesting routing change from Paris to Avord en route to Wiesbaden via Luxembourg. We would like to try the approach at Avord and expect to remain in the area about thirty minutes. Over."

"SAM 26000, this is Paris Control. You are cleared for Avord as requested, then proceeding Wiesbaden via Luxembourg."

"Paris, this is SAM 26000 acknowledging routing change and thank you."

Albertazzie sent word back to Kissinger in the presidential lounge. "We are cleared for Avord and should be on the ground in about thirty minutes."

On the ground, the French directed SAM 26000 to a military "alert" strip away from the terminal. Kissinger and his two aides quickly boarded a waiting French two-engine jet that took them into Villacoublay Airport outside Paris. Dick Walters crowded them into a rented car and sped them over the darkened streets to his Paris apartment where they spent the night.

The plan called for Kissinger to wind up his secret session with the North Vietnamese in time to be back to Avord by three o'clock the following afternoon when the President's plane would return from its overnight stop in Wiesbaden. Once again, Albertazzie had to tinker with the flight plan to mask his side trip into France.

At Wiesbaden, he filed a routing only as far as Shannon "because nobody would question that." He didn't mention Avord.

"I knew Kissinger well enough to know that he might be delayed in Paris or we might be delayed at Avord. And I didn't want Andrews Air Force Base to have us on file with a flight plan from Wiesbaden and then begin to ask, as time went by, where the hell is Albertazzie?"

As soon as SAM 26000 cleared German Control coming out of Wiesbaden, he contacted Paris Control and obtained clearance to fly to Avord. But another deception had to be arranged. After suitable flying time had elapsed to have reached Shannon from Wiesbaden, Albertazzie instructed his chief radio operator, William Justis, to contact Wiesbaden and say that the President's plane was on the ground at Shannon.

That relieved the base at Wiesbaden of any further responsibility for—or interest in—SAM 26000. But Shannon was expecting the presidential aircraft to land at any moment, and it was not in the Irish skies at all but about to touch down at Avord.

"So we radioed Shannon from the plane and advised that we were at Avord. We requested that they not transmit our Avord arrival time to anybody. And we said we would call back as soon as we were ready to depart Avord for Shannon."

The complicated web of truths and deceits apparently satisfied all the flight operations centers that otherwise would have worried about the plane. Wiesbaden assumed it was at Shannon. Shannon knew the plane was in France, so it wasn't worried. And back in the United States, Andrews Air Force Base knew only that SAM 26000 had flown to Wiesbaden the day before on a training exercise and presumably was still there, since no return flight plan had been received. Henry Kissinger had no time for flight details, but he would have appreciated all the fabrications that were being spun in the skies and on the ground to conceal his presence in Paris.

In fact, at Avord on Saturday afternoon, February 21, Albertazzie was sure he would have to engage in even more elaborate prevarications to protect the secret mission. The presidential plane landed promptly at three o'clock and tried to make itself as inconspicuous as possible among the French tanker jets. But Kissinger was nowhere to be seen. Nor was the French military plane that was to have brought him back from Paris. There was nothing to do but wait—and hope the French military personnel would not become too friendly or curious.

One hour passed. Two hours. Albertazzie and the crew began to fret. Something must have gone awry. He reviewed his top-secret guidance and strolled back into the cabin to compare instructions with Diane Matthews, a Kissinger secretary who was also waiting for him to return from Paris. Their information was identical and quite clear. Unless Albertazzie had received a telephone call in Wiesbaden by midday, the pickup time would remain as originally set: 3 P.M. sharp at Avord. To preserve secrecy, there were to be no other calls or messages between Paris and Albertazzie. It was a case of "don't call us, we'll call you."

Three hours elapsed. Still no Kissinger. And no explanation. Albertazzie was worried not only about him but also about his cover for *Air Force One.*

"I was concerned that Shannon or possibly other people were beginning to wonder where in hell we were." He instructed his radio operator to again reassure Shannon Control that the plane was all right. "Tell them we'll be in contact as soon as we're airborne from Avord."

Finally, about six-thirty, just when Albertazzie was beginning to think he might have to break his silence in an effort to check up on Kissinger, the French executive jet whooshed in for a landing. Kissinger and his two aides hurried aboard SAM 26000.

"We're late," Kissinger barked by way of an explanation. "Let's go." The big plane was airborne in less than five minutes.

Before departing Avord, the fuel tanks had been filled by the French military—more than 10,000 gallons worth, for which they refused payment. That kept the bill from hitting the Pentagon and thereby blowing Kissinger's cover. Their generosity also meant the presidential aircraft would be able to fly nonstop back to Andrews Air Force Base.

Heading for home on an easterly course across the English Channel, Albertazzie radioed Shannon once more. He canceled the scheduled landing there and filed a new flight plan directly to Washington. Since the plane was then under Shannon Control, the plan would turn up on the teletype at flight operations at Andrews as a departure from Shannon, not from Avord. It was misleading, of course, but that was the way the regulations could be jiggered. Kissinger's cover would hold up. Nobody in the Pentagon or Foggy Bottom would be the wiser.

The February 20–21 trip set the pattern for all of Kissinger's subsequent secret visits to Paris to confer with the North Vietnamese and, beginning in the summer of 1971, with the Chinese. In all, SAM 26000 and SAM 970 flew thirteen clandestine missions with Kissinger during 1970 and 1971. Some of the Paris sessions lasted nearly eight hours, but the presidential planes always managed to get Kissinger back to Washington within an elapsed time of forty-eight hours.

The world's press and official Washington were astounded when President Nixon himself disclosed the secret talks during a nationwide address on January 25, 1972. Among those who had been kept in the dark were Defense Secretary Melvin R. Laird, Secretary of State William Rogers, and most of the White House staff.

It was a miracle that the secret had held so long. With each successive trip, the circle of those in the know kept widening. Albertazzie estimated that at least forty persons, counting American and French air crews, had assisted in the first undertaking. Subsequent flights, involving Kissinger drops at Stuttgart, Wiesbaden, Frankfurt, and U.S. and Royal Air Force fields in Britain as well as Avord, added to the list of accomplices. Many of them were in the military services of their respective countries, and Albertazzie believes that helped reduce the risk of discovery. "It was a matter of military discipline," he said. "People were told not to talk, not to ask questions. It worked."

Just as Kissinger and Dick Walters had found it necessary to inform key aides on a need-to-know basis, Albertazzie decided that it would be useful to apprise at least one close Air Force friend early in the game. He was Col. John Goodlett of San Antonio, Texas. Goodlett had served with Albertazzie twenty years earlier in Hawaii and in 1970 was chief of the U.S. Air Force command post at Wiesbaden, the nerve center for all American military flights in Europe. "Goodlett's unit monitored everything that happened in an Air Force way," Albertazzie explained.

"I told Goodlett I was going to be running these trips of a highly classified nature involving the national defense and the war in Vietnam. And that if he saw or heard anything that might compromise the mission—if some guy came around asking too many questions—would he please invent a reason to cover my operation. I did that as a precaution in case somebody discov-

288

ered we were in Avord or another French place and began asking the command post for Europe, 'Hey, what's the President's plane doing in France?' Goodlett then could respond by saying, 'Well, we have this reason or that,' and thus keep such questions from going any further."

The clandestine flights to Paris were considerably more ticklish than another famous secret trip by Kissinger—this time to Moscow in April 1972. By then, Kissinger had already made his "belly-ache" flight to China to set up Nixon's visit there in February 1972. The President was preparing for his first Moscow summit meeting later in the year, with the Vietnam war and a strategic arms limitation treaty (SALT) very much on the agenda. The Russians, not wanting to be upstaged by Peking, figured they also merited a taste of Kissinger's secret diplomacy.

The trip began in typical Kissinger fashion the evening of April 19. Slipping away from a splashy cocktail party in Georgetown, Kissinger was whisked by limousine to Andrews Air Force Base, where the presidential jet, four key aides, and Soviet Ambassador Anatoly Dobrynin were waiting. While Kissinger slept and Dobrynin napped and read, Albertazzie pushed SAM 26000 through the night skies over the Atlantic and northern Europe, landing ten hours later at Vnukovo Airport on the outskirts of Moscow. The flight aroused no curiosity in high places because the President was scheduled to fly to Moscow in six weeks. It was customary for a presidential plane and crew to make an advance inspection of the landing facilities at his destination overseas. There was no reason to suspect that Kissinger was aboard.

Unlike the trips to Paris, there was no problem at all in maintaining a blanket of secrecy over Kissinger's presence in Russia. The Soviets were masters of the art. They put up Kissinger and his party in luxurious quarters in Lenin Hills, a secluded, scenic area outside the Soviet capital for VIP guests and Kremlin leaders. Nobody was informed of Kissinger's arrival except the top Russian officials. Kissinger himself insisted that the trip be kept secret from the American Embassy and Ambassador Jacob Beam in Moscow until the eve of his departure four days later. In fact, Kissinger did not even notify Major Gen. Brent Scowcroft, the President's senior military assistant, who was heading up a White House advance team then in Moscow to make technical arrangements for the Nixon-Brezhnev summit in May.

Kissinger's fetish for secrecy created a headache for Albertazzie and the crew. Every day, following every session with Chairman Brezhnev and the Soviet negotiators, Kissinger filed secret cables to the White House over the aircraft's superb communications system. The heavy traffic was handled by operators of the White House Communications Agency, who had flown to Russia with Kissinger. Then, without warning, the plane's encoding computer malfunctioned, making it impossible to communicate in a secure fashion with the White House Situation Room.

Kissinger was furious. The plane was parked in a guarded sector of Vnukovo Airport. There was no way to acquire replacement parts or use alternate equipment. The cables could have been sent from the American embassy in Moscow or over the communications facilities aboard Scowcroft's aircraft. But that would have disclosed Kissinger's presence and he would not hear of it. For a whole day, the equipment was down. Not a coded message went into the White House.

"What will Nixon think I'm doing here?" Kissinger complained. Albertazzie's crew and the communications operators finally managed to solve their problem and thereby ease Kissinger's anxiety. The President no longer might wonder if he was taking a Russian holiday.

In the sky, the pilot's word is law. His passengers may outrank him and may seek to advise him. But their safety and the safety of the aircraft is his responsibility —and his alone. In the exercise of that responsibility, a presidential pilot may find himself in the unenviable position of pitting his judgment against a presidential directive, even in so flagrant a matter as considering whether to unmask a secret diplomatic mission.

That question confronted Albertazzie in March 1970.

Henry Kissinger was due in Paris for another ultra-secret talk with North Vietnamese negotiators. His clandestine meetings since mid-February had gone well and so had the flights. Actually, as Kissinger confided in a rare moment of candor to one of

290

his aides, the flights were smoother than the talks. Up to that point, Albertazzie had been carrying Kissinger on SAM 26000, the primary *Air Force One*. This time he decided to use SAM 970, the presidential backup plane.

"It had been in a maintenance facility in New York for two months on an IRAN basis: 'Inspect and Repair as Necessary.' When it came back to Andrews Air Force Base, I wanted to give it a shakedown flight before I put the President aboard. Kissinger's trip seemed like a good occasion. And the shakedown excuse would be a secure cover for the secrecy we needed."

The plan was to be a carbon copy of the first Kissinger mission of February 20, 1970. He would arrange to be seen in public in Washington, then quietly slip out to Andrews and take off in the waiting presidential jet. Albertazzie again filed a flight plan from Andrews to Wiesbaden, Germany, where U.S. Air Force headquarters in Europe was located. But on the way, by devious design, the flight plan would be altered so that Kissinger could be dropped off at night in Avord.

Kissinger liked SAM 970. Although its tail number was not as prestigious among aviators as the premier presidential plane, SAM 26000, he found its interior accommodations more comfortable for his purposes. And, of course, few Americans or foreigners could tell the difference between the two planes. Both bore identical presidential markings.

But a difference soon cropped up.

Midway across the Atlantic, flight engineer Joe Chappell informed Albertazzie that the plane was slowly losing hydraulic pressure. "He thought it might be a slow leak in the pressure system. When it reached a certain low point on the instruments, he said he would go below into the hold and replenish the system."

It seemed only a minor inconvenience, certainly nothing to become alarmed about. An hour later, Chappell came back on the interphone to the cockpit.

"I've just refilled the hydraulic system, but something's wrong. The fluid doesn't stay there very long."

"Try it again," Albertazzie ordered. "And keep looking for the trouble."

291

Chappel came forward shortly thereafter. "Colonel, we got a real problem. The fluid is going out as fast as I can put it in. In fact, I don't have any more to put in."

Albertazzie swore softly. Hydraulic power on a modern jet does just about everything but fly the plane. It raises and lowers the flaps, assists the steering, operates the landing gear, and provides braking power on the ground.

"We tried playing with the system," said Albertazzie. "We pushed the brakes. Nothing happened. We tinkered with the flaps. No response. We had lost all hydraulic power. From there on it was going to be a case of muscle versus the machine."

Another fact was immediately obvious to the crew. SAM 970 was now more than halfway across the Atlantic. It no longer had enough fuel to return to the United States. It would have to land in Europe—somewhere.

Avord? That was where Kissinger was destined to be dropped. But the French military base had no facilities for handling a crippled Boeing 707. Without repairs, the plane would not be able to depart and that posed a serious risk to the secrecy of the mission.

Albertazzie went back into the cabin to apprise Kissinger of the problem. Kissinger slammed his hand on the table and in Kissingerian fashion, came back with an analysis.

"Albertazzie, you've got two problems. One, what to do with me. Two, what to do with the plane." He remembers offering a suggestion. "Ideally, we will solve both with one solution."

Albertazzie assured Kissinger that the plane could be landed safely, even without a hydraulic system, by mechanically lowering the landing gear and the wing flaps and by skillful use of the engines' reverse thrust to compensate for the loss of brakes and steering. But the landing site could not be Avord. It would have to be some airport with facilities for repairing SAM 970. That meant a commercial airport used by the scheduled international airliners. Shannon? London? Paris? Frankfurt? Rome?

"I don't have to tell you that the President does not want this trip to be compromised, " Kissinger said. "Despite the difficulties, this mission must be preserved. That means, quite simply, that a way must be found to get me to Paris without detection."

Visibly perturbed, Kissinger turned to his deputy, Alexander

292

Haig, who was accompanying him on the Paris mission. "Get word of this back to the President and request instructions," he told Haig.

Nixon, equally perturbed, flashed back a quick answer from the White House: The trip was not to be aborted. It had to be saved at all costs. He urged Kissinger and Haig to contact Dick Walters in Paris to hear what he might suggest. Thus began an urgent flow of coded messages between SAM 970 over the Atlantic and Walters at his office in the Paris embassy, via the Situation Room at the White House.

With less than three hours to go, Albertazzie made the firm decision to risk a landing at Frankfurt's busy Rhein-Main Airport. It had a long runway with arresting gear in event the plane could not be slowed. The U.S. Air Force had an installation there— and that offered a cover for the presidential jet. Lufthansa, the German airline, maintained servicing facilities for its own Boeing 707s at Rhein-Main; the hydraulic problem probably could be repaired there.

And it was not too far from Paris. With help from Walters and help from trustworthy Air Force personnel at Rhein-Main, perhaps Kissinger could still get to Paris without being recognized.

The decision to go to Rhein-Main was quickly transmitted to Walters in Paris, where he had been anxiously deciphering messages from the distressed aircraft. Walters pondered what he could do now to bail out Kissinger. It was eight o'clock in the evening. He was alone, his secretary had left, and the office was closed. As Walters recounted in his memoirs, "I decided the only thing I could do was to go to President Pompidou."

A startled gendarme at Elysée Palace alerted Michel Jobert, Pompidou's close adviser, that Walters was at the entrance. Jobert heard Walters' story and excused himself. Moments later, Walters was ushered into Pompidou's office, where he explained the dilemma taking place in the skies near Europe even as they spoke. Walters described Pompidou's reaction:

"He reached for the telephone on his desk and he called his flight crew at Villacoublay Airport south of Paris, where the [French] President's executive aircraft, a Mystère 20, was kept. After a brief conversation, he said to me, 'Go out to Villacoublay. They will be waiting for you and they will take you to

Frankfurt, where you can pick up Kissinger and bring him back here.'"

Walters drove swiftly to Villacoublay. Pompidou's plane and Colonel Calderon were ready to go. The speedy Mystère jet flashed down the runway and took off for Frankfurt, Germany.

Minutes away from Rhein-Main Airport, Calderon caught up with SAM 970 as Albertazzie was easing the big Boeing into its final approach. Calderon followed him in.

"I had radioed ahead to the Air Force commander of our own operations at Rhein-Main," Albertazzie said. "I told him I was coming in unexpectedly on a classified trip and that I didn't want a lot of attention when we got down. I didn't even tell him we had any trouble aboard. I just said I wanted one man on the field to bring the stairs up to the plane. I said, 'I don't even want to see you there.'"

SAM 970 settled down slowly, making maximum use of the runway's length. As the wheels touched down, Albertazzie pushed the engines into reverse to brake its speed. It worked. Then, putting two engines into forward thrust and keeping the other two in reverse, he varied the power to maneuver SAM 970 off the runway and into a long taxiing run to the Air Force sector of the field.

Pompidou's plane got there first. Walters leaped out of the Mystère and commanded that all the floodlights be turned off.

SAM 970 rolled to a stop. Kissinger, with his familiar glasses off and his coat collar turned up, was hustled aboard the Mystère along with his aides. Calderon ordered the door closed, throttled up the engines, and quickly moved the French jet to a runway. Moments later the plane was airborne for Paris.

Back on SAM 970, Albertazzie removed his headset and sighed with relief. The radio operator sped a coded message to Nixon at the White House. Flight engineers Joe Chappell and Danny Daniels soon diagnosed the difficulty—a badly ruptured hydraulic line. With the help of Lufthansa's service facilities, and by working all night, they could repair the Boeing before it was due to fly to Avord to pick up Kissinger the next afternoon.

Meanwhile, en route to Paris aboard the Mystère, pilot Calderon summoned Dick Walters to the cockpit to deal with a new dilemma. The scene back at Rhein-Main, Calderon observed,

294

had been most unusual, even awkward. It was potentially troublesome for President Pompidou; his plane was not in the habit of making unannounced, nocturnal stops at German airports. The Germans were sure to come around with a lot of questions. What, Calderon asked, should he say?

That problem, Walters noted in his memoirs, was something he had not anticipated. He thought about it silently for a few moments, and then an idea came to him.

"Tell them it involved a woman," he advised Calderon. "They will believe it of the French and be discreet."

Chapter Ten
The Flight That Shocked the World

Albertazzie knew something was afoot the moment Brig. Gen. James Hughes called from the White House.

"Do you suppose you could drive over?" Hughes asked.

The President's senior military aide had used a special "secure" telephone line, a connection over which voices could be scrambled to foil eavesdroppers. "By the way," Hughes added, "keep this to yourself."

Albertazzie invented an excuse to cover his absence from the base and sped down Suitland Parkway, over the South Capitol Street Bridge and into downtown Washington. White House police opened the steel gates guarding the southwest entrance to West Executive Avenue, which separates the Executive Office Building from the White House compound. Albertazzie slid his car into a parking space near the basement entrance to the West Wing of the presidential mansion.

Inside, guards waved him through to the East Wing, where the Military Office was located. Hughes was waiting, but instead of motioning him to a chair, Hughes beckoned Albertazzie out of the office and down a corridor. Soon they were deep below the White House in the "shelter," a hardened concrete-and-steel bunker intended for temporary use by the President and the First Family in the event it became necessary to evacuate them in an emergency.

Albertazzie had been there before. The shelter was a useful hideaway for private meetings—away from the eyes and ears of other White House staffers. Hughes closed the heavy door and pulled up a chair at the table opposite Albertazzie.

"We've got an interesting one this time," Hughes began, a grin spreading across his face. "The Boss is sending Kissinger to China. Secretly. You know a way to smuggle him in? And out?"

"You mean Communist China? Good Lord!" Albertazzie's eyes fairly popped.

Which way to Peking? For most Americans during the last three decades, there was but one answer: You can't get there from here.

Then on February 1, 1969, scarcely three weeks after Nixon's inauguration, an intriguing Oval Office memo found its way to the basement desk of an unsuspecting Henry Kissinger. Unsigned by the President, it said simply: "I think we should give every encouragement to the attitude that this administration is exploring possibilities of rapprochement with the Chinese." But the notion was not to be mentioned out loud. "This, of course, should be done privately and should under no circumstances get into the public print from this direction."

The signals soon became public, although Nixon himself stayed in the background. Before the year was out, the administration authorized American scholars, scientists, and journalists to have their passports validated for travel in mainland China. Tourists were permitted to bring back Chinese goods; naval patrols in the Taiwan Strait were suspended, and Secretary of State Rogers announced U.S. eagerness to resume the ambassadorial talks in Warsaw that had broken off during the Johnson administration. To make sure that Peking got the message, Nixon discreetly told key foreign leaders with access to Mao—French President de Gaulle, Rumania's Nicolae Ceausescu, and Pakistani President Yahya Khan—that the United States desired to "open a dialogue" with the leaders of China.

The Chinese were intrigued by Nixon's overtures, but in no

298

big rush to accommodate him. Eighteen months elapsed before Peking bothered to respond directly, and then it was through a series of ambiguous, unsigned notes to the White House, with Pakistani diplomats playing postmen. Then, early in the spring of 1971, the Chinese electrified the world by inviting an American ping-pong team to tour China—the first official American delegation to set foot on the Chinese mainland since 1949. On April 27, Peking finally sent to the White House, via Pakistan, the private message for which Nixon had been angling for two years. It was an invitation for an American envoy to visit Peking for secret talks.

Nixon decided to send Kissinger.

But how?

Hughes was enjoying Albertazzie's astonishment. "Don't call it Communist China," he corrected. "Kissinger's going to the People's Republic of China."

"I know. It just takes getting used to." Albertazzie leaned back in thought. "It's not going to be easy to get him in and out of there secretly. Maybe harder than sneaking him into France."

"You said it."

"And when does he have to be there?"

"No dates have been set—at least I'm not aware of any," Hughes replied. "But I understand it will be soon, so there's not much time to figure how to do it."

Hughes, it turned out, already had been doing some figuring. Now he wanted the presidential pilot's opinion on what he had in mind, much as the two of them had worked out the secret flights taking Kissinger to Paris to meet with North Vietnamese diplomats for more than a year.

Attached to Special Air Missions wing at Andrews were nearly a dozen Lockheed Jetstars, small, speedy executive aircraft employed by the White House and top government VIPs for domestic trips and courier service. Both Hughes and Albertazzie had been checked out in Jetstars and so were qualified to fly them. There were also five or six high-altitude Jetstars belonging to the Air Communications Service (ACS), each of them outfitted with special communications equipment for testing and calibrating the air-to-ground instrumentation at U.S. air bases around the country. Each plane normally required two pilots, a flight mechanic, and a technician. That left no room for passengers.

Hughes's idea was a simple one. Under the guise of a training mission, one of the ACS Jetstars would be quietly dispatched to Japan. Kissinger would discreetly disappear from Washington and fly secretly to Japan aboard one of the jet transports in the SAM fleet. Or he could make an open diplomatic trip to Japan and then drop out of sight there for a few days. Either way, the plan called for Kissinger to link up secretly in Japan with Hughes and Albertazzie. Using the special Jetstar, and with Kissinger occupying the technician's seat, they would fly him quickly across the East China Sea to Shanghai, or Peking, or wherever the meeting with the Chinese leaders was to take place. After his talks, Kissinger would exit by reversing the procedure. If everything worked out on schedule, Kissinger would be absent from Washington about four days.

From a pilot's standpoint, Albertazzie thought it sounded like a workable scheme. But diplomatic complications and security considerations caused the plan to be scrubbed during ensuing days.

One obstacle was that, in 1971, Japan had not yet established diplomatic relations with China. And the Chinese, with their exquisite attention to the niceties of protocol when it suited them, were expected to frown on a flight plan originating from an airfield in Japan. Colonel Haig, Kissinger's deputy on the National Security Council, posed another problem: A lone Jetstar penetrating Chinese air space might easily be mistaken for a hostile aircraft by the ever-watchful Chinese Air Force. Besides, there was no way of knowing whether Premier Chou En-lai, who had arranged the Kissinger visit, had taken his own military establishment into confidence on the secret contacts with the White House. After all, President Nixon was keeping the Pentagon in the dark. Might not Chou be doing a similar thing in Peking?

But it was Kissinger who raised the ultimate and conclusive obstacle. The President, he said, was not yet ready to apprise the Japanese government of his delicate overtures to Peking. For one thing, the Japanese government was notorious for "leaking like a sieve" to its own press corps. The risk of publicity was too great to take. Secondly, the Japanese leadership would go into shock at the audacity of the Nixon-Kissinger opening to China; Tokyo already was apprehensive of Washington's modest public moves to lessen tensions with the People's Republic. To let the Japanese in on the big secret would arouse fears of damage to Japan's own relations with the United States. In their anxiety, they might well create enough public and private fuss to abort the entire mission.

The Chinese may have sensed the dilemma they had handed Nixon. While Hughes, Albertazzie, and Haig continued to fashion—and discard—various plans for clandestinely depositing Kissinger on Chinese soil, the President got another message on May 31 from China via the Pakistani ambassador in Washington. The Chinese leadership was pleased with Nixon's choice of Kissinger as his envoy; the dates for his visit would be July 9–11, the site would be Peking—and the travel arrangements were to be handled by the Pakistanis.

Hughes and Albertazzie greeted that word with sighs of relief. They had found no way to put Kissinger into China without the whole world discovering it. Now the government of Pakistan would handle it in concert with the government of China, the two being in good standing with each other. All that remained to be done now—Albertazzie stressed the word *all* with wry understatement—was to get Kissinger to Pakistan by July 8 and arrange for him to quietly drop from sight for the next two or three days.

The planning proceeded on three levels. The President, Secretary of State Rogers, and Kissinger put together an eleven-day diplomatic mission that would take Kissinger to Vietnam, Thailand, India, and neighboring Pakistan. By design, it was to be an open trip so as to avoid suspicion of its real purpose. President Yahya Khan of Pakistan, meanwhile, secretly worked out with Chou En-lai in Peking the scheme for smuggling Kissinger from Pakistan into China. Hughes and Albertazzie were given the responsibility for selecting the aircraft and crew that could adequately support the public portion of Kissinger's mission, while simultaneously providing secure communications with the Oval Office regarding his clandestine entry into China and his return home.

301

From a technical standpoint, two planes were eminently suited for this delicate enterprise. One was *Air Force One* (SAM 26000), with its unsurpassed communications capability. The other was SAM 970, the shorter Boeing 707 that served as the presidential backup plane. Both could offer the President and Kissinger the most sophisticated electronic equipment for exchanging top secret messages.

But from a public relations viewpoint, both aircraft were ill-suited for this mission. Kissinger was not supposed to attract extraordinary public attention. If he were to travel in one of the two primary presidential planes, the mission would automatically take on the high-level significance that Nixon and Kissinger wanted to avoid. The world's press corps had to believe the trip was just an ordinary exercise in diplomacy.

Albertazzie had an idea.

"How about one of the executive C-135s assigned to SAC, TAC, and CINCPAC?" he asked Hughes. "They've got the communications capability we're looking for. And they don't wear the White House label. (SAC = Strategic Air Command; TAC = Tactical Air Command; CINCPAC = Commander-in-Chief, Pacific.)

Hughes agreed. With his authorization, Albertazzie went to Langley Air Force Base in Virginia and arranged to "borrow" the converted C-135 jet transport of the commanding officer of the Tactical Air Command. Special Air Missions at Andrews Air Force Base assigned a pilot with C-135 flying experience and a flight steward who had traveled previously with Kissinger. To handle message traffic, the White House Communications Agency chose one of its top communicators. None of the crew and none of the Air Force brass were aware that the real purpose of the trip was to position Kissinger to make his covert entry in the People's Republic of China. To ensure secrecy for the unusual mission, it was given the code name "Project Polo," in honor of Marco Polo, the Western explorer who "discovered" China in 1271.

On July 1, Kissinger left Andrews and headed for Saigon for talks with President Thieu and Ambassador Ellsworth Bunker. That visit made splashy news in the United States, including a major segment on the CBS Evening News with Walter Cronkite and a page-one story in *The New York Times*. Four days later, Kissinger arrived in Bangkok for private talks with Thai leaders. Kissinger had little to say to newsmen there. The story dropped off the front page. New Delhi was the next stop. After seeing Prime Minister Indira Gandhi, Kissinger was badgered by reporters demanding to know if he would be seeing Le Duc Tho, the top North Vietnamese negotiator, when he got to Paris. Kissinger fudged his answer; the *Times* settled for a short Associated Press account on an inside page. Unable to extract anything dramatic from Kissinger, the press contingent rapidly melted. By the time he arrived in Islamabad, the new capital of Pakistan, on July 8, only three newsmen were dogging his trail.

"I had brought the press to tears," Kissinger remembers, "never saying anything of interest to them."

Now began one of the slickest deceptions since the days of Houdini. It was masterminded by Pakistan's President Yahya Khan and executed by Foreign Minister Sultan Mohammed Khan, with a supporting cast starring the U.S. ambassador to Pakistan, Joseph S. Farland, and several dozen Pakistani extras. Four men were going to vanish from sight for nearly three days—Kissinger and three of his traveling aides: staff assistant Winston Lord, and two Asia experts, John Holdridge and Richard Smyser.

The disappearing act commenced immediately after Kissinger paid a ninety-minute courtesy call on President Khan. By prearrangement, word went out that Kissinger was exhausted from his long trip. The formal dinner scheduled in his honor that evening was canceled; this, too, was part of the plan. Khan announced that Kissinger would rest up in the nearby mountain resort of Nattria Gali.

A motorcade of limousines, escorted by motorcycles and conspicuously flying American and Pakistani flags, soon began winding out of Islamabad and up the mountain road to Nattria Gali.

The following day, July 9, the office of President Khan announced that Kissinger had been seized with "a slight indisposition," a polite euphemism for an intestinal upset common in Asia.

As part of the masquerade, a Pakistani physician was sum-

303

moned to the posh, secluded bungalow assigned to Kissinger on the mountaintop. But Sultan Mohammed Khan had carefully ascertained in advance that this doctor had never laid eyes on Kissinger. Little did the good doctor know that the American he examined and treated was actually a security agent who had indeed contracted stomach flu.

The Pakistani ploy didn't stop there. During the next two days, high-ranking government officials were instructed by President Khan to drive up to Nattria Gali to chat with Kissinger and wish him well. Foreign Minister Khan and Ambassador Farland received the innocent callers, told them Kissinger was napping, and thanked them profusely on Kissinger's behalf for driving out.

Kissinger, in fact, had never gone there. He never felt better in his life.

Following his courtesy call on President Khan, he was secluded in the presidential guest house in Islamabad to await the next step in his secret journey to China. At two-thirty in the morning, Sultan Mohammed Khan arrived in his own car, a modest Toyota, and drove Kissinger to the airport. Khan skirted Kissinger's plane, the U.S. Air Force C-135, which was prominently parked at the terminal, and drove out to the far end of the field. There waiting was a Boeing 707 jet bearing the insignia of the Pakistan International Airline (PIA).

Khan escorted Kissinger aboard to meet his welcoming party, four ranking Chinese officials sent to Islamabad by Chou En-lai three days earlier. Moments later, Kissinger was joined by his three aides. The American quartet, plus two Secret Service bodyguards, would be the first U.S. officials to enter China in nearly a quarter century.

"I kept pinching myself," Kissinger told us later. "It did not seem possible that I could be making such a trip."

Shortly after three o'clock, the PIA jetliner hurtled down the dimly lit runway, banked to the northeast, and charted a course over the snow-capped Himalayas directly for Peking. Kissinger would get there at noon, the hour set by Chou En-lai.

The departure attracted scant attention, since PIA regularly flew to China. It was one of the few airlines having entry permission from the People's Republic. European businessmen frequently traveled via PIA. Kissinger and his companions easily could have passed for international sales representatives going to a trade meeting in China.

But the carefully constructed cover was nearly blown by one of those odd coincidences that dog the best of plans. As British journalists recount the story, there just happened to be at the Islamabad airport a Pakistani named Mohammed Beg, who was a stringer for the *Daily Telegraph* in London.

"Isn't that Kissinger whom Sultan Mohammed Khan just put on the airplane?" Beg inquired of an airport official.

The official nodded casually.

"Isn't that plane going to China?" Beg asked.

Again the official nodded.

"Why is Kissinger going there?"

"I haven't the faintest idea," the official replied.

Beg hurried back to his Islamabad office and wired a bulletin story to the *Daily Telegraph*, describing what he had seen and heard. In London, a busy night editor read Beg's copy several times and tossed it aside. "That damn Beg," he groused. "He must be drinking again. Imagine, Henry Kissinger flying to China! Impossible!"

On July 11, Kissinger wound up his talks with Chou En-lai in Peking and boarded the waiting PIA jet for the return trip to Islamabad. He had been in China forty-nine hours, totally without contact with the President in Washington. Before departing the White House, he and Nixon had agreed that if the Chinese were prepared to invite Nixon on a presidential visit in the next few months, Kissinger would send an urgent one-word message immediately upon his return to Pakistan.

Moments after the PIA jetliner landed, Kissinger hurried over to his U.S. Air Force jet, still waiting on the tarmac at Islamabad, and handed the White House Communications Agency operator a secret cable to be flashed directly to the Western White House in San Clemente, where Nixon had gone for a working vacation.

In California, Alexander Haig took the decoded dispatch and rushed to the waiting President. "We've got a message from 'Polo,' " said Haig.

"What does he say?"

Haig grinned. "The word is 'Eureka!' "

Nixon grinned back. He stood up and strode around the room, rubbing his hands together. "Eureka!" he repeated. "Eureka!"

Planning for "Polo II" began almost immediately after Nixon had announced to an astonished world on July 15 that he would visit Peking before May 1972 to confer with Chinese leaders "to seek the normalization of relations between the two countries." In his address, televised live from a Los Angeles studio, the President disclosed that arrangements for the presidential trip had been worked out in secret talks in Peking between Kissinger and Chou En-lai.

At Andrews Air Force Base, pilot Albertazzie patted the shiny fuselage of *Air Force One* and urged the ground maintenance crew to give the plane loving attention. Before long, it—and he—would be in China, too. At the Western White House, there was talk that the President might go as soon as autumn 1971. That meant that "Polo II," the advance trip to work out the actual arrangements, would have to take place within a matter of weeks.

"We'll be ready whenever you give us the word," Albertazzie told General Hughes, Nixon's military assistant.

But two events conspired to push Nixon's trip off the 1971 calendar and into 1972, thereby delaying Polo II as well. One was Nixon's decision, on August 2, to buttress the U.S. position in Peking by announcing that America was discarding its twenty-two-year opposition to mainland China's admission to the United Nations. At the same time, Nixon made clear, the United States would oppose any effort to deprive its old ally on Taiwan, Nationalist China, of U.N. membership. Peking opposed the "two-China" policy. But before the U.N. could move the issue to a vote in September, a dramatic leadership convulsion shook Peking and directly threatened Nixon's trip.

Defense Minister Lin Piao, once Mao Tse-tung's heir apparent, launched a bold bid for power, using Chou En-lai's overture to Washington as the rallying issue for China's unhappy radicals. But Mao sided with Chou and snuffed the coup. Lin tried to flee the country by seizing a Chinese jet transport and flying to the Soviet Union. The Chinese later said he was killed when his

306

plane crashed in the Gobi Desert of Mongolia. Peking accused Lin of plotting to assassinate Mao.

During the tense days of late September, the Chinese government canceled all flights, put off the traditional October First parade in Peking, and prepared for what looked like another internal upheaval. Then, just as suddenly as it had erupted, the political storm blew over. Kissinger and Nixon breathed easier once again. The President's history-making trip was still on track.

On October 2, the White House announced that Kissinger and an advance party would go to China on October 20 "to make concrete arrangements" for the President's eventual visit. This time the trip would be made in the presidential backup plane, SAM 970, with stops in Hawaii and Guam before flying into Shanghai and then Peking. The route was the same that Nixon later would take, thus giving *Air Force One*'s flight crew, the Secret Service, and the White House Communications Agency a chance to familiarize themselves with facilities and physical surroundings at each stop.

It was a hectic time of preparation for Albertazzie. He hadn't the foggiest notion of airfield conditions, instrumentation, or navigation systems used by the Chinese on the mainland.

"The Air Force had only old data on such stuff as radio frequencies, approach and landing procedures, and the like," he said. "It was terribly outdated and just about useless.

"In addition to learning the flying procedures in and out of the Chinese airports, I needed to know whether auxiliary ground power was available and whether it was compatible with our Boeing 707 at each place. And whether they had suitable refrigeration facilities for food supplies, the right kind of fuel, and safe areas for parking *Air Force One* and allowing our own Air Force guards to protect it."

Albertazzie obtained classified aerial photographs of the Chinese airfields that had been taken clandestinely by high-altitude SR-71 "spy planes," plus satellite photographs. Albertazzie was shocked to find China's "state of the art" so primitive.

"The Russians, before the split with the Chinese, were supposed to be keeping them up-to-date on aviation technology," Albertazzie said, "but from the material given to me, it was pretty clear that the Soviets really had been keeping the Chinese in the Dark Ages.''

In the end, Albertazzie's best sources turned out to be the commercial airlines that were flying 707 jets into Shanghai: Pakistan International Airline and Air France. To his delight, Albertazzie discovered that at least Shanghai's landing procedures were identical with that of other major airfields handling international air traffic.

Peking was something else. Its airport regularly served only internal Chinese traffic, and the Chinese were flying Soviet-built aircraft.

"It has outmoded Russian facilities," Albertazzie explained to Kissinger at one point. "If the weather gets bad between Shanghai and Peking, I'll have to rely on the Chinese ground control system and I won't be familiar enough with it to use it." Fortunately, the weather cooperated when *Air Force One* made its Polo II trip in October. For Nixon's trip the Chinese Air Ministry agreed to put English-speaking air controllers in the Peking tower to help talk *Air Force One* down if the weather closed in.

Kissinger was positively euphoric as the advance party of Polo II neared China aboard the presidential plane. He was in charge of arranging the most historic summit since World War II. But this time, unlike his first visit, he had a purposeful agenda and everyone aboard had an assigned role to play. Kissinger came up into the cockpit to share his expansive mood with Albertazzie. He climbed into the jump seat (actually the observer's seat) behind Albertazzie and began his customary bantering.

"Do you understand Chinese cloud formations?" Kissinger jibed.

"I do now that you're here to talk us through," Albertazzie shot back with a grin.

He never knew quite how to take Kissinger. At times he could be extremely uptight and most unreasonable. But Albertazzie also knew him as a man with a puckish humor—one of the few on the White House staff. During Nixon's first overseas trip as President, a visit to Europe in 1969, Kissinger had sauntered into the cockpit while Nixon was still on the tarmac outside saying goodbye to his hosts. When Nixon seemed to be taking an unusually long time to get aboard, Kissinger poked Albertazzie's back. "Why don't we go? I'm on board," he urged. Albertazzie threw him a questioning look.

"What's the matter, Albertazzie?" Kissinger cracked. "Don't you want to become famous?"

Now, with the China coast coming into view and Kissinger growing more ebullient by the moment, Albertazzie had a challenge for him.

"Dr. Kissinger, would you really like to make an impression on the Chinese?" he asked.

"What do you mean?" Kissinger parried.

"Well, there's going to be a big delegation on the field to meet us, including some important people you met here before," Albertazzie explained. "So right after we land and while we're taxiing up to the ramp, I'll get out of my pilot's seat and you climb in. The co-pilot will handle the taxiing. Then, when we come to a stop and cut the engines, you can open the pilot's window and wave to the welcoming delegation. The Chinese will think you flew the airplane in!"

"A marvelous idea!" Kissinger responded. "I'll do it."

But when the President's plane touched down at Shanghai, Kissinger was back in his own seat in the cabin. Later, when Albertazzie needled him about losing his nerve and an opportunity to become truly famous, Kissinger's face grew sober.

"Albertazzie," he said, "if I thought this administration had a sense of humor, I would have done it."

The first planning session with the Chinese began shortly after the big Boeing arrived in Peking at 11:20 A.M. on the 20th of October. They gathered at a long table in a conference room, the Chinese on one side, the Americans on the other. While Kissinger met with officials of the Chinese Foreign Ministry and Chou En-lai regarding an agenda for the President's private talks, White House Appointments Secretary Dwight Chapin took charge of arranging the matters of schedule, security, housing accommodations, ceremonies, and protocol. Besides Albertazzie, the group included Robert Taylor, chief of the White House Secret Service detail; General Albert Redmond of the White House Communications Agency, who worried about keeping Nixon in touch with the White House, the Pentagon, State Department, and American military commanders around the world;

Tim Elbourne, advance man for the White House Press Office, who was responsible for press arrangements; and General Hughes, White House military aide.

The leader of the Chinese side was Han Hsu, the chief of protocol who later went to Washington as chief of the Peking mission there. Also present were the vice minister of public security; the chiefs of information and telecommunications; and a pleasant chap who introduced himself to Albertazzie as "Mr. Chung." He turned out to be the personal pilot for Premier Chou En-lai—and he spoke English.

"We began very cautiously at first," said Albertazzie. "Since the Chinese were our hosts, we waited to hear what they had in mind for the President's visit. But after much polite sparring back and forth, it soon became obvious that they were waiting for our side to offer suggestions.

"Chapin finally said, yes, we have prepared some briefing books for a presidential visit, one of five days' duration, another of seven days. He tendered copies across the table to the Chinese. Whereupon they smiled, announced it was time to adjourn and that we would meet again the next day. It was clear they wanted time to go through the briefing books by themselves and consult with the Chinese leadership."

So it went, a group meeting every day, plus sessions between each American and his Chinese counterpart to work out detailed procedures for the President's upcoming visit. And every day the Chinese took the Americans on tours of Peking's sights and plied them with nightly banquets and entertainment, including the Chinese opera.

"Their hospitality was unbounded," Albertazzie said. "There were seventeen in the official party, but the Chinese also included the sixteen members of *Air Force One*'s crew in the festivities."

Not a word of publicity attended their presence in China. Not even Kissinger's name appeared in the Chinese press. The American advance party was quartered in an attractive guest compound, a ten-acre park surrounded by a high wall with barbed wire along the top. Armed soldiers guarded the gates and stationed themselves inconspicuously throughout the grounds.

"While strolling leisurely across the yard one day, a couple of

310

us started to cross an arched footbridge over a lovely pond," Albertazzie said. Out of nowhere popped a Mongolian guard brandishing an AK-47 automatic rifle. He held up his hand, indicating we were not to go any farther. We smiled at him and turned back. We heard later that there were other foreigners in the same compound. The Chinese did not want us to mingle."

The seclusion policy extended as well to their automobile trips across Peking. As soon as the Americans entered the vehicles assigned them, the Chinese escorts drew curtains across the windows.

"They told us it was to avoid large crowds and demonstrations," Albertazzie said. "But the word must have gotten out. Whenever our car stopped, ordinary Chinese would come right up and peer inside at us."

Despite their pre-China fears, Albertazzie and his *Air Force One* crew discovered that the Chinese were eager to adapt to modern aviation techniques even though they were putting up with antiquated Soviet equipment.

"They were able to provide almost everything we requested for handling *Air Force One* and our supporting aircraft, including ground facilities and security arrangements. Matter of fact, they sometimes exceeded our requirements."

Whenever the President's plane is on the ground, for example, its own Air Force armed guards maintain a twenty-four-hour watch around the perimeter of the parked aircraft. That can be an ordeal in bad weather. But the Chinese did something no other country had ever done. Anticipating that Nixon would make his Peking visit in the middle of winter, when the weather there is much as in Des Moines, Iowa, they provided enclosed and heated guardhouses for *Air Force One*'s security men.

Kissinger extended the advance party's stay by two days, primarily as a symbolic act, while the U.N. in New York was voting to admit Peking as a new member. The additional time allowed Albertazzie to further assess Chinese aviation proficiency—an important matter inasmuch as Chung had told him that the President would be expected to travel aboard Chinese-operated Russian aircraft on the planned flights from Peking to Hangchow, Mao's favorite winter resort, and then to Shanghai.

"I knew, as a matter of course, that I would recommend to the

311

President that he use *Air Force One* inside China," said Albertazzie. "That was our customary procedure in most countries, including those in Europe. But I knew that if the President decided to fly on Chou En-lai's plane as a matter of protocol, I really would not have to worry with Mr. Chung in the cockpit."

Chou's personal plane was an Ilyushin-18 turboprop, similar in appearance to the American *Electra*. "But the Chinese were quite aware of American flying procedures—and they didn't, thank God, fly like the Russians."

Indeed, had the Chinese turned out to be imitators of the Soviets, Albertazzie was prepared to plead personally with Nixon that he refuse to fly aboard their Soviet-made aircraft. To buttress his argument, the presidential pilot had obtained a confidential memo from Air Force sources detailing some of the horror stories of Russian flights bearing high-ranking Soviet diplomats to the United States, Canada, and Cuba. Portions of the memo went as follows:

CONFIDENTIAL
SOVIET FLIGHT PROCEDURES
1. Below-standard procedures utilized by Soviet VIP crews are continually being observed. . . .
2. On a flight carrying Foreign Minister Gromyko to the U.S., the Soviet navigator began using *not* a navigational chart but a *road map* of the New England states, and refused to use the navigation chart that [the American escort pilot] offered. On an earlier flight, one of our escort pilots observed the Soviet navigator using an ESSO road map. . . .
4. On a weather divert from JF Kennedy International to Boston's Logan International, the Soviet aircraft descended 300 feet below the ILS glide path. . . . Only the last-minute application of power prevented the flight from terminating in Massachusetts Bay. . . .
6. On a Gander (Newfoundland) to Havana flight, the flight . . . descended 3,000 feet below assigned altitude without prior clearance. He returned to assigned altitude only after the escort pilot threatened a possible fighter intercept. The Cuban escort refused to return with the same Soviet crew.
7. Poor fuel management aboard a TU-104 resulted in [the escort pilot] declaring an emergency and requesting the landing runway [at JFK International] be reversed to preclude engine failure over

a populated area. Soviet crew agreed to ditch the aircraft on Jones Beach if the initial landing at JFK could not be made. The aircraft landed with 10 minutes fuel on board; only suitable alternate was Bangor, Me., 30 minutes away. . . .

10. While flying an IL-62 to JFK, the co-pilot pulled out a hand-drawn copy of the VOR approach . . . the navigator changed VOR stations. . . . Control said aircraft was two miles off course. At that point, an argument erupted between pilot, co-pilot, and navigator. . . . Approach procedures were completely disregarded.

11. Returning from New York to Moscow, the Soviet crew was unable to start #4 engine. They began discussing a three-engine takeoff. . . . I asked if this had been done before; the Soviets replied they had made a three-engine flight from Africa to Moscow. I informed the Soviets I would not go along under such unsafe conditions.

12. On a flight from Toronto to Havana with Soviet Premier Kosygin aboard, the two HF radios malfunctioned and for two hours the aircraft was out of radio contact. As it was [also] out of VHF radio range, position reports could not be made until approaching Miami.

CONFIDENTIAL

But while Albertazzie was prepared to accept the President's decision to ride on Chinese aircraft inside China, the usual precautions were ordered. On each leg, Peking-Hangchow and Hangchow-Shanghai, *Air Force One*'s backup plane SAM 970 would be standing by, ready to substitute for Chou En-lai's IL-18 in the event of mechanical difficulties before takeoff. The White House planes would be making the internal trips anyway since they had to transport many of the technical and security personnel and the communications equipment required to support a President away from home. *Air Force One* would take off first, followed by Nixon in the Chinese plane. But, of course, if anything went wrong while the Nixons were airborne in a foreign aircraft, there would be little that Albertazzie or any other American could do.

Additionally, the Chinese agreed to "fix up" the IL-18 so the President could keep in touch with the outside world while flying with Chou. A White House Communications Agency specialist would be on board to handle urgent messages. The Chinese con-

313

sented to let him use one of the plane's antennae to transmit directly to *Air Force One*'s communications center. From there, Nixon's message traffic could be sent directly to the White House or to the Pentagon—and vice versa—in the event of an international crisis.

The American press corps, the Chinese decreed, also would be transported in Chinese aircraft once they arrived on Chinese soil. The big Boeing 707 charter planes of Pan American and Trans World Airlines that would fly the press to China were not to be permitted to travel beyond Shanghai, the port of entry. It was a matter of Chinese pride and protocol. Actually, as it turned out, the Pan Am and TWA planes were not even allowed to remain in Shanghai during the President's visit. They were ordered to return to Guam and wait there until it was time to pick up the press contingent in Shanghai for the homeward flight.

Despite their supposed inscrutability, the Chinese could scarcely restrain their curiosity about the presidential plane. Only Peking's officialdom could get near the gleaming silver, white, and blue 707. It was parked in a secluded area of the capital's airport and under close guard by Air Force police and further cordoned off by stern-faced Chinese soldiers. Albertazzie sensed that Chung, Chou En-Lai's personal pilot, and his own interpreter, "Mr. Lee," were dying to go aboard to inspect the presidential plane they had heard so much about. Whenever they were in the vicinity of the aircraft, Albertazzie noticed, his Chinese companions cast admiring glances at SAM 970 and plied him with questions about its interior facilities.

"I offered several times to give them our usual 'show and tell,' " said Albertazzie, "but they steadfastly refused, smiling and shaking their heads as if to say 'Gee, we'd love to, but we don't dare.' They were like kids eyeing a dish of candy, but who had been warned not to touch."

Then Kissinger invited Premier Chou to tour the handsome craft. The seventy-two-year-old Chou was as curious as any of his subordinates and quickly agreed.

"Seeing that, I renewed my invitation to Chung and Lee," Albertazzie said. "They accepted with alacrity. Suddenly I understood why they had been hanging back. It wasn't permissible until Chou himself had done it."

The most difficult negotiations during the advance party's visit to Peking centered around the American press group that would be accompanying President Nixon. The Chinese simply could not grasp the scope and size of the media operation that the Americans were proposing. They were not sure they could physically accommodate so many persons—Elbourne of the White House Press Office had glibly tossed out a figure of "three or four hundred" that had left the Chinese gasping. Hotel facilities suitable for Westerners were in short supply in Peking and Hangchow, the two prime places Nixon would visit. Besides, the Chinese government did not allow foreigners to wander around willy-nilly, not even visitors from socialist countries in Africa and eastern Europe. It insisted upon small, manageable groups—a few dozen at a time—and always assigned government guides and interpreters to accompany them everywhere. The scale of the American proposal was beyond anything Peking was prepared to handle.

To complicate matters, Chinese officials simply could not understand the competitive nature of the American press nor its need for massive communications facilities to instantaneously transmit words and pictures to the United States on such a big story. Three separate television networks, plus something called Public Broadcasting? Two American wire services, plus scores of individual newspapers and magazines that insisted on providing their own coverage? Crowds of photographers and technicians and people running around with walkie-talkies? Miles of cables and wires and darkrooms and studios and control rooms? Banks of telephones and Telex machines and operators? The Chinese experience with their own press was a matter of several major newspapers, one radio network, and a budding television operation, all owned and operated by the government. Even to cover Chairman Mao (who certainly ranked above Nixon in Chinese eyes), it didn't take more than a handful of reporters and cameramen. Still, the Chinese wanted to be generous to their American guests. How about bringing in a press contingent of ten?

"Ten!" The tempestuous Elbourne nearly leaped across the table at Tin Sui, the dour chief of the Ministry of Information.

"Don't bother taking me back to the White House with that

kind of proposal," Elbourne disconsolately announced later to the other members of the American party. "Just let me die right here in China."

Everyone in the group knew instinctively that Elbourne was right. The President of the United States could not make a journey as historic as a trip to China with the kind of press coverage the Chinese envisioned. The Chinese correctly had surmised that Nixon didn't like the press. They had incorrectly surmised that he didn't need it. Thus began an arduous negotiating process that continued all week, through a second advance trip in January 1972 and almost up to Nixon's departure from Washington in mid-February.

Gradually, the number of American press crept upward—to twenty-eight, to eighty, and finally to eighty-seven.

Even so, it was woefully small. More news people than that usually traveled on Nixon trips inside the United States. The White House had received more than 2,000 applications from news organizations for the China trip, several hundred of which represented major publications and broadcasting operations. Besides, as Press Secretary Ronald Ziegler knew, the China trip would occur during a presidential election year. Cutting the China press list to eighty-seven would make a lot of news organizations very unhappy with the Nixon White House.

In the end, it came out as astute correspondents predicted. ABC, CBS, and NBC networks received the biggest share—thirty-seven slots for correspondents, camera crews, and producers. Naturally, the top television names were included—Walter Cronkite, Barbara Walters, Eric Sevareid, John Chancellor, Harry Reasoner, plus three network vice presidents who listed themselves as producers. Public Broadcasting got one slot—for a radio correspondent. Associated Press and United Press International were allowed three writers and two photographers each. The remaining spots went to twenty-one newspaper reporters, six magazine writers, two magazine photographers, four radio broadcasters, three columnists, a man from the Voice of America, and two photo darkroom technicians.

But getting a minimum number of correspondents into China was only part of the negotiating difficulties with the Chinese. How to get the Nixon story out of China—promptly, not days later? The television networks wanted to broadcast live. The daily press needed ample telephone and Telex lines around the clock. Peking's existing links to the Western world were totally inadequate for the task, consisting of a few antiquated commercial telegraph circuits and several broadcast frequencies of poor quality. There was almost no way to transmit a timely story from there to here, certainly not in the fashion required by the American news media and expected by the American people.

To overcome the communications gap, the White House advance party came up with an ingenious solution. The U.S. government would acquire a wide-body Boeing 747 and, in conjunction with American Telephone & Telegraph, International Telephone & Telegraph, and the three networks, would transform the jumbo jet into an elaborate broadcasting facility complete with newsroom, studios, and electronic gear. The giant aircraft then would be flown to China and parked at Peking's airfield. From there, the words and pictures of Nixon's activities in China would be beamed to the communications satellite in orbit over the Pacific and then relayed directly to the United States. The crash project would cost approximately $80 million, a tidy sum for covering a presidential trip of one week's duration. But who would quibble over costs for such an historic event?

The Chinese, to say the least, were intrigued. Not even the Russians could boast of such attention from the United States. But the Chinese had one reservation. The People's Republic would have to insist upon the right to purchase the Boeing 747 and all the equipment installed in the plane.

They were reminded that $80 million was a lot of money, even for so fancy a facility. And what would the Chinese government do with it after President Nixon had departed?

Ah, the Chinese smiled, you Americans have missed the central point. The money and the future of the plane are of no importance. What was important was the *sovereignty* of China, which the President at least would be acknowledging by making his visit to Peking. It would not be proper for a foreign nation to broadcast directly from China over the foreigner's own communications system. Indeed, that would be a serious breach of China's sovereignty. Therefore, China would have to own the

317

Boeing 747. Then it would be a *Chinese* broadcasting facility. And China would be happy to pay for it—with American dollars or gold. How soon would the White House like the money?

Now it was the Americans' turn to smile, but only faintly. General Redmond and Albertazzie exchanged worried glances. They were greatly relieved when Chapin, as head of the advance party's negotiating team, told the Chinese that, er, we'll have to get back to you on that.

Chapin was responding out of normal caution to a proposal that had not been anticipated, and therefore had not been cleared by the White House. Besides, the question of sovereignty added a delicate dimension to the advance party's assignment. Most countries were usually so delighted to have a presidential visit—or were so awed by the prospect—that Americans had grown accustomed to handling travel arrangements pretty much their own way. But there were also practical reasons for hedging on the plane sale.

In order to assure flawless broadcasting to the United States, the Pentagon planned to install the latest voice-transmitting equipment aboard the Boeing 747, sophisticated electronics not readily available for ordinary commercial broadcasting. The plan made sense, so long as the plane and its facilities remained in the hands of the U.S. government. But it made no sense if the package was sold to the Chinese and found its way, as it surely would, into the possession of Peking's intelligence apparatus.

Even the plane posed a problem. On board the jumbo jet would be an inertial navigation system like the one aboard *Air Force One* and similar to the brain center of the Minuteman intercontinental ballistic missile. "We would have immediately lifted the Chinese out of the electronic Dark Ages," said Albertazzie.

(After the President's visit and as part of the decision to move toward "the normalization of relations" with Peking, the Nixon administration approved the delivery of ten Boeing 707 jet transports to the People's Republic of China. The Chinese agreed that the planes' black canisters containing the heart of the inertial navigation system, would remain sealed. In event of malfunction, they were to be removed and sent to Japan for servicing by authorized technicians. That somehow was deemed to be a suffi-

318

cient security measure, although U.S. officials had no way to enforce it. One of the 707s, incidentally, was used by the Chinese to pick up former President Nixon at Los Angeles in 1976 for his private visit to Peking. And to fly Vice Premier Teng Hsiao-ping to America for his 1979 tour and visit with President Carter.)

Since the plane deal could not be consummated, the White House and the Chinese government finally worked out an alternate scheme for transmitting the Nixon story. The Chinese would construct and *operate* their own communications center. It would relay radio, television, telephone, and teletype signals to a mobile ground station they would bring over under lease from Western Union International. That terminal, in turn, would feed the coverage to the mid-Pacific satellite, which would beam it to a ground station at Oakland, California. From there it could be instantly transmitted to any point in the United States and the rest of the world. The White House quickly came up with the blueprints for a two-story communications center and gave them to the Chinese. With a speed that probably couldn't be matched in America, the Chinese began building the structure in a matter of weeks. It was ready in January 1972. About eighty American technicians from the networks and the Hughes Company satellite division flew to Peking to set up more than thirty-two tons of communications equipment needed to dispatch the pictures and words of the Nixon trip to the outside world. The group and the gear flew over on Trans World Airlines, thus giving TWA the distinction of being the first American commercial airline to fly into the People's Republic of China. Before departure, Albertazzie briefed TWA's senior pilot, Captain Marvin Horstman, on Chinese aviation procedures.

With that decision out of the way, it then became possible for the White House and the Chinese to agree on the total number of Americans who would be accompanying Dick and Pat Nixon. It was a modest contingent by U.S. standards, but a sizable armada nevertheless, one that would have awed Marco Polo. "Things more strange come into this town . . . than into any city of the world," the amazed Polo had chronicled in his diary 700 years ago. "Everyone from everywhere brings them for the lord who lives there, and for his court."

There would be 38 persons in the official White House delegation, including the Nixons, Henry Kissinger, and Secretary of State Rogers; 52 support persons, including Albertazzie, *Air Force One*'s crew, the President's valet and Mrs. Nixon's hairdresser; 45 members of the White House Communications Agency; 12 men to assist the Chinese in operating the leased satellite ground station, 16 members of the White House Press Office, 29 Secret Service agents and, of course, the 87 members of the press. The total came to 279, a figure that represented considerable Chinese generosity. When Chou En-lai and Kissinger had met secretly in July 1971 to agree on a presidential visit, the Chinese assumed the President and his lady could get by with about 50 attendants. They had not reckoned with the power and majesty of the presidency and how it translates into a body count.

If the White House had been given its way, the presidential entourage would have numbered nearly 500, including an additional 100 members of the press, mostly American and some foreign. As it was, several thousand foreign journalists had beseeched the Chinese Ministry of Information for permission to enter the country on their own in order to witness the Nixon spectacle. Except for the handful of foreign correspondents already based in Peking, the Chinese answered all other supplicants with two words: So sorry.

As it was, the American contingent would require a small fleet of aircraft. Besides *Air Force One,* the Washington airlift would comprise the presidential backup plane, SAM 970, two air force C-141 jet cargo planes carrying support and security personnel and tons of equipment ranging from copying machines to the President's yellow legal pads, plus the Pan Am and TWA 707s chartered by the press corps.

One is tempted to imagine that advance parties on presidential trips deal mainly in matters of protocol and high policy. But that is a pleasant myth encouraged by those who have to go through the process. Most of the time is consumed with determining the right number of hotel rooms (and which hotels), the availability of telephones, meals, transportation to and from the meeting places, including ceremonial stops, as well as the selection of a pressroom and working space for turning out thousands of pages of speeches, announcements, and schedules. White House communicators need to know precisely where the President is going to be (the exact room or vehicle) at every minute, so they can keep him in touch with Washington and the world outside.

The Secret Service needs to know all that and more. What is the detailed route through the streets for every presidential movement outside his quarters? Will there be crowds—and where? What is the host's plan for crowd control—and can the President live with it? Will the President be on foot or in a vehicle—and where and for how long and how great a distance? When can we walk the route to see if we'll okay it? And if we won't, what are the alternatives? Oh, yes, we need to check the limousines in which the President will be riding and those near him. And we need our own security people around his vehicle an hour beforehand. We want to check the food preparation service. Who are the waiters? We would like to know which bathrooms are being reserved for his use. Can we station agents there?

Security agencies of most countries are accustomed to such precautions. As a matter of fact, the U.S. Secret Service tends to feel more comfortable about a Presidential trip to a totalitarian nation than to a Western democracy. A police state can keep its populace under strict control. And an American President usually inspires a warm and friendly response from subjugated people—he is a symbol of freedom and liberty; their dreams of a happier life may be riding on the outcome of the visit.

It was too much to hope that the Chinese masses would see Nixon in that light. For nearly a quarter century, they had been drilled into believing that American imperialists were the mad dogs of the earth, a potential threat to China itself. The Secret Service ascertained that Nixon would not be allowed to mingle with the ordinary people of Peking; indeed Chinese authorities would keep the public off the streets he traveled and well back from every intersection along his route. This was not to be a triumphal trip by Richard Nixon.

All this was eminently satisfactory to the Secret Service; it would make their job easier. But the image makers at the White House were disappointed. They would have preferred the media attention that would result from a magnificent public outpouring for Nixon, preferably in Peking's gigantic Tien-An-Men Square.

The conflict between the publicity-conscious and the security-conscious was natural enough, but it also could be acrimonious.

As presidential pilot, Albertazzie had his own list of details to work out. *Air Force One* and the presidential backup plane, SAM 970, required safe parking areas at each of the cities Nixon would visit—Peking, Hangchow, and Shanghai. The proper fuel mixture had to be available, and Albertazzie had to test it and have it stored in sealed tanks, either underground or in transporter trucks. Auxiliary ground power units had to be provided so the crews could perform their maintenance work and preflight preparations. Telephone ground lines to the aircraft were required. Fresh water and ice had to be on hand.

Albertazzie also had a couple of sensitive matters to take up with the Chinese. One that soon surfaced was the need for a mutual understanding of what would constitute "arrival time." Diplomatic protocol demanded that the President arrive precisely at the moment the Chinese were expecting him. To arrive early or late—even if the gap amounted to just a few minutes— could be an embarrassment to both sides. It might well mar the atmosphere of the visit.

The White House customarily designated the time of arrival as the moment *Air Force One* came to a stop at the red carpet and the President was ready to leave the plane to meet his host. The Chinese, it turned out, regarded arrival time as the moment when the plane's wheels touched the runway; their definition didn't allow for the five or six minutes of taxiing time to the ceremonial site. So a compromise was deftly fashioned. The schedule would show the time that *Air Force One* was to land, thus satisfying the Chinese, and the time that Albertazzie would stop the plane before the waiting Chou En-lai, thus satisfying the White House.

Compromise was in order, too, on a second problem involving the two planes' crew members. They would not be allowed to wear their Air Force blues in China. The Chinese disliked the idea of foreigners walking around in military uniforms, for it brought back too many memories of the old days of foreign domination. But the Chinese said it would be perfectly all right for Air Force guards to carry their customary weapons while patrolling the cordoned perimeter around *Air Force One* and SAM 970, provided the arms were not openly displayed.

It wasn't that the White House or the Chinese government anticipated trouble during the Nixon visit. That point was made perfectly clear to Albertazzie by the slight, elderly head of the Chinese civil aviation agency, who was his constant companion.

"Surely, in a society of 800 million people, you must have some discontented people," Albertazzie had commented during one of their social encounters.

"Oh, yes, we have some," came the reply through an interpreter. "We just don't have them around here during your visit."

Albertazzie determined through the ever-present interpreters that the old man was not an expert on civil aviation but an "administrator" of its bureaucracy. He had been with Mao Tse-tung and Chou En-lai on the famous "Long March" of the 1930s, when China's future Communist leaders and their ragtag followers were fleeing both the Japanese invaders and Chiang Kai-shek's Nationalist army. So he had survived. And being a survivor of the Long March had given him prestige and a place of importance in Mao's China.

But the old man displayed a keen interest in modern flying procedures. He constantly asked Albertazzie questions, and especially sought his opinion on which Chinese airfield offered the best facilities—Peking's or Shanghai's.

"I kept ducking the question because I sensed a hook in it," Albertazzie said. "Then I learned that Peking Airport had been built with help from the Russians, whereas the Chinese themselves had constructed the big one at Shanghai and were immensely proud of it—although both seemed to have been built from the same set of plans.

"So the next time Mr. Ma—as I knew him—asked the big question, I was ready. 'Oh, Shanghai is much superior,' I told him. He was delighted with my answer and constantly repeated it to everybody at every opportunity—including Premier Chou."

Albertazzie and his *Air Force One* crew members were surprised by the absence of air traffic between Shanghai and Peking, China's major cities. There were only three civilian flights

323

a week. Shanghai's terminal was huge, with many shops and several restaurants. Peking's was similar in layout but smaller.

"But all of us noticed the one thing that was missing—no airline ticket counters for Chinese travelers, and nobody waiting around to board."

Although the U.S. Air Force had not asked them to "spy" during their time inside China, the crews of *Air Force One* and SAM 970 naturally kept their eyes open during several "proficiency flights" they took around the Peking area. They saw a few civilian IL-18 turboprops and one Vickers Viscount flown by the Chinese government airline, but spotted no Chinese Air Force planes. Nor did they see any Soviet Aeroflot transports, an indication that the ideological rupture with Moscow extended even to airline travel between the two Communist giants. They identified two other IL-18s, one bearing the tail insignia of North Korea and the other of Cambodia. On the ground between Shanghai and Peking, they detected evidence of several concealed airfields and anti-aircraft missile sites.

The proficiency flights were intended to gather operational data and to familiarize the crews with Chinese takeoff and landing procedures for the President's visit.

"It was apparent to us, and soon apparent to the Chinese— because we convinced them—that the Soviets had been giving them junk," Albertazzie said. "By our standards, the Russian navigational aids in China were vintage 1949–50. The Chinese air routes between cities were still keyed to radio beacons, or homers, as we call them. When we first arrived, our Chinese escort pilots and navigators would not allow us to use *Air Force One*'s sophisticated navigation system, because they had no experience with such modern equipment. So we flew on radio curves from station to station, much as we used to do in the United States many years ago."

Albertazzie and other members of the White House advance team, however, were struck by the "work ethic" of the Chinese and their meticulous attention to detail. One Peking sight that daily impressed them was the magnificent Great Hall of the People, a cavernous structure of immense rooms and auditoriums that served as the center of governmental and Communist Party activity. It had been erected within one year during Mao's "Great Leap Forward." Every adult in Peking had contributed at least one day's manual labor toward its completion. The advance party got to see a lot of it (as would President Nixon), for it was the site of many of their meetings and banquets.

One of the Great Hall's marvels was its huge domed ceiling, adorned with many thousands of small incandescent lights. Try as they did, the Americans were never able to spot a single burned-out bulb.

"I think I know how you achieve that," Albertazzie jokingly remarked to his interpreter, Lee. "You have assigned one person to watch each bulb—so you have thousands of people keeping an eye on the Great Hall all the time."

Lee laughed appreciatively, but his pride turned to chagrin one evening when Albertazzie finally spotted an unlit bulb and pointed it out to him. Lee excused himself momentarily as they entered the lobby of the Great Hall and later rejoined Albertazzie to escort him to the mezzanine where a receiving line was forming for the night's banquet.

"When we reached the mezzanine, I turned back to look once more at my prize find," Albertazzie said. "I couldn't believe what I saw. A light bulb was shining brightly there again!"

Albertazzie developed a genuine liking for Lee. He spoke English fluently and was obviously accustomed to Westerners and Western ways, having served in Chinese government posts in Paris and Stockholm. But he refused to accept a parting gift that Albertazzie tried to present him in appreciation for his assistance during the advance party's trip.

"In China, I am the host and you are the guest," Lee told Albertazzie. "If I ever come to America, then I will be able to accept your hospitality."

On the final day, Albertazzie was busily engaged in departure preparations aboard SAM 970 when Master Sgt. Joe Lopez, the plane's chief guard, tapped him on the shoulder.

"Mr. Lee is outside and would like to see you," Lopez said.

"Tell him to come aboard," Albertazzie replied.

Moments later, Lopez returned without Lee. "The Chinese guards won't let him through," he reported.

Puzzled, Albertazzie left the plane and walked beyond the security cordon to his waiting interpreter. Lee had a small gift for him, a token of their friendship.

"Why won't your guards let you come aboard?" Albertazzie inquired, noting that Lee had been on the President's plane many times during the week.

Lee shrugged. "Policy," he said, steering the conversation away from the subject.

Albertazzie did not pursue it, but later, as SAM 970 winged its way homeward, he hit upon the answer. The Chinese obviously had observed their easy friendship. What if Lee had come aboard and asked for political asylum?

"The implications of such an act were devastating," Albertazzie said afterward. "What would we have done? What would the Chinese have done? An incident like that might have blown the whole Nixon trip. I don't believe Lee had any such notions, but the Chinese apparently decided not to take any chances on a possible defection."

The Chinese were not the only people concerned about security. The American intelligence community mounted an extraordinary "listening" campaign in the weeks preceding the President's visit to assure itself of the purity of China's motives in inviting him. The Central Intelligence Agency, the Department of Defense, and the Secret Service were concerned not only about what might happen *to* the President in China but also about what might happen elsewhere in the world *while* he was there. He was, after all, the Commander-in-Chief of the armed forces; his responsibilities would be traveling with him to one of the most secretive and unpredictable countries on earth.

The *possibility* of Nixon's being held hostage was more than a figment of imagination among intelligence agencies, even though its *probability* was unthinkable and therefore heavily discounted by Asia specialists in Washington. Some contingency plans were actually pondered, however, including the feasibility of mounting a rescue attempt.

The Pentagon eventually opted for a more rational but nonetheless significant security measure. It was in the secret guise of a training mission. A high-level Air Force memorandum conveyed the decision: ". . . During the period from 16 February

326

to 29 February (1972) NEACP [National Emergency Airborne Command Post] will deploy two aircraft to the Pacific area to conduct extensive communications training and exercise of National Military Command Center procedures.'' The two planes were C-135s, elaborately outfitted as airborne command posts and known as "Doomsday planes," the type the President would use to ride out a nuclear attack on the United States and from which he could direct America's worldwide military forces. Operating from American bases on Okinawa, the two aircraft would maintain a continuous orbit outside the territorial limits of the People's Republic of China during the entire time of Nixon's visit, monitoring the flow of communications from the President and his top aides inside China and "standing by" in the event of any emergency there or anywhere else.

The justification was that if for any reason the President needed an airborne command post, one would be in his immediate vicinity and not half a globe away. The decision didn't allay the fears for his safety, but the Joint Chiefs of Staff at least felt better. They were doing what they could to backstop the Commander-in-Chief during his unorthodox visit inside China.

Home! The advance team of Polo II could hardly wait to get there. They had tasted a small slice of China, dealt with its bureaucracy, marveled at its human density, learned to use chopsticks, admired its ancient arts and sights, and were awed by the discipline and dedication of the people. The People's Republic of China was more than a government, it was a religion. Chairman Mao was more than the head of the country, he was a god. People spoke of him and quoted him as comfortably as Western Christians spoke of Jesus.

And the advance party had tales to tell! Tales of people who were well-fed and smiling and courteous, who dressed alike and who thought alike and who owned a watch and a bicycle and considered themselves well-off. Richard Nixon's advance men had lived a week among people who deferred to their elders, who didn't demonstrate against the local White House, and who arose at four in the morning to do the tasks the state assigned them, from sweeping the streets to slopping the hogs to running the country. How could all this be explained to family and friends in America? Indeed, how could it all be reduced to sterile White House memos that began with "To" and "From" and would serve as guidance for a President soon to journey to this strange country?

The trip home aboard SAM 970 was filled with relief and regret. Relief at escaping the grimness and earnestness of China, relief that they could eat American food—with forks and knives—once again, relief over conversing with people without needing interpreters. And regret for having been in China so briefly, for not having had time to see more of the country, for having to leave just when they were beginning to savor the delights and understand some of the contradictions of China.

Chapin, as chief of the arrangements group, was anxious to summarize the work of the team, to note its accomplishments, and to underline the issues that would need further refining and negotiating. Consulting with the others and organizing his notes, he hoped to have at least a rough draft ready for Haldeman, the White House staff chief, when the plane landed in Washington. Henry Kissinger, meanwhile, had moved into the presidential lounge with his own assistants to prepare for the President a concise outline of his week's talks with Chou En-lai and the leaders of China. Sometimes sitting, sometimes pacing the floor, Kissinger kept dictating from his notes and from his intuition. His would be a long report and neatly organized, complete with sections and subheadings and options on this and alternatives on that. Kissinger, like Chapin, was in no mood for chitchat and relaxation. The first advance trip to China was over but the real trip—the President's—was still ahead. Indeed, it seemed to both of them that another advance party would have to go into China around the first of the year to finish the task. There were still a lot of loose ends to tie down concerning the Nixons' schedule and the press arrangements. (A second advance team eventually went to Peking in January 1972 to do just that.)

Early on February 17, 1972, they rolled the big blue and silver Boeing, SAM 26000, out of the hangar at Andrews Air Force Base. They had waxed the wings, polished the windows, put out the candy dishes and the matchbooks, and stowed the food, including thirty-year-old Ballantine scotch from the White House pantry.

They also had put aboard a supply of chopsticks.

Ten minutes after takeoff, President and Mrs. Nixon were strolling jauntily down the aisle, shaking hands and chatting with most of the fifty-two persons aboard. There was only one thing to talk about: China. After 11,500 miles and overnight stops in Hawaii and Guam, they would land in a vast, Communist country that America did not even recognize diplomatically.

Nixon was euphoric. One of the seven members of the press pool showed him a China portfolio with the label of its source on the frontispiece—the Central Intelligence Agency. "This will probably prove how little we know about China," Nixon cracked.

The President bragged of his proficiency with chopsticks, but doubted that Henry Kissinger had ever used them before his secret trip to China seven months earlier. En route, Kissinger and Secretary of State Rogers ducked in and out of the Nixon suite, helping him devise America's emerging policy toward the People's Republic of China. Would they be dealing only with Premier Chou En-lai, Kissinger's new diplomatic friend? Or would they, as Nixon hoped, also plumb the thoughts of Mao?

Air Force One touched down on Chinese soil at 8:55 A.M. February 21, 1972. The stop at Shanghai's Rainbow Bridge Airport was just long enough for everyone to stretch their legs, sip hot tea, and take aboard a Chinese navigator and radio operator as escorts for the hour-and-forty minute hop to Peking.

Nixon, peering through the window, got his first glimpse of the sprawling Chinese capital at 11:25 A.M. as his plane descended through a wintry overcast. From the cockpit, Pilot Albertazzie sighted the field. The place looked almost deserted. Acres of barren concrete stretched everywhere. He radioed a Secret Service advance man who was positioned on the windswept field near the gray, boxlike terminal building.

"That is affirmative," the agent repeated. "No crowds."

Assembled near the terminal was a knot of Chinese officials headed by Premier Chou, plus a Liberation Army band, a military honor guard of fierce-looking men bundled up in fur hats and greatcoats, and the American press corps that had flown in earlier. Affixed to the terminal building and dominating the scene was a thirty-foot high portrait of Chairman Mao, flanked on either side by a scarlet Chinese flag and the Stars and Stripes.

Albertazzie guided *Air Force One* into this bleak Chinese moonscape and cut the engines. An expectant hush settled over the field. No one spoke. No one moved. All eyes were fixed on the gleaming craft that had just landed. Then the door slowly opened and, for an instant, no one would have been surprised to see a helmeted spaceman step into view.

Instead it was Richard Nixon. He was hatless. He was smiling. He was in Peking.

Chapter Eleven
On The Horizon

The "Aeroplane" was seven years old in 1910, when Teddy Roosevelt decided to give it a whirl. That marked a red-letter day in the history of aviation, and not merely because TR became the first of the American Presidents to leave the ground in a heavier-than-air machine. On the same afternoon, October 11, and over the same field outside St. Louis, another plane managed to set a new American endurance record by staying aloft for three hours, eleven minutes, and fifty-five seconds.

Roosevelt, fifty-one years old and nineteen months out of office, placed his hand on the strut of a canvas, wire, and wood contraption at Lambert Field, Kinloch, Missouri, and proclaimed the airplane to be "a practical and safe vehicle of transit." The occasion was an air meet of the Aero Club of St. Louis, and Colonel Roosevelt's pilot was Arch Hoxsey, one of the intrepid pioneers of aviation, who had opened the show with a nervy, ninety-mile nonstop flight from Springfield, Illinois. Hoxsey's craft was a Type B pusher, built by those Dayton Bicycle makers, Orville and Wilbur Wright, who had achieved the world's first airplane flight at Kitty Hawk, North Carolina, on December 17, 1903.

331

The daring and the excitement of those early days leaps from the yellowed files of *Aero* magazine for October 15, 1910, describing Teddy Roosevelt's first ride in a flying machine:

Although he had repeatedly declined invitations to ride in an aeroplane at Mineola, L.I., and in Europe, Col. Roosevelt settled himself comfortably on one of the seats of the Wright soon after his arrival, and while Hoxsey handled the operating levers, rode for more than three minutes at an average altitude of 50 feet above the field, rising at times to an elevation of 200 feet.

That Col. Roosevelt greatly enjoyed his brief experience in the air as a guest of Hoxsey could not be plainer evidenced than through the incidents leading up to, during and after the flight with the aviator. Shortly after the colonel reached the aviation grounds, among the first to be presented by President A. B. Lambert, of the Aero Club of St. Louis, was Hoxsey. The latter advanced to the side of the car, placed one foot on the running board and shook hands with the former President.

"Col. Roosevelt, our birthdays fall on October 27," he said, "and as a result, I feel that I have somewhat of a lien on your indulgence. I want you to take a short spin with me in the air. You can, with perfect safety, trust yourself in my hands."

Col. Roosevelt pushed his hat back on his head and asked, "Now?"

"Yes," replied Hoxsey, "this is as good a time as we can ever get. It is calm, and ideal flying machine weather. Will you go?"

In an instant Col. Roosevelt had assured him that he would, but cautioned Hoxsey to proceed about it as secretly as possible, wishing to avoid the crowd. Accompanied by the colonel, Hoxsey walked swiftly over to the machine. Announcing all in readiness, the colonel experienced some little difficulty in getting through the many strands of wire which brace the plane to the seat. This finally accomplished, he was ready.

His heart beat harder and faster when Col. Roosevelt entered the machine than it did just before he rose into the air on his Springfield–St. Louis journey. When the machine had risen about 200 feet, Hoxsey says he looked at Roosevelt, and the latter had his hat off, waving at the crowds below. The aviator says he leaned over and yelled to him not to pull any of the cords, to which Col. Roosevelt instantly replied, "Nothing doing!"

"He then replaced his hat on his head, smiling contentedly," said Hoxsey. "In passing over the ship Doughnaught, [a mockup of a naval vessel] the colonel looked at me and yelled with all his might, at the same time pointing to the make-believe ship, 'War, army, aeroplane.' I nodded my head.

"At no time did I circle, in flying, closer than 200 feet to the ground, and at no time did I permit the aeroplane to get anywhere but where I could have landed instantly had anything happened.

"I realized the tremendous responsibility that rested upon my shoulders. I knew that had I injured Col. Roosevelt in any way, or lost control of my machine, my whole reputation as an aviator would have been blasted forever, and I was determined to land in absolute safety."

Scarcely seventy years have passed since that primitive event, yet in terms of aeronautic progression, it amounts to an eon. Hoxsey fretted under the responsibility of landing his famous passenger in absolute safety; pilots of the presidential jets are so accustomed to the safety of their big craft that they almost take it for granted. The accent now is on smooth performance over long distances at great speed and high altitudes. The goal is an aircraft so superbly tailored to a President's needs that it can truly serve as a White House in the sky.

The transition from propeller-driven aircraft to turbojets was a giant stride toward that objective; it impressed even the placid Dwight Eisenhower, the first President to fly a jet on White House business. The next generation of presidential aircraft may actually achieve it.

What will the next *Air Force One* be like?

A clue certainly exists in the giant, widebody Boeing 747, and the similar Douglas DC-10 and Lockheed L1011, already transporting hundreds of passengers on long-range commercial flights. Three of the jumbo 747s have been acquired by the Air Force and converted into national airborne command posts in event of all-out war. President Carter took a ride in one in 1977; the Pentagon, for the first time, gave a clutch of reporters a rare tour of its interior. Aside from its elaborate electronics communications and battle-planning facilities—which would not be on an *Air Force One* in any event—reporters were impressed with its spaciousness and the variety of its accomodations. Without breaching national security, it is useful here to describe some of the quarters aboard a "Doomsday" 747:

333

The command authority room in the forward section, where the President would work, relax, or sleep, is a comfortable compartment containing several small desks, two bunk beds, a gold-upholstered sofa, and four high-back seats. Connecting with it is a storage room and a commodious restroom, plus a presidential galley for meal preparation and seats for flight stewards and two Secret Service men.

To the rear of the presidential quarters lies a conference room, featuring a large rectangular table, a chair for the President at the head of the table, and eight other chairs, four to a side, for key assistants. A built-in projection system allows conferees to look at movies, slides, or charts. Aft of the conference room, a larger briefing area provides seating for twenty-one persons, a head table for three, a lectern, and another projection system.

In the mid-section of the 231-foot aircraft, a wide area houses the consoles and twenty-nine personnel stations for the officers and men who would run the communications systems in wartime. Separate compartments, farther back, allow for radio equipment, additional seating, and eight more bunks. Below the main deck are electronic maintenance stations and storage rooms. A "Doomsday" 747 can stay aloft seventy-two hours with aerial refueling. A five-mile long copper antenna can be trailed behind the plane for communicating with American nuclear submarines patrolling the world's seas.

Almost twice as wide as a Boeing 707 and nearly ninety feet longer, the Boeing 747 suggested itself long ago as an ideal *Air Force One* for presidential use. But a study conducted for the White House during the Nixon years came to the conclusion in 1970—the year the 747 first entered commercial service—that a new Boeing 707 would more adequately serve the President.

"We concluded then that the 707 was the proper aircraft because it could go anywhere a President might wish to go and it could carry the number of people a President would want with him. It was a comfortable plane possessing the proper communications, it could be supported with existing equipment, and could land, take off, and be serviced at most major airfields in the world," said Albertazzie.

The 1970 study also looked into the feasibility of a supersonic

334

Air Force One, a sleek, spectacular airplane that would be capable of flying several times faster than the speed of sound. In the late 1960s, the Soviets had begun developing the Tupolev Tu-144, a 100-passenger transport capable of roaring through the air at 1,550 miles an hour. It held prospects of flying from Paris to New York in a little over two hours. And, of course, the French and the British were test-flying the beak-nosed Concorde. It possessed about the same speed and passenger capacity as the Tu-144 and in 1976 would inaugurate supersonic air service to Washington from Paris and London.

In 1970 the United States was pushing its own supersonic transport development through contracts with the Boeing Company. Then in 1971 the project collapsed when Congress, after bitter debate, refused to give Nixon additional funds for the SST. But suppose, for the sake of examining all the options, that the SST project had stayed alive and that Boeing this year was about to roll out of its Seattle factory a supersonic transport every bit as nice and as fast as the Concorde. Would it then be a useful *Air Force One*?

For a President who wants to get to London, Paris, Moscow, or Los Angeles in a hurry, a 1,600-mile-an-hour aircraft would be ideal. But what would he do with such a presidential aircraft the rest of the time? At present, an SST could not be employed to fly to Americus, Allentown, or Akron, nor to Xenia, Yarmouth, or Zanesville. Only faraway places with adequate runways and special ground support facilities can handle such a craft. Moreover, flying speeds are not set by the manufacturers of airplanes, nor even by the pilots, but by the national and international aviation control agencies. The setting of speeds and flight paths is especially essential over congested areas to avoid either overtaking other planes or being overtaken.

Then there is the matter of on-board room for passengers and fuel. A Concorde or Tupolev-type *Air Force One* would give a president even less space than his present Boeing 707. And while swifter, the SST's nonstop range would also be less.

For all of these reasons, a supersonic *Air Force One* is not yet a practical option, certainly not to replace the existing 707s. Presidents must lead, but they must not race too far ahead of the people they serve. If and when U.S. airlines begin using supersonic transports for commercial air travel, it would be more practical for a president to charter one for those few occasions when he needed an SST to serve as a temporary *Air Force One.*

The ideal airplane for full-time presidential use should be an all-purpose craft, possessing the speed and range that can take him wherever he wants to go in a reasonable amount of time. It ought to be commodious enough to comfortably carry the necessary staff members and provide the working facilities required while airborne and on the ground. And, of course, it should be an aircraft capable of being serviced at a majority of airfields in the United States and abroad.

These practical standards for future presidential air travel are held by the men who fly presidents and some officials of such supporting agencies as the Secret Service, the National Military Command Center in the Department of Defense, the White House Communications Agency, the National Security Council, and of course, the Air Force. The consensus thus focuses on a long-range, wide-body aircraft of the type now in service—the three-jet DC-10 of McDonnell Douglas, Lockheed's three-jet L-1011, and the four-jet Boeing 747.

In terms of presidential travel, it would amount to a quantum jump from the Boeing 707, a leap perhaps greater than the switch from the piston-engine Lockheed Constellation of Eisenhower's time to the intercontinental Boeing 707 that became the first jet-powered presidential aircraft during the Kennedy era.

The wide-body airplane is nearly twice as roomy as SAM 27000 or SAM 26000. It thus could overcome some of their interior shortcomings while offering self-containment advantages for communications, security and command post functions now lacking in the 707s. At the same time it could land and take off at most airfields capable of handling the present presidential planes.

Pilots and flight crews become downright enthusiastic whenever they contemplate such an *Air Force One.* "From the standpoint of the White House and the crew, my guess is that it would be just about the answer to everything," said Col. Lester McClelland, presidential pilot for Ford and Carter.

Albertazzie, McClelland's predecessor, concurs. "A wide-body aircraft with a split-level configuration would also permit a nice separation of crew and presidential staff functions, while augmenting the space needs of both. And some of the presidential support agencies would be able to eliminate a lot of the on-the-ground work that now has to be done at every stop."

What the pilots and crews foresee in the next *Air Force One* is a craft that offers the President a compact version of many facilities of the West Wing of the White House. No longer would it be merely a mini-Oval Office in the sky, with cramped space for the First Family, airborne conferences, staff work, and crew operations.

The wide-body airplane, for example, offers a level immediately above or below the cockpit that could house a self-contained communications center duplicating most of the key functions of the White House Situation Room—and do it on an around-the-clock basis whenever the President travels. Such a communications center, plus use of additional space in the plane's belly for computerized coding and decoding equipment, would greatly reduce—if not eliminate—the present necessity of installing a temporary communications center in a hotel, an American embassy, or other ground location wherever the President stops.

"You could have full security at all times, thereby reducing the risk of foreign electronic surveillance and penetration," observed Albertazzie. "And you would have instant mobility if the President had to leave the place in a hurry."

The airborne communications nerve center, a vital requirement for a President who cannot escape his national security responsibilities, could have as many communications lines as the current signal board in the White House. And it could house a telescoping antenna that would provide a ten-mile radius for the "page boy" system for maintaining liaison with key White House aides at every destination.

With such an elaborate communications system in the aircraft, it would then be possible for the Secret Service to operate its local command post from the parked *Air Force One,* instead of having to set up a temporary base at a ground location. That would be a tremendous advantage, especially whenever a President travels abroad.

When Nixon made the first presidential trip to the Soviet

337

Union in 1972, for example, the White House Communications Agency and the Secret Service had to set up advance facilities for supporting and protecting the President in each of the cities he visited—at locations specified by the Russians. Moreover, when the President departs, it usually takes hours for the temporary facilities to be dismantled, crated, and put aboard one of the other aircraft in the presidential fleet.

The space afforded by a wide-body also would permit a compact medical dispensary aboard the President's plane, something that is nonexistent in today's 707s. If the President or someone in his entourage became ill or suffered an injury, prompt medical attention could then be provided aboard *Air Force One*, in the air or on the ground, leaving only serious cases to be treated at a hospital. A White House physician always travels on the President's airplane, but his present-day equipment is basically limited to what he can carry in his doctor's valise or stash in the aircraft's first-aid cabinet.

One feature the presidential crew wants on the next *Air Force One* is a place to rest when off duty—something lacking on SAM 27000 and SAM 26000. The need is particularly acute on long overseas flights lasting ten and eleven hours. On today's presidential plane, the pilot, co-pilot, and navigator have no place to sit except in the cockpit. On a wide-body, however, small but comfortable crew's quarters could be provided on another level, aft of the flight deck and opposite the communications center. It should contain a lavatory, two chairs, and a couple of Pullman-style bunks.

For a President, the great advantage of a wide-body airplane would lie in the opportunity for greatly expanded working and living space—for himself and for his staff. Because of the upper and lower levels provided by the wide-body's unusually deep fuselage, nearly all of the middle level's 2,300 square feet of main deck space can be devoted to working offices and compartments for the President and his traveling entourage. That is more than twice the total floor space of a Boeing 707, and the equivalent of an office suite 21 feet wide and nearly 110 feet long. There are almost unlimited possibilities for dividing it up. Here is one aircraft designer's interpretation of how this immense amount of space could be utilized to serve a President and his staff:

338

•A presidential bedroom near the nose section. The suite would be large enough to hold twin beds with built-in bedside tables and lamps, two lounge chairs, a small table, a built-in dresser, television console, and closets. Adjoining the bedroom would be a dressing room with lavatory and shower. No previous or existing presidential airplane has ever provided comparable sleeping quarters for a President and the First Lady.

•An executive office, 21 by 24 feet, twice as spacious as the presidential working quarters on today's *Air Force One*. Its features would include a full-size desk and presidential chair, a sofa, a square table and four chairs for top-level conferences, built-in storage cabinets and television set, and a telephone console connecting the President with Washington and any place on earth. This suite would be an airborne Oval Office, capable of serving a President almost as adequately as his office in the White House.

•Immediately to the rear, over the wings, a fully equipped galley. It would include all the facilities of a modern kitchen in a space almost twice as large as the galley on today's *Air Force One*. In the corridor outside the galley would be chairs for two Secret Service men on duty outside the executive suite, plus the stairway leading to the operational level. Just to the rear of the galley is a Secret Service compartment for eight more agents.

•Behind the security compartment, an 18- by 25-foot conference dining room. It would feature a rectangular table with seating for eight, a sofa for four, perimeter storage cabinets, television console, wall maps, and film projection facilities. This suite would be similar to the Cabinet Room in the White House, while also permitting "working" dinners for the President, key members of his staff, and other government officials. On long flights, this room undoubtedly would be the most useful space aboard for large meetings. Again, nothing like it exists on today's *Air Force One*.

•A national security suite for senior American diplomats, defense officials, and ranking foreign guests. The compartment, about the size of a cozy den in a typical home, would offer the privacy conducive to confidential discussions and recommendations vital to a President traveling abroad.

•Aft of the wings would be the main staff suite, featuring two

339

large working desks with four chairs apiece, four secretarial stations with electric typewriters and copier capability, plus six additional chairs for presidential aides working on individual assignments. The compartment would be large enough for staff briefings, meals and relaxation.

•The rear compartment would provide seating space for about thirty-eight more persons—guests, additional staff members, Secret Service men, *Air Force One* security guards, and the press pool of reporters. Another galley and a bank of lavatories would occupy the tail section.

The acquisition of such an aircraft would drastically alter the concept and improve the caliber of presidential air travel. Earlier in this book, the point was made that the President and White House staff members do less work aloft than might be supposed—often because of limitations of space and airborne working facilities. Some decisions are made, yes, and some things accomplished while hurtling across the skies. But most of the creative, productive work of the presidency usually awaits the President's return to Washington. It should not have to be that way.

A wide-body jet aircraft, with room for additional staff members and a physical division of labors and functions, would tremendously enhance the working environment and the working potential of an airborne president. At the same time, the capacity of a larger aircraft for housing a self-contained communications center and command post would reduce the dependence of support agencies on temporary ground installations at every destination, thereby saving expense and effort while improving presidential security control and national security coordination. Presidential travel by air could then finally become more than a matter of merely getting from here to there.

One day soon the President of the United States, this one or the next, will step aboard such an *Air Force One* and soar away to a distant land. On that day, America will be able to hail a shining new presidential aircraft, the eighth in a proud line. And one thing more: the advent of a "Flying White House" magnificently worthy of the name.

340

Bibliography

Christian, George. *The President Steps Down*. New York: Macmillan, 1970.

Cormier, Frank. *LBJ: The Way He Was*. Garden City, N.Y.: Doubleday, 1977.

Dean, John. *Blind Ambition*. New York: Simon and Schuster, 1976.

Dickerson, Nancy. *Among Those Present*. New York: Random House, 1976.

Donovan, Robert J. *Conflict and Crisis*. New York: W.W. Norton, 1977.

Eisenhower, Dwight D. *Mandate for Change*. Garden City, N.Y.: Doubleday, 1963.

————. *Waging Peace*. Garden City, N.Y.: Doubleday, 1965.

Gallagher, Marv Barelli. *My Life with Jacqueline Kennedy*. New York: David McKay, 1969.

Kalb, Marvin, and Bernard Kalb. *Kissinger*. Boston, Massachusetts: Little, Brown, 1974.

Manchester, William. *The Death of A President*. New York: Harper & Row, 1976.

McGovern, James. *To the Yalu.* New York: William Morrow, 1972.

Miller, Merle. *Plain Speaking.* New York: Berkley Publishing; G.P. Putnam's Sons, 1973.

Nessen, Ron. *It Sure Looks Different from the Inside.* Chicago, Illinois: Playboy Press, 1978.

O'Donnell, Kenneth P., and David F. Powers with Joe McCarthy. *"Johnny, We Hardly Knew Ye."* Boston: Little, Brown, 1970.

Rather, Dan, with Mickey Herskowitz. *The Camera Never Blinks.* New York: William Morrow, 1977.

Reeves, Richard. *A Ford, not a Lincoln.* New York: Harcourt Brace Jovanovich, 1975.

Roberts, Charles. *The Truth about the Assassination.* New York: Grosset & Dunlap, 1967.

Safire, William. *Before The Fall.* Garden City, N.Y.: Doubleday, 1975.

Smith, Timothy G. *Merriman Smith's Book of Presidents.* New York: W.W. Norton, 1972.

terHorst, J.F. *Gerald Ford and the Future of the Presidency.* New York: The Third Press, 1974.

Thomas, Helen. *Dateline: The White House.* New York: Macmillan, 1975.

Valenti, Jack. *A Very Human President.* New York: W.W. Norton, 1975.

Walters, Vernon A. *Silent Missions.* Garden City, N.Y.: Doubleday, 1978.

White, Theodore H. *Breach of Faith.* New York: Atheneum Publishers; Reader's Digest Press, 1975.

Woodward, Bob, and Carl Bernstein. *The Final Days.* New York: Simon and Schuster, 1976.

Youngblood, Rufus W. *Twenty Years in the Secret Service.* New York: Simon and Schuster, 1973.

Index

343

344

345

346

347